KING OF CAPITAL

KING OF CAPITAL

SANDY WEILL

AND THE

MAKING OF CITIGROUP

Amey Stone and Mike Brewster

John Wiley & Sons, Inc.

ISBN 0-471-21416-7

Printed in the United States of America.

10 9 8 7 6 5 4 3 2 1

To our parents:
Jackie and Lanier Stone
Ann Brewster and Bob Brewster

When beginning this book, we first had to decide which Sandy Weill we were going to concentrate on: Weill the corporate titan; Weill the philanthropist; Weill the entrepreneur; or perhaps Weill the manager.

We decided to focus on Sandy Weill the dealmaker. By dealmaker, we mean someone who not only negotiates a merger, but also carries out its goals. It is this aspect of Weill's career that puts him in a class with few other CEOs.

By focusing on deals, we show how Weill evolved over the course of his long career as the size and scope of the deals grew. In a single generation, with no personal connections or family money to speak of, Weill built one of the biggest brokerages in the United States—Shearson. Then he did it all over again, creating Citigroup, one of the world's most profitable financial services institutions. To help readers who aren't familiar with the scope of his career, we included a long introduction that sketches the major events.

This is not the authorized biography of Sandy Weill, although he did meet with us at the end of the project to answer some questions and gave us access to several of his top executives for interviews. Nonetheless, we did not have an opportunity to ask Weill everything we'd have liked to. When we quoted Weill from a secondary source, we footnoted it. When we quoted him directly, we made it clear in the text that he made the comment during our interview.

Most of the material in this book was generated from approximately 60 interviews conducted between July and December 2001. All the people quoted directly, without a footnote, were interviewed by us. We also gathered material from official documents, such as congressional testimony, court filings, and annual reports. A number of people we interviewed asked not to be named or spoke to us only on background.

Weill remains at the peak of his career. There is likely no other job as well-suited to him as his current one as head of Citigroup. To have written a biography of Weill any earlier would have risked leaving out the climax of his amazing career—a risk we still run with this book.

ACKNOWLEDGMENTS

Writing this book would have been much more difficult without the help of our researcher, Paul Rogers, who—along with being an excellent reporter and editor—possesses the patience and diplomatic skills to work closely with a husband and wife team. We'd also like to thank Lauren Cooper, who searched tirelessly to find photos that capture Weill and his era. Courtney Rowe also offered research assistance, as well as her support. Our readers, Suzanne Woolley and Bill Schwartzman, offered invaluable suggestions for revising our manuscript.

Friends, colleagues, and family members too numerous to mention volunteered their ideas and encouragement. We'd like to give special thanks to Bob Arnold and the staff of *Business Week Online,* David Shook, Weld Royal, Dermott and Elizabeth Morgan, Julie Tilsner (for those immortal words that kept us going), Jean Bergstresser, Evan Simonoff, Kerry Capell, Andy Wickstrom, Kathy Bonadie, Rebecca Hefter, Randy Fuller, Joyce Magruder, Irene Sitbon, Seth Kaufman, Jackie Mroz, Sam Freedman, Nate and Frances Burke, and Dee Stearns. We also extend our thanks to Citigroup's public relations staff, especially Jennifer Scardino and Leah Johnson, who set up several key interviews for this book.

A special thanks also goes to the authors of some excellent books that greatly helped us understand the context and import of Weill's career. In that regard, we'd like to thank Jon Friedman, co-author with John Meehan of *House of Cards*; David Rogers, author of *The Future of American Banking*; and Tim Carrington, author of *The Year They Sold Wall Street*.

Finally, we'd like to thank our agent, Susan Barry, who helped us through the agonizing and exhilarating process of writing our first book, and Jeanne Glasser, our editor at John Wiley & Sons, who can spot a good story when she sees one.

CONTENTS

1812	The future Citicorp is founded, under the name City Bank of New York.
1908	Etta Kalika, Sandy Weill's mother, emigrates to the United States with her family.
1933	Sandy Weill born in Brooklyn; Glass-Steagall Act passed.
1947	Weill sent to Peekskill Military Academy; he graduates four years later.
1951	Weill starts at Cornell University with plans to major in engineering.
1955	Weill graduates from Cornell, marries Joan Mosher, and lands his first job as a runner at Bear Stearns for $150 a month.
1957	Marc Weill, Sandy and Joan's first child, is born; two years later, Jessica is born.
1960	Weill, with three others, starts Carter, Berlind, Potoma & Weill.
1970	Weill's firm acquires the older, more established brokerage firm Hayden Stone.

1970-1980	Weill's firm acquires H. Hentz & Co., Shearson Hamill, and Loeb Rhoades.
1981	American Express acquires Shearson Loeb Rhoades.
1983	Weill is named American Express president.
1984	John Reed becomes CEO of Citicorp, replacing the legendary Walter Wriston.
1985	Weill resigns from American Express, along with protégé Jamie Dimon.
1986	Weill acquires control of consumer finance company Commercial Credit.
1988	Weill acquires Primerica Corp., including Smith Barney.
1992	Weill acquires a 27 percent stake in Travelers Insurance.
1993	Weill recaptures Shearson from American Express.
1993	Weill buys the remainder of Travelers and assumes the Travelers name.
1997	Travelers buys Salomon Brothers.
1998	Citigroup merger announced; Reed and Weill to become co-CEOs.
1999	Repeal of Glass-Steagall Act legitimizes Citigroup's structure.
2000	Weill wins power struggle with Reed, who agrees to step down as co-CEO in April.
2001	Citigroup continues international expansion, acquiring Mexico's Banamex.
2002	Sandy and Joan announce a $100 million donation to Cornell's Weill Medical Center, their second such gift to the school.

Introduction: Meet Sandy Weill

Calling Sandy Weill a dealmaker is a little like calling Warren Buffett an investor, Bill Gates a techie, or Al Dunlap retired. The statement is true only so far as it goes.

Every now and then, someone redefines the meaning of success—or failure—through the sheer enormity of their achievements or shortcomings. Weill, the chairman and CEO of Citigroup, the largest financial services firm in the world, more than redefined "the deal"; he has come to embody it. And the deal, more so than many other aspects of business, is exhilarating: midnight oil is burned, careers are made and destroyed, stock is swapped, and fortunes made.

Deals are so addictive, in fact, that Weill—who turned 69 in March 2002—keeps making them. He built two business empires literally from scratch, the first culminating with the brokerage house Shearson and the second with financial giant Citigroup. Weill, through a keen eye for value, pure will, and boundless energy, may have fathered more corporate births and presided over more corporate deaths than any other single business executive. Along the way, Weill fired more friends than some people ever make, made more mistakes than most people have ideas, and experienced more triumphs than most people dare dream of.

Fiercely intelligent? Amazingly ambitious? Certainly, and so are most of his competitors, peers, and would-be successors. What separates Weill from his fellow CEOs is a laser-like focus on boosting the bottom line, a keen eye for hiring talented and loyal lieutenants, and prodigious amounts of raw energy and drive.

"I have never met anyone in my life who was better at forcing things to be accomplished—setting a goal and getting it done," says Charles Prince, Citigroup's chief operations officer and one of Weill's most trusted advisors. How does he do it? "Well, he drives us all nuts," says Prince, laughing. Rather than reading memos and reports, Weill favors walking down the hall and asking 20 employees the same question, taking in all their responses, and then making a decision. "He has a 100 percent hands-on focus. And no detail is too big or small."

Weill's associates marvel at his facility with numbers and ability to make difficult decisions quickly—so quickly that he has been called rash and ruthless. "Sandy can tumble numbers in his head like most of us tumble words," says George Murray, who worked with Weill throughout the 1970s. Murray remembers:

We would sit in a room, eight or ten of us, trying to figure out what would happen if we did something. Six people would say, "Give it to my staff and we'll meet next Tuesday." With Sandy, the numbers would go into his head and immediately he knows the answer. That's where, in my view, the tag 'ruthless' comes into play. He's just so far out in front of everyone else. It's not a matter of being ruthless, it's, "Let's not waste a lot of time and let's get the thing done."

The Legend

Earlier in his life, few people would have imagined that Weill would later be called ruthless. Cowed by neighborhood bullies as a child, hazed as a military school plebe, intimidated by Arthur Carter's personality at the brokerage firm of Carter, Berlind, Weill & Levitt (CBWL), Weill has become the most daring deal-maker and assembler of companies on the business landscape.

Today, it is safe to say that Weill is a legend ("for better or worse," his one-time protégé Jamie Dimon, now CEO of Bank One, once put it[1]), both on Wall Street and in executive board-rooms all over the world. During his nearly 50-year career, Weill changed the shape of the business world—but not by dispensing financial wisdom like Buffett, nor by pioneering innovative products like Gates, nor through revolutionary management principles like Jack Welch. Instead, Weill created successful businesses out of smaller, seemingly unworkable pieces; filled product vacuums no one else even realized were void; and forced issues that no one else had the gumption to tackle.

Take, for example, the Financial Services Modernization Act of 1999, a piece of legislation that was passed on the heels of the most audacious deal in Weill's career—the epic 1998 merger of Travelers Group and Citicorp. (Weill was 65 when the deal was completed, an age at which most corporate executives choose to retire or have already been pushed out the door.) The deal was a direct challenge to the decades-old legislation that prohibited companies from selling insurance, issuing securities, and providing banking services under one umbrella. Weill lobbied incessantly—even placing a call to President Clinton just before the deal was announced—until he got what he wanted. A little more than one year after the controversial merger was completed, the financial services laws he had defied were rescinded.

Colleagues say that Weill always comes out on top in various business (not to mention legislative) encounters largely because he is a superior tactician. One high-ranking Citigroup executive likens Weill's strategy to a champion chess player. (Weill, incidentally, plays chess only with his grandson.) Weill, he says, always "thinks three moves ahead," taking pains to conceal his ultimate goal. Each move appears to be independent, without major significance, until the opponent is boxed in. Weill used this strategy most famously in besting his former co-CEO John Reed, who retired in April of 2000, leaving the bank he had run since 1984 to his rival.

Not surprisingly for someone who has waged and won so many corporate battles, the business world is littered with former colleagues and partners who aren't so enamored of Sandy Weill. Former partners and protégés who seem to have mixed feelings about him include: Arthur Carter, publisher of the *New York Observer;* Arthur Levitt Jr., former Securities and Exchange Commission chairman; James Robinson, former CEO of American Express; Bank One CEO Dimon; and Reed.

But there are many others, especially brokers who have experienced his hard-nosed entrepreneurial style, to whom Weill is a hero. In an interview with the authors, Weill said he has three heroes: Isaac Stern, one of the twentieth century's foremost violinists whom Weill worked with on restoring Carnegie Hall in the mid-1980s; Tubby Burnham, who took a young Weill under his wing at the brokerage Burnham & Co.; and former New York Jets owner Sonny Werblin, a Weill friend and client for years, about whom Weill says, "I thought he was a great dreamer. He had a lot of life and he really made things happen."

Weill amassed a great personal fortune, estimated in 2002 to be $1.4 billion.[2] Recently, there has been a backlash concerning CEO pay, and in 1998, the year he made $168 million, he was frequently chided in the press for being overpaid. He shrugged it off. After all, throughout his career, Weill championed the concept of employee stock ownership. It's a philosophy that made him and many of his long-term employees very rich.

It was also a key to motivating people, according to Ed Budd, CEO of Travelers when Weill acquired it:

> One of the traits that people don't fully appreciate about Sandy is that he really wants people to have fun working. People know he is intense. They know he is demanding. But when we would have issues and problems to solve, Sandy would say, "We have to give everybody more stock. They have to have more fun around here." He believes a company has to make some money and people have to be rewarded.

Sandy and Joan, who married in 1955, have rewarded themselves with an eight-acre estate in Greenwich, Connecticut (with an 8,000-bottle wine cellar), a penthouse apartment on Park Avenue in Manhattan, and an Adirondack retreat, which they enhanced with a glassed-in swimming pool with a view of Upper Saranac Lake. Despite the trappings, it is unlikely that money is today a primary motivator for Weill. "It's just a way of keeping score," says Richard Bove, a long-time banking analyst with the research boutique Hoefer & Arnett, who has worked with Weill in the past.

Indeed, Sandy and Joan devote considerable time now to giving their money away. The Weills have made two separate $100 million pledges to the medical school of his alma mater, Cornell, which has been renamed the Joan and Sanford I. Weill Medical College. He is also chairman of the board of Carnegie Hall and founder and chairman of The National Academy Foundation, a nonprofit organization that helps steer high school students toward careers in finance, information technology, and travel and tourism.

Weill has also ensured that Citigroup reflects his commitment to philanthropy. For instance, after the September 11 terrorist attacks on the World Trade Center and the Pentagon, Citigroup established a $20 million college fund for children of the victims.

The couple's charitable work makes them a fixture on the New York City social circuit. For example, on December 2, 2001, the couple, resplendent in black-tie and evening gown, were featured in two photos from separate events in the Sunday Styles section of the *New York Times*.

Weill seems to love the limelight, be it the Citigroup annual shareholders meeting, a Carnegie Hall fundraiser, or one of his annual "surprise" birthday parties arranged by Prince, Citigroup's COO. It wasn't always that way. Profound shyness, in fact, prevented Weill from taking center stage early in his career. "He could not get up and speak before 20 branch managers," says George Murray. "He just couldn't do it." At first, that is. Ultimately, Weill forced himself to get up and speak publicly, and eventually excelled at it. "It was painful," Murray says, "but he made himself do it."

High school friend Winston Kulok says, "Sandy was very likeable, very affable. He was a very self-contained guy from the start. Because of his reputation, people think he's a shark. I never saw him that way at all."

In fact, a constant refrain from business associates is that Weill is decidedly *un*shark-like in his personal manners, working style, and everyday demeanor. Even his infamous outbursts and penchant for berating peers and underlings, while distasteful, reveal not shark-like calculation but grizzly-like passion and aggressiveness. With his plainspoken style, Weill has been underestimated for much of his career—to his great benefit.

On Wall Street, where family connections, advanced academic degrees, and classic good looks go a long way, Weill never had these advantages. In the corporate suite, Weill was neither a precocious wunderkind like Reed nor a patrician chief executive like Robinson. He is neither tall nor svelte. Although he works out with a personal trainer several mornings a week and boasts excellent health, he struggles to keep his weight in check. An old joke about Weill is "If you happen to notice his waistline expanding, you can bet he's working on a big deal."

Weill insists that a key to his success has been his honest and straightforward (although not unemotional) approach to deal-making. Often, he has walked away from negotiations, when he felt the other side was attempting to strong-arm him. Weill says that even then, the door to opportunity never really closed. "I would think that if you went and spoke to the people we did our deals with, 99 percent of them, or maybe 100 percent would think they were treated very well, that it was fair, that we kept our word, and they would do another deal with us," Weill told *Directors and Boards* magazine in 1998. "And I think that if you don't leave that kind of impression, the next deal is not going to be there."[3]

Business: A Family Affair

Weill, perhaps more so than any other CEO, integrates the personal, professional, and social. The approach has worked on many levels: Coworkers become part of the family, loyal to Weill and ready to support the next acquisition plan he hatches. Also, he has employed both of his children at high levels of Citigroup, though each has left in recent years.

The involvement in Weill's business dealings of the popular and charming Joan (personal acquaintances invariably describe her as "terrific," while the word used most often for Sandy is "tough") has softened some of her husband's harder edges. Unlike many successful business executives, whose marriages crumble under the work and stress, Sandy and Joan's marriage has endured, perhaps because Joan Weill is a true partner. E. D.

Donahey, the exwife of Weill's son, Marc, describes Joan as Sandy's "partner in all respects."

Not only does Joan excel at all the traditional duties of a corporate wife, but she is also a reliable sounding board. "I think there are very few major business decisions that he doesn't ask her opinion on," says Prince.

The workplace as hearth and home has manifested itself in many ways for Weill, from Joan's involvement with important business decisions to the photograph of his boyhood home hanging on his office wall to his affinity for office fireplaces (he now mocks the endless media references to them with a cardboard fireplace in his office at Citigroup).

Mixing work and family isn't always the best recipe, however. Weill's daughter, Jessica Bibliowicz, left Citigroup in 1998, partly because she clashed with her father's protégé Dimon. Marc Weill, formerly head of Citigroup's investment business, took a leave of absence in July of 2001 and has not returned. According to the *Wall Street Journal*, Weill asked Marc, who served on Citigroup's management committee, to seek help for a drug addiction.[4]

Outside of the office, colleagues suspect that Weill has few interests. Those hobbies Weill does enjoy usually combine work and play. He is an avid golfer and frequently flies business associates down to Augusta National Golf Club, the annual site of the Masters tournament and the most exclusive country club in the country. Weill's aptitude for the game falls somewhere between that of near scratch golfer Jack Welch and hopeless hacker Bill Gates.

In perhaps his one concession to age, Weill is less passionate about the game of tennis these days, but was a champion player as a youth and continued to play with business associates through much of his career. One Shearson branch manager, several years younger than Weill, recalls playing tennis with him a few times in the 1970s. "He was just as you'd imagine—very competitive, but levelheaded, not in any way a poor sport," he says. Joan also plays tennis, but like many married couples, they apparently found playing tennis together trying. "We prefer to keep the marriage going," was how Joan once put it.[5]

Boyhood

Various journalists have tried to dismiss Sandy Weill's rags-to-riches story, which is essentially how he has portrayed his upbringing in interviews over the years. While he did not have a hardscrabble boyhood, the fact remains that Weill grew up in a modest house in Bensonhurst, Brooklyn, with his grandparents—who fled Russian-occupied Poland after the Jewish pogroms of 1905 to 1907—as well as his parents, a sister, an aunt, and an uncle.

Journalists have credited Sandy's father, Mac, with stoking Sandy's hunger for business success. But it was Philip Kalika, Sandy's grandfather, who seems to have really planted this seed, founding and running a dressmaking company for 40 years. In the Kalika home, business was clearly a family affair, and Philip helped Mac launch his own dressmaking business, Kalika & Weill.

This family atmosphere continued after Weill was sent to Peekskill Military Academy, where the boarding school culture mixed school work with athletics and marching drills. Academic or disciplinary problems were solved over dinner at teachers' on-campus homes. PMA, with strict discipline and a clear system for rewarding accomplishment, was a formative experience for Weill.

Weill made his way through Cornell—joining the tennis team, playing poker with his fraternity brothers, and majoring in government—and then embarked on his career. He got off to a slow start. Established Anglo-Saxon and German Jewish firms on Wall Street rejected Weill's application to their training programs.

After starting as a low level messenger on Wall Street and then working for five years as a broker, Weill started his own firm in 1960. Even then, he immediately showed an ability to surround himself with extraordinarily talented individuals. Among his early partners were current entrepreneur and publisher Arthur Carter, Broadway producer Roger Berlind, businessman Marshall Cogan, and former SEC chairman Arthur Levitt.

A Career Overview

Weill's firm, CBWL—or "Corned Beef With Lettuce" as it was derisively referred to by some—employed an unusual recipe for success. Small, contained, and well-capitalized, the brokerage bucked the Wall Street trend of overexpansion and inefficient back office operations. Weill was fortunate that his firm started on Wall Street at a time when there was ample opportunity for new companies, as some bloated old-line partnerships were starting to buckle under their own weight.

In 1970, CBWL's bid to buy the 100-year-old brokerage firm Hayden Stone was approved only hours before the patrician firm was to be dissolved for insolvency. Weill and his partners purchased a firm 10 times their size. The once-tiny firm became an acquisition machine, and the Hayden Stone deal became the prototype: Buy a struggling company with a prestigious name on the cheap, adopt its brand name, close underperforming divisions, integrate its operations into the existing infrastructure, and slash costs.

Weill became CEO of Hayden Stone in 1973, in the midst of one of the toughest times the securities industry has ever known. But by running a fine-tuned, well-capitalized operation, Weill was able to seize opportunities as larger firms floundered. The firm doubled in size after the 1974 purchase of Shearson Hamill. It doubled again when Shearson Hayden Stone purchased Loeb Rhoades in 1979, becoming Shearson Loeb Rhoades.

After 14 deals, CBWL had become Shearson, the second-biggest brokerage on Wall Street. In an interview, Weill describes his evolution as a businessman this way:

> My original interest was retail when we started the company, retail customers. But then it broadened out into doing research and then it broadened out into doing investment banking. Then it broadened out into trying to build the company rather than just working on deals for other clients.

Weill decided to sell Shearson to American Express in 1981, joining the AmEx management team and becoming a millionaire many times over. But as third in line to CEO James Robinson III, he became, in a phrase he made famous, a "deputy dog."

In 1983, Weill was named president of American Express. But it was the wrong job for Weill, who felt he didn't have enough to do. He chafed under Robinson, struggled to get deals done, and handed off his beloved Shearson to protégé Peter Cohen, losing his power base within the firm. Eager to run the show again and realizing he had little chance of supplanting Robinson in the near-term, Weill quit in 1985.

Weill left American Express accompanied by Dimon, his number-crunching right-hand man. They started looking for the right opportunity to build another empire. Weill tried to take a shortcut back to the top, offering to run the struggling Bank-America in early 1986, but his bold and unconventional bid was never taken seriously by the bank's board.

Instead, in 1986 Weill became CEO of Commercial Credit, then a failing consumer credit company based in Baltimore.

The deal seemed below Weill's station. "No one would have thought Commercial Credit could ultimately become the parent company of something like Citigroup," recalls analyst Bove. "The fact that he saw the opportunity in that company just blows my mind."

During the next 12 years, Weill dazzled the business world, as he turned around Commercial Credit and used it as a base for building a massive financial services conglomerate. In 1988, Weill purchased Primerica, which owned the retail brokerage Smith Barney, putting him back in the securities business. Then Weill acquired part of Travelers Insurance and bought back the ailing Shearson from American Express. The rest of Travelers soon followed, and in 1997 Weill acquired the volatile investment bank Salomon Brothers. Amazing as this litany of purchases was, it would all prove just a warm-up for what was to come.

The merger of Citicorp and Travelers (or, as one former Citigrouper put it, "the so-called merger; it was a takeover of Citicorp by Travelers") shocked the business world when it was announced in the spring of 1998, a time of tremendous global consolidation in the financial services industry. Not only was it monstrous in size—at $70 billion it dwarfed any other deal in history—but it was in clear violation of federal securities law. Furthermore, the co-CEO structure Weill and Reed adopted to get the deal done struck most observers as unworkable from the start.

They were right. Even though Reed and Weill's relationship started smoothly enough, tension quickly pervaded the offices of the co-chairmen. Weill was hands-on, Reed was aloof. Reed was intellectual and visionary, Weill was hard-nosed and bottom-line oriented. Efforts to work together, including bringing in former Treasury Secretary Robert Rubin as a third voice in the offices of the chairmen, ultimately failed. Finally, following a historic Citigroup boardroom showdown in early 2000, Reed resigned and Weill took up the reins on his own.

With full control, Weill has remade Citigroup in his image, claiming that "our core competency is acquisitions." As he said in his "Chairman's Letter to Shareholders" in the 2000 annual report, "Few companies that have led the world in earnings would be described as a work in progress. The fact is, we are."

As always, the key to Weill's acquisitions is that he is a fiscal conservative. But there is the possibility that Weill's inability to resist a good deal may come back to haunt him. In September 2000, Weill closed his most controversial acquisition at Citigroup, a deal to buy Associates First Capital. The company has been accused in the past of preying on low-income families with high-interest loans. (Citigroup has since denied that Associates was involved in predatory lending.) He has also expanded aggressively into emerging markets by buying Banamex, Mexico's number two bank in 2001, at a time when the global economy was weakening.

Belief in Weill's judgment, however, is an article of faith in the financial services industry. Thomas Hanley, a longtime banking analyst now with Friedman, Billings, Ramsey & Co., is betting that both deals will ultimately prove a triumph for Weill. "This is one shrewd man," Hanley says. "I go back a long way and I've never met anybody like him. He's awesome—in his power, his managerial skills, but also in his shrewdness."

Citigroup Today

Citigroup reaches across the financial world in a way no single institution has ever done. The firm operates in more than 100 countries, has 250,000 employees, and holds assets in excess of $1.5 trillion. In 2001, worldwide revenues approached $84 billion and profits neared $15 billion, making it one of the most profitable corporations in the world.

In such a huge company, problems inevitably arise: Citibank, albeit before Weill's era, was linked to scandals such as money laundering for Russian mobsters and helping the brother of former Mexican President Carlos Salinas salt away millions of ill-gotten gains.[6] Weill has had trouble retaining key executives at Citigroup, something analysts who follow the company have fretted about. Several key individuals, most notably Dimon—fired by Weill and Reed—but also CFO Heidi Miller and co-COO Jay Fishman have left in recent years. Citigroup also faces intensive global competition, regulatory and legal hurdles, overlapping and obsolete technology platforms in some subsidiaries, and intense media and government scrutiny.

There are those who believe that the very *existence* of Citigroup poses a major risk to the United States and its citizens. According to this argument, huge global banks like Citigroup have become "too big to fail." If Citigroup somehow teetered toward bankruptcy, the thinking goes, the U.S. government would be obliged to stave off widespread financial panic by bailing it out, leaving taxpayers to foot the bill.

As long as Weill continues to manage these risks as well as he has, he will likely remain at the helm of Citigroup. Each day he strides into 399 Park Avenue at 7:30 A.M. wearing a business suit and a bright, umbrella-print necktie, ready to strike a deal. It's clear that Weill relishes the action, challenge, attention, and celebrity of the top job—and has little intention of stepping down anytime soon.

"He's not going anywhere—unless something extraordinary happens," says Jeff Lane, CEO of the money management firm Neuberger Berman and former Weill lieutenant. "And as an investor in Citi, I'm not sure it's in my best interest to have him go anywhere."

The Past Is Gone.
The Future Is Limitless

Their respective presentations delivered, their visions for the future of Citigroup outlined, Sandy Weill and John Reed sat alone together, tensely watching television at Citigroup's 399 Park Avenue headquarters in New York City. The day was Sunday, February 27, 2000. Weill and Reed, co-CEOs since the historic merger of Travelers and Citicorp 16 months earlier, had called a special board meeting because their vastly different styles and disintegrating relationship were hurting the company. Even Citigroup's largest shareholder, Prince Alwaleed bin Talal of Saudi Arabia, had recently expressed concerns that the two couldn't work together. The joint leadership arrangement was clearly failing and Weill and Reed each came to the meeting with a solution to the problem.

Reed, 61, made his presentation first. His view was that the time had come to find a successor. He and Weill had forged a new company out of the merger and should gracefully bow out together. Weill, 66, told the board that he wanted to stay and put his imprint on the sprawling firm. Anyone who knew Weill or followed his career might have predicted that would be Weill's take on the situation.

Forty years earlier the Brooklyn-born, scrappy Weill had started a small brokerage firm with three other brokers. Now, after a lifetime of deals and achievements he stood on the verge of running—on his own—the Holy Grail of financial services. Reed, the cold, brilliant engineer, was no stranger to board-room duels, of course; he had run Citicorp for 14 years before the merger with Travelers. But he had never faced an adversary like Weill.

Over the past several months, the relationship between Weill and Reed had become so strained that they could barely tolerate one another's presence. Now, awaiting their fate together, Weill and Reed took solace in one of the few things they had left in common: golf. Superstar Tiger Woods was playing Darren Clarke of Northern Ireland head-to-head in the World Match Play Championship. In match play, the winner moves on to face the next challenge; the loser goes home.

Reed and Weill, embroiled in their own high stakes match, weren't the only ones nervously waiting. Ex-Treasury Secretary Robert Rubin, who had been hired at Citigroup several months earlier to act as a peacekeeper of sorts between Weill and Reed, sat in another room watching the New York Knicks play the Philadelphia 76ers. Rubin, perhaps suspecting that his judgment would be called on to help make the final decision, steered clear of Weill and Reed.

Back in the boardroom, director Franklin Thomas led the debate, which dragged on for over eight hours. The board was having so much trouble deciding what to do that at it one point a director proposed that Rubin, the former head of Goldman Sachs, take the CEO job. He refused, saying the company would best be served with Weill at the helm.

"It was very tense," Weill said in an interview with the authors. "I think we tried to make it less tense, but obviously it was tense and nobody knew what was going to happen." At one point, Weill and Reed were summoned individually to the boardroom. "One of the directors asked John to go in and then one of them asked me to go in and they asked me some questions," Weill says. When Reed was called into the boardroom, Thomas asked him if he would stay on for a year in a ceremonial chairman post. Reed declined. For the second time that afternoon, the board had one of their proposals turned down.

Eventually, the board was running out of scenarios, save one: Weill would lead the company on his own. A board member entered the room where the two co-CEOs watched the golf tournament and told them that Weill would soon take over as sole chairman and chief executive officer of the massive financial services conglomerate. Reed would resign. Just like that it was over.

A statement was released in Reed's name announcing his resignation: "My decision was a deliberate one that I have discussed fully with the board, and I leave the company knowing we have put into place a truly outstanding management team and a sound strategy."

"It was obviously a very emotional time and John was a perfect gentleman," Weill said in an interview. "He was extremely cooperative, a great gentleman."

Weill's graciousness notwithstanding, his triumph was nothing short of astounding. It had been under two years since he first thought seriously about buying a bank. Now he had displaced one of the most well-known and highly respected bankers in the United States and was running the country's biggest financial services company. As Winston Kulok, a high school friend, puts it, "Think about it. A regular guy from Brooklyn outfoxed John Reed."

A Done Deal

Weill's favorite response to inquiries about the co-CEO arrangement during the prior 16 months—"I'm a lot happier with John in the organization than not"—belied his ambition to run the company his way. To Weill, Reed and other managers of the former Citicorp must have stood as living symbols of fiscal laxness: a culture defined by ubiquitous and costly bank branches dotting the streets of major cities, excessive spending on experimental technologies, generous benefits, and few restrictions on business travel and expenses. Once firmly in control, Weill set about doing what he always had done after a merger: putting his people in place, cutting costs, and dismantling perceived boondoggles.

Even though few on Wall Street expected the co-CEO arrangement to work, given Weill's age and Reed's tenacious hold on power, few industry executives, members of the press, or even executives involved in the deal would have bet that Weill would ultimately ascend to the top spot. Even more to the point, perhaps no one quite understood that for Weill, this huge merger was not the peak achievement of his long career, but instead something closer to his heart: a chance to reinvent himself once again.

In the spring of 1998, even as details about the upcoming merger with Citicorp percolated in his head, Weill summed up his feelings about achievement:

I don't view anything we have done, any acquisition, any achievement, as an end, only as a building block for the future. We always get to a point and throw the rope out a little further and then throw it out a little further again. You can't stop doing that. You can't stop looking ahead, thinking a little bit about doing something differently. You've got to look at something as a building block for the future. Not the end in itself, but as a way to create a new future.[1]

A Talent for Reinvention

Throughout his life, Weill has never hesitated in creating a new future for himself. If you were to draw an arc of Weill's nearly 50-year career, an accurate picture would consist not of one great, glorious sweep, but a series of slowly building peaks and modest valleys marking Weill's many victories and occasional setbacks. The graph would show that Weill has had his share of slumps, particularly in the mid-1980s when he quit as the president of American Express and took nearly a year to find his next deal.

But if you examined the chart a little closer, you'd find a sharp spike after every setback, an indicator that after defeat Weill came back more determined than ever, even if it meant starting over from scratch. It is this legendary ability to create—a new company, a new persona, a new brand—that distinguishes Weill from less celebrated CEOs.

The talent for reinvention is often viewed as a quintessentially American trait. But Weill's gift was brought to the shores of America from Russian-occupied Poland and handed down to him by two remarkable people—his maternal grandparents, Etta and Philip Kalika.

Coming to America

In the first decade of the twentieth century, Jews in Poland faced a deadly new strain of anti-Semitism and grew more and more desperate to escape.

Spurred by the first Russian Revolution, the pogroms of 1905 to 1907 terrorized Jewish residents in hundreds of towns and cities in Russia and "Congress Poland," the area of Poland incorporated into the Russian Empire when the country was partitioned late in the eighteenth century among Russia, Austria, and Prussia. Numerous Jewish families were massacred in Poland during this extraordinary outburst of hatred. The number of Jewish emigrants from the Russian Empire to the United States jumped from 74,000 in 1904 to more than 100,000 in 1906 and 1907.

Philip Kalika and Riwe Schwartz came from the small village of Sierpc, 70 miles northwest of Warsaw. Sierpc was one of the few Jewish strongholds in rural Poland, which at the time was 90 percent Catholic. With just 7,000 people at the start of the twentieth century, Sierpc lay within the heart of Congress Poland. So Philip and Riwe, despite their Polish ancestry, were not Polish but Russian citizens.

Philip and Riwe married and Philip immigrated to the United States and established his own dressmaking company. Philip sent for his wife and their three young children in 1908. Riwe and her children made it to Liverpool, England, most likely by train, where they boarded the Umbria, one of the oldest and by far the slowest steamships in the famous Cunard line. After a 10-day journey, the Umbria arrived at New York Harbor on June 11, 1908, one of 23 steamships and merchant ships that landed there on that busy day. It was still daylight when the Umbria made port with Riwe, her children, and the other 383 passengers.

They had started a new life in the United States, and neither Philip nor Riwe ever went back to Sierpc again. During the Holocaust, the Nazis went from village to village in rural Poland rounding up Jews, killing many and shipping others off to the death camps. Today, according to official records, the Jewish population of Sierpc—like many Polish towns that once had significant Jewish populations—is zero.

When Riwe arrived at Ellis Island for processing, she had $1.50 to her name. Accompanying her were her six-year-old son, Lieb, three-year-old daughter, Ettel, the future mother of Sandy Weill, and two-year-old daughter, Rachel. Like many immigrants, they Americanized their first names. Riwe became Rebecca, Lieb became Louis, and Ettel became Etta. Philip and Rebecca had two more children in the United States, Irving and Rose.

As did many Polish immigrants in New York at the time, the Kalikas settled in Brooklyn, eventually buying a large home in Bensonhurst in 1919. The purchase must have been a triumph. The large, two-family structure has a crow's nest on the third floor and a small front yard and a larger side yard. Throughout his career, Weill has kept a photo of his childhood home in his office.

On February 27, 1926, Philip incorporated his company, P. Kalika, and named himself and three others as directors. Louis, now 24, joined his father in the business, as did two others, a married couple from Manhattan. The articles of incorporation for the Manhattan company described its purpose as the "business of jobbing, manufacturing, producing, repairing, buying, and selling and otherwise dealing in all kinds of wearing apparel." The four directors divided 350 shares of common stock at $100 apiece, giving the company a value of $35,000. It was certainly an odd board of directors: a father and son and a married couple. Yet, P. Kalika became a very successful business, and Philip's death on April 29, 1954 warranted an obituary in the *New York Times*. Making business a family affair worked for Philip Kalika, and he would pass that ethic on to his grandson, Sandy Weill, who would later use it to his great benefit.

Lessons Handed Down

Weill grew up in the same house as his grandparents, and surely knew well their story of fearlessness, ambition, and pursuit of a better life. In an interview, Weill affirmed that his grandfather was an important figure in his childhood.

What did he learn from Philip Kalika? Perhaps to be decisive and unsentimental about change, even when personal allegiances came into play. Perhaps he learned to be generous to his greater community. Perhaps he learned to integrate family and business, which he carried to his own life by so heavily involving his wife and children in his business dealings. But most of all, perhaps he learned to let go of the past and start anew—something Weill has managed to do countless times in his career.

It is likely that Etta, Sandy's mother, learned from Philip and Rebecca—her parents—as well. She went to school, started a career, and became a U.S. citizen as soon as she could. On her application for citizenship in 1923, Etta listed her profession as "bookkeeper." She was slight, just five-foot tall and 100 pounds, with brown hair and brown eyes. It would not be long before she would meet and marry Max Weill, generally known as "Mac," with whom she would have two children, Helen and Sanford. To say that her son, born on March 16, 1933, would inherit Etta's apparent affinity for working with numbers would be an understatement.

Banking and the Great Depression

The early months of 1933 marked the nadir of the Great Depression and the worst period in history for the nation's banks. Unemployment peaked at 25 percent, and the nation's economic output had dropped by nearly a third. During the first few days of March, a particularly dramatic bank run took place in Michigan, with depositors resorting to panic unseen since the first decade of the 1900s—showing up at their bank and demanding cash. Like Frank Capra's widows and farmers populating the fictional Bedford Falls in *It's a Wonderful Life,* they formed long lines at their local branches to collect their savings.

No institution epitomized banking's troubles more than the National City Bank, the precursor of today's Citibank, which opened in 1812. In February 1933, the bank's president, Charles Mitchell, soon to face tax evasion charges, was the Senate Banking Committee's lead witness in hearings to gauge the culpability of the industry in bringing about the Depression. Although historians today find many other causes for the length and severity of the Great Depression—including some ill-advised moves by the new Federal Reserve, which hiked interest rates instead of cutting them—banks then bore the brunt of the blame, for transgressions both real and imagined.

Mitchell and other prominent bankers were forced to resign. They were pursued with criminal charges. One Senator from Montana proposed that the best way to clean up the banking industry "is to take these crooked presidents out of banks and treat them the same as they treated Al Capone when Capone avoided payment of his tax."[2]

When Franklin D. Roosevelt took office on March 4, 1933, restoring order to the nation's banks was his first priority. To halt the number of failing institutions, President Roosevelt took the unprecedented step of closing all American banks on March 6. His plan to certify the soundness of every bank was welcomed after more than three years of perceived inaction on the part of the Hoover Administration. Before they could open, banks were required to have their soundness affirmed by federal or state authorities.

Banks were eventually punished harshly through legislation passed later in 1933. The landmark Glass-Steagall Act—enacted the year Weill was born—was one of the defining pieces of financial legislation in American history. More than just a law, the Act was a regulatory broadside at the banking industry. It divided the financial world into investment banks, which underwrote and traded securities, and commercial banks, which took in deposits and lent companies money.

The law would stand essentially unchanged for 65 years until Weill devised the epic merger that created Citigroup and pushed Congress to repeal the anachronistic legislation.

Depression-Era Baby

Despite the gloom of the era, on March 16 good news leapt off the pages of the morning papers. The majority of the nation's banks had been successfully certified and reopened. In New York, for example, out of the 585 banks that were members of the Federal Reserve, 473 had reopened.[3] Also, Congress passed the "beer bill," ending prohibition by legalizing the sale of beer and wine with low alcohol content. This news was met with spontaneous celebrations around the country.

For Etta and Mac Weill, however, the glad tidings on this clear, cold day in Brooklyn, New York, had much more to do with the birth of their first child, Sanford I. Weill. Etta gave Sandy the middle initial without it standing for any particular name. "How did it happen?" Weill said in an interview. "Maybe the same way it happened to Harry S. Truman. My mother wanted to name me after somebody whose name started with an 'I,' but she couldn't think of a name she liked. So she gave me the initial with the idea that after I was 21 I could choose whatever middle name I wanted." Weill never did get around to it.

The addition of a new baby made for close quarters. The Weill family shared the large house on Bay 26th Street with the extended Kalika clan (both the 1933 and 1939 Brooklyn city directories show that living in the two-story home were Mac and Etta, Philip and Rebecca, Etta's sister Rose, and Etta's brother Irv, a student at that point). Sandy's birth also must have added pressure on the family financial situation, which was still tenuous in 1933. At that point, Mac longed to start his own business. While the Depression had ground industry to a stop in much of the country, Brooklyn was still an industrial giant. The teeming borough had more than 37,000 stores, 5,000 manufacturing plants, 26 freight terminals connecting to 14 railroads, and piers berthing ships from more than 70 steamship lines. There was business to be done, and Mac was ready to make his fortune.

Dressmaking: The Family Business

It was his father-in-law's dressmaking connections that would help Mac launch his first business. Louis Kalika and Mac started Kalika and Weill Dress Manufacturers together in 1936. The business operated out of 501 Seventh Avenue, in the heart of the garment district. The fact that Weill's father got his start from his father-in-law should be no surprise. Not only were many immigrant Jews at that time involved with the "rag trade," but Polish Jews were particularly known for comingling family, business, and religious ties.

That first year in which Kalika and Weill started doing business was a tumultuous one for the dressmaking industry. Just five days after the company opened, one of the biggest nationwide garment strikes in history took place. Despite President Roosevelt's request to the nation to avoid labor unrest during the Depression, 10,000 garment workers went on strike on November 10 as part of a coordinated campaign for higher wages and better working conditions. On the same day in Washington, D.C., the International Ladies' Garment Workers Union committed $500,000 to organize a nationwide lobbying campaign for labor legislation. Garment workers, mostly women, were extremely low paid. In one November strike that year in Bayonne, New Jersey, workers' demands included a 35-hour work week, a minimum of $44 per week for cutters, $1.25 an hour for pressers, and 85 cents an hour for operators.

The turbulent time was a harbinger of sorts for Mac Weill's business career. Mac was in and out of business, as well as in and out of trouble, during Sandy's childhood. Kalika and Weill Dress Manufacturers eventually became Hilma Women's Dresses, with Mac as president. In 1944, when Sandy was 11, Mac pled guilty to wartime price gouging, violating federal Office of Price Administration rules. Hilma Women's Dresses had overcharged retail shops $8,129 on "materials for women's low-priced dresses."[4] Mac received a $10,000 fine—which he managed to pay in three installments over several months—and a suspended three-year prison term. The real financial toll on Mac and his family, however, resulted from a civil action by the retailers who bought the materials. On April 12, 1944, Mac settled out of court, agreeing to pay the shops a sum total of three times the price he had overcharged them, which came to $24,389.16. Mac soon left the dressmaking business for good.

Mac Weill may have been a victim of bad timing or bad luck, or he simply may have been a bad businessman. But one thing is clear: Sandy Weill's business approach and success more closely resembles his maternal grandfather's than his father's. Weill retained great affection for his father throughout his life, even employing Mac part-time after he had retired. But if he learned anything from his father, it was most likely what not to do.

Weill—by every account—is straightforward in both his business dealings and his personal life.

Shaped by Military School

Weill has characterized his Brooklyn boyhood as rough-and-tumble. He delivered newspapers and played stickball. It was obvious even then he liked winners. His favorite baseball team was the New York Yankees, who played in the Bronx and inevitably clobbered "Dem Bums" from Brooklyn in the World Series year after year. He has said he was a mediocre student in the public schools he attended, was a "sissy," and that his mother would rescue him from fights on the streets of Bensonhurst. Weill said that avoiding rather than embracing confrontation, as he now so famously does, only "postponed the inevitable."[5]

But those days ended when, perhaps because of Mac's arrest or perhaps because of Mac's new steel-importing venture, the family moved to Miami Beach, Florida, in 1945. Weill later described the move as a disaster and said he did poorly in school there. After two years, the family moved back to Brooklyn, settling in their own house on 12th Avenue, near the boundary of Flatbush and Borough Park.

In the fall of 1947, Weill was sent to Peekskill Military Academy (PMA), a well-known boarding school not far from the U.S. Military Academy at West Point. The school's slogan was, "Quit You Not."

Peekskill is a town on the Hudson River about 30 miles north of New York City. Arriving students and their parents would drive into the center of the town, turn on Hudson Avenue at the train station, drive up the hill two miles or so from the river to the gates of the school. The yellow bricks that, for a time, adorned Hudson Avenue inspired former PMA student L. Frank Baum's famous Yellow Brick Road in his novel *The Wizard of Oz*.

The 53-acre campus, which closed in 1968, is today occupied by the town's public high school, an institutional gray building without charm. PMA's five impressive brick buildings, all but one of which was razed in 1969, were centered on the northern and western edges of the campus. The teachers at PMA lived in a row of well-kept cottages along the eastern edge of the campus. While very little physical evidence remains of PMA, the most important feature of the school to many alumni still stands. The iconic figure of PMA was the Old Oak, where an American spying for the British was hanged on January 27, 1776. The historic tree, which stands at what was the center of the parade ground, is today fortified by supporting cables.

Military school may seem a strange choice for a middle-class Jew from Brooklyn. But it was not necessarily seen as punishment, and many students, like Weill, were sent there because of family discord. "I think she [Etta Weill] thought this was a place to get a good education and maybe learn about life," says David Miller, who was one year behind Weill at PMA. "In those days, military education was not viewed as something punitive. The classes were small, and you got a ton of one-on-one attention."

Stuart Fendler, one of Weill's roommates at PMA, says that many of the boys sent to PMA were in need of either reining in or building up. "We went there because every kid was a problem," he says. "I was a hyper type of kid. Sandy's parents had a marriage that wasn't going too well." Miller recalled that Weill's mother sent Sandy to PMA so he would be removed from the marital discord at home. Mac and Etta Weill's marriage would eventually unravel completely during Weill's last year of college.

The time period in which Weill attended PMA, immediately following World War II, was marked by intense Cold War rhetoric, and the military aspect of such a school was taken very seriously.

In the strict military regime in place at the school, the boys wore their uniforms at all times. In fact, they were not even allowed civilian clothes on campus. The youngest students at the school— seven- and eight-year-olds—were given toy rifles made out of wood so they, too, could practice the drills and maneuvers. First call was at 6:45 A.M., reveille at 6:55, morning formation at 7:05, and breakfast at 7:15. Classes ran until 3 P.M., followed by athletics and additional military activities from 3 P.M. until 6 P.M. After dinner, students were in study hall from 7 P.M. until 9 P.M., then had an hour of free time before lights out at 10 P.M.

According to fellow students at the school, Weill embraced the routine. He thrived under the regimented system of defined activities and a strict system of tangible awards for every achievement. As plebes, though, the first hurdle was the brutal hazing by older cadets. "At that time there was some very serious hazing," Fendler says. "Sandy shrugged it off. He hung right in there."

The four years he spent at PMA were defining ones for Weill. He found a niche in several activities at the school, and excelled academically. Perhaps most important, he was rescued from having to watch his parents' marriage deteriorate. It seems Weill found a second home among the students and teachers at PMA.

Tennis Champ and Drum Major

Weill quickly made a name for himself in the classroom, on the tennis court, and as a drum major in the band. He developed an uncanny ability to assess his surroundings and do what it took to rise to the top—a skill that came in handy in the business world.

"Sandy was smart. He looked around and figured out how to get ahead here," David Miller recalls. "There were three big things: grades, sports, and the band. Sandy got good grades. But Sandy wasn't much of a musician, and he didn't play contact sports. So he decided to get ahead by doing whatever he could in these areas." For example, he took up the bass drum. "It's not too hard to bang that drum, but he kept good tempo," says Miller. "I can still see him leading the battalion. He was a very determined type of person."

Weill himself believes that PMA was a major influence on him. He said in an interview, "The academy was great for me. The discipline was important and the success I had there did give me a lot of confidence."

A significant achievement was Weill's tennis prowess. PMA prized athletic skill, with swimming the most important sport (amazingly enough, the tiny school produced several national champions and a 1964 Olympic gold medalist). No swimmer, Weill knew that he had to develop some kind of athletic skill. Ironically enough, after two years spent in Florida without picking the sport up, Weill chose to devote himself to tennis. His senior year he won the Westchester public/private school championship, and was invited to try out for the Eastern U.S. Junior Davis Cup team.

"We both picked up the game at the Academy," Fendler said. "We just hit ball after ball. We'd just keep playing. I could never beat Sandy in tennis. I wanted to beat Sandy in everything we did. But I couldn't." That competition extended to academics, which came easily to Weill in his new environment. As Fendler recalls, "He got the As, I got the Bs. He wasn't a grind either; he didn't study much at all." Weill earned high honors in algebra, geometry, science, Latin, and French. As a senior, he was one of five students named to the National Honor Society.

Weill emerged as one of the leaders of the school, becoming an "officer" in both his junior and senior years. He was a second lieutenant his junior year and a first lieutenant his senior year. Only eight students in the school served as officers at any given time, making student officer positions both coveted and respected. Weill later said about the school, "I tried harder because of the discipline and competition."[6]

Weill would later mirror the PMA approach of providing tangible rewards for achievements when running his own business. "It wasn't like other schools," his friend Fendler said. "Everything was based on achievement. If you accomplished something, you were awarded a rank. The discipline, the military atmosphere, it just formed you."

Being an officer also meant that Weill had to be, at times, fairly stern and serious with his non-officer classmates and the underclassmen. The student corps, though it had an adult commandant, was largely self-governing, according to several PMA graduates. That meant Weill, like the other officers, inspected other students' uniforms, made sure they attended formation, and held room inspections. If someone failed an inspection, Weill handed out a demerit, which the unlucky student would have to work off by shining a brass doorknob or other such task.

But Weill had a sense of humor as well. As a member of the yearbook staff his senior year, "Duck" Weill (as he signed himself) penned the senior class "Last Will and Testament," a humorous send-up of his fellow graduates.

Searching for Lox in Peekskill

Another aspect of the PMA culture was that teachers were encouraged to open their homes to students. For Weill and Fendler, tennis coach and language teacher Clair Frantz became a trusted and respected mentor. Frantz was an accessible male presence for Weill, who often went to his on-campus home for dinner. "Sandy's father was sort of an aloof guy," Fendler said. "I think Sandy really connected with Clair Frantz."

Weill also became a leader among the small coterie of Jewish boys at the school, recalled Winston Kulok, a student at PMA two years younger than Weill. Kulok has fond memories of Weill leading trips into town where the boys, craving lox, would buy pickled salmon. That night, Weill would soak the fish in a pail of water, dumping out the salty brine and repeating the process again and again until the fish at least approximated the taste of the lox available in Brooklyn.

Along with authentic Brooklyn lox, Weill must have missed his parents as well. Friends cannot recall Etta ever coming to the school, but on occasional Sundays (every one of which was a visiting day), Mac Weill would drive up to Peekskill, watch Sandy play the drum in the formal parade, and take his son and Fendler out for lunch. The hulking image of Weill's father still remains with Fendler. "He'd walk up the hill, this big guy smoking cigars," Fendler recalls. "He seemed a hard, serious guy."

Despite the closeness and camaraderie at PMA, none of his fellow students guessed that Weill would eventually vacation with U.S. presidents and take private jets all over the world. While he was well-liked and respected as one of the school's officers, he was not, for example, voted "Most Likely to Succeed," but instead earned the moniker "Mr. Five O'Clock Shadow." Kulok says he saw signs of Weill's drive back then, but it was understated. "He had ambition," says Kulok, "but it didn't sit on him like a deformity."

Fendler, too, says he didn't foresee Weill's great business success as a youth, but once his friend started to achieve in the corporate world, he knew it would be smart to invest in whatever company Weill was running. "I didn't really expect this kind of business success," Fendler says. "But whenever Sandy got to be the head of something, I'd buy it. When he bought Primerica, I'd buy it. I've got a ton of Citigroup stock. My father would buy the stock, too, because he met Sandy at the school, and he was impressed by him."

Poker Games and Government Studies at Cornell

Weill graduated third in his class from PMA in 1951. Intrigued by the dawn of the Space Age, Weill decided to pursue engineering. He was admitted to both Harvard and Cornell, but he decided on Cornell. "It had an engineering school and Harvard didn't," he said in an interview.

In one way, Weill's military surroundings followed him to Ithaca. As a land-grant college, Cornell was subject to requests by the government to supply things such as space for military training. First-year male students, including Weill, lived in the barracks that had been built for training soldiers during World War II, perhaps lending him some continuity from PMA.

The early-1950s was a golden age of sorts for Cornell. The school was far more progressive than other Ivy League schools. Women were admitted to the school and, according to several classmates of Weill's, blacks and Jews were more welcome than they were at universities such as Harvard, Yale, or Princeton. Cornell was academically rigorous, with a notoriously difficult engineering program. During Weill's years there, the school lured some of the intellectual giants of the day to its campus. For example, Vladimir Nabokov, the Russian novelist most famous for writing *Lolita,* taught a wildly popular literature course.

The rigorous Cornell engineering program proved difficult for Weill. He struggled with physics and nearly flunked out before switching to government, which he later called "a good bullshit major."[7] (John Reed, incidentally, had little trouble earning his undergraduate degree in physical metallurgy from MIT, and then went on to earn a master's at the school.)

Weill's years at Cornell, while academically undistinguished, served as an intermission of sorts between the intense military academy experience and what would be an even more intense working life. According to his senior yearbook, Weill played on the varsity tennis team at Cornell and served in student government. He joined a fraternity, Alpha Epsilon Pi, made up predominantly of Jews. Though he never lived in the fraternity house, Weill was active in both its community service programs and its all-night poker games.

The big difference in those days between Cornell and the other Ivy League schools was that Cornell admitted women. Weill had at least one steady girlfriend during his first two years at Cornell, but on a blind date on April Fool's Day in his junior year, he met Joan Mosher, an education major at Brooklyn College. Slender, with auburn hair, an engaging smile, and a quick wit, Joan quickly captured Sandy's heart.

Marrying Joan—A Key to Weill's Success

While Sandy and Joan's relationship was just getting started, Weill's parents' marriage came to an end. His father left his mother for a younger woman in February 1955, his senior year in college. Weill would always recall this as a traumatic event. He left school to try to convince his father to return to his mother and, as a result, failed to take a cost-accounting exam. Without enough credits to graduate, he would not receive his diploma until September. Indirectly, his father's situation led Weill to the brokerage business, because his delayed graduation cost Weill an assignment in the Air Force.

Joan Weill would reflect that Mac's desertion of Etta taught Sandy to always value loyalty. To this day, one of Weill's dominant characteristics as a manager is that he surrounds himself with people who are intensely loyal to him. Not surprisingly, Weill is also known for discarding close associates who show any sign of disloyalty.

This difficult time for Weill did nothing to endear him to his future in-laws. In what now seems one of the all-time great father-in-law misjudgments, Joan's father was worried about Sandy's future prospects. He was concerned that Sandy failed to graduate with the rest of his class at Cornell and was also troubled by the failure of Sandy's parents' marriage. The Moshers urged Joan to break off the relationship.

Joan was undeterred and in June 1955, Joan and Sandy were married in a Conservative Jewish ceremony. Weill's father, who was married for the second time the day after Sandy's wedding (he would ultimately be married a third time), did not attend the ceremony. There was a small reception at the Essex House in Manhattan. Perhaps as a peace offering, Joan's parents gave the young couple $3,500, just about all the money the newlyweds had. Their honeymoon was a one-week stay at the Concord Hotel, a famed Borscht Belt resort in the Catskill Mountains.

Even though he had just been married, the summer of 1955 was a strangely aimless time for Weill. He had no degree, no job, and no immediate prospects. His college friends had all graduated, and many of his fraternity brothers had gone into the military—the plan that Sandy had to scrap. Sandy had plenty of work ahead of him to impress his in-laws, with whom he and Joan lived after their marriage.

Weill began to look for a job. He finished his coursework in the fall of that year, becoming the first in his family to earn a college degree. Although he had little money and hadn't had much luck with his job search yet, Weill had made what some consider to be one of the most significant business decisions of his life: Marrying Joan. From that moment on, Joan proved a major asset to what would become a remarkable career. As Weill confirmed in a recent interview, "I think my greatest accomplishment was marrying my wife."

The Best and Brightest

Y ou would expect a firm of Citigroup's size and status to attract some of the top corporate talent in the world. But its board of directors, chaired by Weill, is particularly noteworthy. Weill has surrounded himself with a "Dream Team" of behind-the-scenes players and well-known stars, corporate titans and not-for-profit executives. Trusted friends of Weill mingle with former allies of Reed.

Many CEOs try to stock their boards with pliant insiders and unknown deferential lightweights. Not Weill. Today's Citigroup board looks like a guest list for a White House state dinner, surely intimidating for someone uncertain of his own skills. Weill doesn't have that problem.

Just after the Travelers-Citicorp merger in 1998, the board numbered 19, consisting of nine members from Travelers, eight from Citicorp, Weill and Reed. As of December 2001, the Citigroup board still numbers 19, but with just a few holdouts left from Citicorp. Some of the board's powerful corporate leaders include: AOL Time Warner CEO Richard Parsons, Colgate-Palmolive

CEO Reuben Mark, retired Chevron Chairman Kenneth Derr, and AT&T Chairman Michael Armstrong, a mainstay of Weill's boards for years.

Some influential Washington insiders are also included on the board. Ann Dibble Jordan is an accomplished consultant who sits on various boards and happens to be the wife of Bill Clinton buddy Vernon Jordan. Professor John Deutch of MIT served as one of Clinton's CIA directors. Former President Gerald Ford, an honorary member of the board, first teamed up with Weill when he joined the Shearson Loeb Rhoades board in 1980. When Weill sold Shearson to American Express in 1981, AmEx accepted Ford as an adviser to the AmEx board. Ford and Weill, who have vacationed together, are said to be good friends.

The board's most plugged-in luminary from inside the Beltway is former Goldman Sachs chief and ex-U.S. Treasury Secretary Robert Rubin. Since joining Citigroup, Rubin has proven himself a breed apart from other corporate executives—Weill among them—by playing a role in shaping national economic policy and actively weighing in on much broader public issues than Citigroup's quarterly results. After the 2001 terrorist attack on New York and Washington, for example, Rubin met with Congressional leaders to help shape the fiscal stimulus package. Weill's recruitment of Rubin is a rare case of a CEO bringing in someone who has a profile higher than his own.

A. Michael Lipper, founder of Lipper Analytical Services and a long-time business acquaintance of Weill's, gives the board high marks for its relationships in Washington. "Rubin is respected in Washington, Ford has good relations with Republicans, while Sandy is in with the Democrats," Lipper says. "The Citigroup board is also known for understanding Congress, which was very important with Glass-Steagall."

Perhaps a Citigroup shareholder at the company's 2000 annual meeting gave Weill the ultimate compliment concerning his twin abilities to choose the best people *and* convince them to work with him. "Only a great leader chooses greatness," she said. "You have been able to get Mr. Rubin for your board and to have President Ford. What else can I say? What an honor."[1]

Great Individuals, Yes, But a Great Board?

While the Citigroup board is certainly star-studded, that doesn't necessarily mean it is the best watchdog for Citigroup's shareholders, believes Nell Minow, editor of the Corporate Library, a research firm that tracks corporate governance issues. "It certainly is chock full of superstars, but that doesn't make them superstar directors," Minow says. "There are some very impressive people who are great achievers in their own right, but they aren't well-known for really holding a CEO's feet to the fire."

One criticism of the board is that it has not seemed to push Weill on the issue of who will succeed him as chairman of the company. Weill's critics on this issue were somewhat mollified by the January 2001 promotion of Robert Willumstad to Citigroup president, a move that many perceived as naming him Weill's heir apparent. For his part, Weill often sidesteps the succession issue. "In this day and age, if a company doesn't have a succession plan in place all the time, they [the directors] are failing in their single most important job," Minow asserts. "A lot of CEOs have a succession policy that says, 'I'm not going to die.' That's just not good enough."

Despite the controversial issue of who Weill's successor will be, Citigroup's talent pool runs deep. In fact, a defining trait of Weill's career is that he has always sought to surround himself with the smartest people he could find, from Jamie Dimon to Robert Rubin to, yes, John Reed.

Despite the many successful people Weill has worked with throughout his career, perhaps the most compelling collection of individuals that has ever surrounded Weill remains the small coterie of partners he left behind years ago. Weill and his former partners at the firms Carter, Berlind, Potoma & Weill and then Cogan, Berlind, Weill & Levitt achieved more together than any of them thought possible. Apart, their respective careers since have left indelible impressions on the worlds of finance, media, theater, and public policy.

It could be said that the members of Citigroup's board—accomplished as they are—resemble an aging all-star band on yet another world tour. But the four young entrepreneurs who cooked up Corned Beef With Lettuce were unknowns embarking on an incredible adventure, and each would rise to impressive heights. If the financial world had a Beatles, they would have been it.

First, Some Experience on the Street

During the summer of 1955, jobless and casting about, Weill made a list of industries of interest to him and companies that he would apply to for a job. His first encounter with a brokerage is described in Tim Carrington's *The Year They Sold Wall Street:*

> One day, near Forty-First Street and Seventh Avenue, he noticed an office of the old securities firm of Bache & Company. He had never seen the inside of a brokerage office, and since the street window was darkly tinted to ensure that customers had privacy from passersby, he wandered in. What he saw was confusing: brokers picked up telephones, filled out slips, rushed back and forth across the room. Yet there was an undeniable surge of energy in the place that appealed to Weill.[2]

Weill applied at Bache for its broker's training course, but was not hired. He was also turned down from broker training programs at Merrill Lynch and Harris.

At that time, Wall Street was sharply stratified by class and religion (not to mention race). Firms with Anglo-Saxon roots, like J.P. Morgan, and successful German-Jewish investment banks, such as Goldman Sachs and Lehman Brothers, hired mainly from within their ranks. That left Weill, the middle-class Brooklyn-born son of Eastern European Jews, with little immediate opportunity. But it also made his later success at breaking through those barriers all the more sweet.

"Our Crowd" Was Not Weill's Crowd

Most people view the phenomenon of business leaders achieving celebrity status as emerging in the 1980s. During this infamous "decade of excess," certain investment bankers, junk bond artists, and CEOs performed audacious acts of business derring-do, made astronomical sums of money, and became household names. Long before that, however, the founding families of Wall Street's leading firms achieved nationwide fame. Jay Cooke, who sold Union war bonds during the Civil War, Joseph Seligman, patriarch of the premier 1800s investment bank J&W Seligman & Co., and—the most influential Wall Streeter of all time—J. P. Morgan personified wealth and power in a country unaccustomed to seeing such riches. Though envied and vilified by many Americans, these men and their families became leading philanthropists, endowing major universities and cultural institutions such as the Metropolitan Opera and the Metropolitan Museum of Art. Unsurprisingly, they formed the cultural and social elite of Manhattan throughout the nineteenth and early twentieth centuries, until the end of World War II.

One trait many of these nineteenth-century tycoons shared was that they started with next to nothing. Unlike Europe, the United States did not have an entrenched, ruling aristocracy in the early 1900s. Rags-to-riches stories, while rare, did occur. Many of these fortunes grew out of Wall Street, which operated as a relative meritocracy. At that time, anyone who was smart enough, lucky enough, and worked hard enough just might make it on Wall Street.

Many WASPs did, but so did many Jews. The self-congratulatory term "Our Crowd" was coined by the influential German Jews in New York, who started firms like Goldman Sachs, Lehman Brothers, Kuhn Loeb, and Salomon Brothers.

Wealthy, well-educated, and cultured, the German Jews held themselves apart from the city's less refined Eastern European Jews, including Polish immigrants like Weill's grandparents. The wealthy German Jews lived far from Philip and Rebecca Kalika's Bensonhurst, both literally and metaphorically. They resided in antique-filled apartments on Fifth Avenue or luxury town houses on Manhattan's Upper West Side. They gave generously to the arts and to universities, and formed exclusive social clubs, such as the prestigious Harmonie Club in Manhattan (which Weill himself later joined).

After World War II, the distinctions between the "Our Crowd" Jews and the Eastern European Jews began to blur. Although the German-Jewish Wall Street firms had seemed unassailable for generations, "the walled citadel couldn't survive in the post-World War II economic environment and self-made men like Sanford Weill were there to pick up the pieces," Judith Ramsey Ehrlich and Barry J. Rehfeld wrote in their best-selling 1989 book *The New Crowd*, which described this change.[3]

Weill's New Crowd

Like many of the newcomers to Wall Street in the mid-1950s, Weill belonged to the "New Crowd," the sons of working- or middle-class Eastern European Jewish families headed by a typically self-employed father. Their parents spent long hours toiling as shopkeepers or cab drivers, and made it clear to their children that they were expected to go to college. Like Weill, many of these children were the first members of their family to do so.

When Weill made the rounds of Wall Street after college in 1955, the older firms were clinging to power, and still weren't a place of opportunity for outsiders. Even as late as 1961, a year after Weill started his own firm, the young economist Henry Kaufman declined to pursue a coveted position at Smith Barney because he was warned by a mentor that he would never be able to climb to senior management because of his religious affiliation. In his memoirs, nearly 40 years later, Kaufman would observe that now, "the religious barrier to advancement in Wall Street has nearly disappeared." To illustrate this, he noted that Smith Barney is now owned by Citigroup, which is headed by a Jew, Sandy Weill.[4]

Weill's rejections by the dominant Wall Street firms explain his loyalty to people who gave him a chance, such as I. W. "Tubby" Burnham, who mentored Weill when he was a young broker. Weill would return the favor years later in part by bringing Burnham's firm in on underwriting deals in the early- and mid-1960s. In later interviews, Weill referred to Burnham as "one of my heroes."[5]

A Start at Bear Stearns and an Education with Tubby Burnham

One can't blame everything on the exclusionary policies of the Our Crowd and Anglo-Saxon brokerages and banks. Perhaps with a finance degree or at least a rudimentary knowledge of Wall Street, Weill might have fared better on the job market.

Weill admits to a total ignorance of banking and finance when he launched his career. For example, after his marriage, he deposited wedding gifts in a savings bank and tried to get checks for the account. "I didn't know that savings banks didn't allow you to write checks," Weill later told *Business Week*. "That's how much I knew."[6]

The Weills were living off wedding gifts and cash Weill had saved from his Bar Mitzvah when he was finally hired as a runner by Bear Stearns for what was, even then, the paltry wage of $150 a month. A typical entry-level position on Wall Street, the job entailed literally running, order slip in hand, from the broker who took the order to buy or sell stock, to the trader, who executed the trade. Weill thrived on the energy of the trading floor and was eventually promoted to broker. Weill later told a reporter, "I remember thinking that if I had $10,000, I could buy all the stocks that I'd ever want to buy."[7]

In 1958, Weill was hired at Burnham & Company by Tubby Burnham, the firm's founder and a Wall Street legend. Burnham & Company, located at 60 Broad Street, later acquired Drexel Firestone, a Philadelphia investment bank, and became Drexel, Burnham, Lambert, today most often remembered for launching Michael Milken and his band of junk bond kings.

In the late 1950s, Burnham & Company was a prestigious, if not huge, brokerage house. Weill, at Burnham's urging, spent much of his time in the back office, where he learned how to track and clear orders. Weill also worked as a "board marker" for Burnham, writing out the latest stock prices on a big bulletin board so the brokers could quickly glance up and see the latest prices. Years later, after he started his own firm, Weill is said to have spent hours each day studying the stock ticker, perhaps just happy he didn't have to write all the prices down.

Weill may not have realized it at the time, but these low-level jobs gave him a better fundamental education of how the business of issuing and trading securities really worked than he would have gotten as a broker-trainee at a bigger firm. It was this decidedly nonglamorous administrative experience that taught Weill to take behind-the-scenes operations seriously. Back-office efficiency was the key to much of his firm's early success, including the Hayden Stone acquisition in 1970.

It's clear that Weill developed his core philosophy of running a business partly from Tubby Burnham—keep costs low, avoid unnecessary risks, and keep an eye on the details. He learned to spot the tiny red flags that could turn into big problems for a brokerage firm, such as clients buying too much stock on margin (they then might not be able to pay back the firm if the borrowed shares fell sharply), or traders placing big bets that stocks would go up, exposing a firm to significant potential losses. These lessons would serve Weill well throughout his long career, as he would make sure employees of his firm didn't take the kind of risks that caused other firms to blow up, such as when the brokerage firm Bache backed the Hunt brothers in their 1980 attempt to corner the silver market. Bache ended up so damaged that the owners sold the firm to Prudential.

It was also the late 1950s when Weill, still in his mid-20s, had growing responsibilities at home. His son, Marc, was born in 1957 and two years later came Jessica. Weill, encouraged by Joan, would soon step out from under Burnham's shadow and, with a few associates as partners, go into business on his own.

Four Young Entrepreneurs

The Sandy Weill who would eventually create Citigroup began to emerge when he started his own brokerage firm in 1960. The initial drive to start something new came from Arthur Carter, a charismatic young broker from Woodmere on Long

Island—Joan Weill's hometown—who lived across the hall from Weill and his family on Atlantic Avenue in East Rockaway. Weill had, up to this point, shown little stomach for entrepreneurship, and Carter had a much more adventuresome spirit. Weill's conservative nature held him back for some time before making the leap with Carter. He was ambitious, but his aspirations were modest. He felt he and Joan would be living like kings if they had enough money to buy a deep fryer and a slide projector.[8]

Weill was 27 and Carter was 28. Though Weill agreed to join in the new firm, he insisted that a third person share the risk. Carter did one better; he arranged for two more brokers to join them: Roger Berlind, 29, an old friend of Carter's from Woodmere, and Peter Potoma, 32. Those two had already discussed breaking away from their current firm, Eastman Dillon, and starting their own firm. When Berlind signed up, Potoma was invited to join the firm as well.

On May 3, 1960, the partners went to the County Clerk's office in downtown Manhattan and registered the name of Carter, Berlind, Potoma & Weill. From that point on, Weill would never send out another resume. The four partners managed to scrape together $215,000 from various sources as their seed capital. Weill turned to his mother, for example, for at least some of his $30,000 stake. The four partners bought a seat on the New York Stock Exchange with $160,000 and with the rest, they hired a secretary and rented a fifth-floor office at 15 Broad Street from Burnham. It was also decided that they would clear their trades through Burnham's back-office operations. Each partner received a base salary of $12,000, which was a major pay cut from the $25,000 Weill had earned the previous year as a broker working for Tubby Burnham.

Each of Weill's new partners came to the firm after working at one of the Big Board brokerage houses. All were well-educated and seemed to have more outside interests than Weill, particularly in the arts. Carter had majored in French literature at

Brown University and was a talented enough pianist to consider turning professional. Berlind, who served in the Army after graduating from Princeton, had tried professional song writing in New York after leaving the service. But he had little success. As he told the *Wall Street Journal* in 1984, "some friends took pity on me" and helped him get a job at the firm Eastman Dillon.[9]

Potoma, an Italian steelworker's son and the only non-Jew of the founding four partners, had attended Harvard Law School, but quit after two years. He was the most seasoned broker of the crew and the firm registered its New York Stock Exchange seat in Potoma's name. Potoma took Weill under his wing, teaching the indifferent dresser how to polish his appearance, convincing him to buy a three-piece suit, and giving him a hat and black umbrella to make him seem older than 27.

Each of the four was also fairly well established in his personal life. All were married. Berlind, the frustrated songwriter, and his wife lived on East 55th Street in Manhattan. Potoma and his wife were also Manhattan residents, with a Park Avenue apartment. Weill and Carter were neighbors until Carter and his family moved to the Long Island town of Manhasset.

The founders of Carter, Berlind, Potoma & Weill could not have picked a better time to start their firm. The stock market boom of the 1960s was about to begin. With the power of the old-line firms dissipating, there was plenty of room for a group of aggressive, ambitious brokers to make inroads on Wall Street. And ambitious they were.

A New Kind of Firm for a Changing Wall Street

In 1960, the individual investor was just emerging as a force in financial markets. Retail brokerage, as the business geared to managing accounts for individuals is known, had traditionally been viewed as a backwater of the investment business. Even today, many finance professionals see the real business of Wall Street as buying and selling massive amounts of securities for giant corporate pension funds or masterminding deals between companies. It was even more true back in the early days of Carter, Berlind, Potoma & Weill. Then, most big brokerages simply weren't set up for selling stocks to the public, but sought what is known as "institutional" business—handling the accounts of pension funds or large money managers.

But Weill, who had learned from Burnham to focus on the business dynamics of retail brokerage, realized that doing many little trades for individual investors could be just as profitable as arranging a handful of deals for large institutions. It was also less risky and provided more consistent earnings. The nature of retail brokerage and its focus on connecting with customers also played to Weill's strengths. As a former college athlete and fraternity member, Weill knew how to connect with men who wanted to play the game of buying and selling stocks.

Lipper, a junior analyst at Burnham & Company in the early 1960s, worked down the hall from the fledgling brokerage and observed firsthand the workings of Weill and his partners. Lipper describes the atmosphere as "intense and competitive," punctuated by occasional bursts of laughter. Since the frugal Tubby Burnham wouldn't pay for a quote machine (presumably he still had young brokers scrawling stock quotes on a blackboard), Lipper used to walk down the hall to the office that Carter, Berlind, Potoma & Weill rented from Tubby to look at their ticker. At one point, Lipper even entertained the thought of going to work with the dynamic young firm, but he felt that their requirement that all four partners approve each piece of research before it went out to clients would be unworkable. As Lipper foresaw, having four partners share decision-making responsibility would ultimately create tension—and in more than just research.

The energy Lipper witnessed among the young entrepreneurs manifested itself in several ways. One was in their marketing tactics. The young partners bucked tradition and ran print newspaper advertisements as part of their effort to attract middle-class clients who were just getting interested in the market. Their message in an October 11, 1961, ad for the firm in the *Wall Street Journal*—the word "Investments" followed by the name of the firm—made up in brevity what it lacked in creativity.

The firm quickly made a name for itself, attracting retail clients and also scooping up small underwriting deals that larger firms may have passed on. A February 28, 1961, tombstone display advertisement in the *Wall Street Journal* announced the sale of 60,000 shares of an Omaha, Nebraska, company called Tip Top Products and lists the underwriters as Carter, Berlind, Potoma & Weill. Not coincidentally, Burnham & Company is also listed as one of the four underwriters of the same offering.

The firm was effectively under the radar of the large Wall Street firms at that point. Roy Smith, a former Goldman Sachs partner who is now a professor at New York University's Stern School of Business, recalls half-jokingly that Weill, "started out as a kind of runty little nobody. Big shots like me from Goldman Sachs, our guns couldn't train that low."

The first year, the firm recorded sales of $225,000, thanks in part to the bull market and tireless efforts of the partners who worked around the clock building the firm. The four raised their salaries to $18,000. Joan and Sandy went house-hunting and purchased a $60,000 Colonial home in Brookville, Long Island, in the spring of 1962. Carter, Berlind, Potoma & Weill was doing so well out of the gate that on January 31, 1961, the firm added a director of retail sales, Julian Robinson. The launch had been a smashing success—until it faced its first scandal in early 1962.

The governors of the New York Stock Exchange accused Potoma of "free-riding," or buying and selling securities for his own account by using clients' money to make the initial purchase. In this scheme, the securities are sold, the client's account is replenished, and the broker keeps any profit. The Exchange said that Potoma was "guilty of conduct inconsistent with just and equitable principles of trade."

None of the other partners was implicated, and Potoma, at age 34, "retired" from the firm in April 1962. Three months later, he was suspended from the New York Stock Exchange for one year. Potoma's name was dropped from the firm and his seat on the stock exchange was taken over by the newly hired Robinson.

Although the firm avoided major scandal, the incident shook Weill. Understandably, he was worried about the reputation of the firm and the investigation's effects on the firm's clients. Weill's father's arrest, which drove Mac Weill out of the garment industry in 1944, also couldn't have been far from his mind. Weill obviously would have dreaded a similar fate. Now that Potoma, who had been the most experienced stockbroker of the four, was gone, the power in the firm inexorably shifted toward Carter, who had the clearest vision of the firm's future.

Carter Emerges as the Firm's Leader

As its stock brokerage business took off, Carter, Berlind & Weill challenged the big firms in performing research. In 1962, an 18-page analyst report on Famous Artists Schools, Inc., published by Carter, Berlind & Weill, earned the firm its first mention in the *Wall Street Journal*'s prominent "Abreast of the Market" column.[10] Though coworkers of Weill would later say that he was never very interested in the benefits of a strong research department, perhaps now he saw how it could generate good publicity.

With Potoma gone, the firm had room for new partners and found the perfect hire to raise its profile and restore its credibility in November 1963—Arthur Levitt Jr. Not only was Levitt the son of the New York State comptroller, but he would prove so squeaky clean that he would go on to become one of the most admired securities regulators of the twentieth century. Like Weill, Levitt had been rejected for several Wall Street jobs. Unlike Weill, however, Levitt had dabbled in other professions, serving as a newspaper reporter for the Berkshire *Eagle,* working in promotions for *Time,* and selling tax shelters. Thanks to his well-known father, Levitt had connections the other partners lacked and, by his name alone, added some clout to the firm. At about the same time, Marshall Cogan, a Harvard Business School graduate, also joined the firm. A Boston native, Cogan had always wanted to work on Wall Street. Younger than the others, with a quirky personality, Cogan, too, had difficulty finding a job before joining Carter, Berlind & Weill.

Evidence points to Carter as the firm's top decision maker in its early years. One Carter acquaintance from those years told a reporter, "Actually, Arthur wasn't the most important partner, he was just the loudest."[11] Loud or not, Carter acquired the mantle of leadership, setting the tone and pushing the other partners to succeed. Carter kept a "little black book" listing the commissions generated by each partner every day and scolding them if they didn't meet their quota. He led a weekly firm meeting that often took place over a steak dinner. These highly charged sessions were described in *The New Crowd:*

> On the surface at least, the conversation revolved around business. But these evenings were closer to an exercise in sibling rivalry. Pressured by Carter, who played the role of the eldest brother, each partner maintained a separate account of his output in the office. . . . in the fraternity-like atmosphere, Weill was lampooned as the partnership's proletarian Brooklynite who couldn't make a good impression on the firm's

clients; Berlind was ribbed because he had gone to the whitest of the white-shoe colleges and had almost forgotten how to be Jewish; Levitt was derided for coattailing the success of his famous father; and Cogan was put down as a hysterical mass of tics, wild gestures, and hysterical outbursts. Carter, who typically escaped criticism, orchestrated the high-volume banter.[12]

Carter was also the one who was asked to sit on corporate boards, as he did with Studebaker. And when the partners incorporated on January 21, 1965, it was Carter who wrote his name down as "President" on the business certificate. The certificate of incorporation states that the company's business includes "brokerage of securities, investment advice, and general business attendant to membership in national securities exchange." It is clear from that broad language that the young firm could have gone in many different directions.

Fighting for the Soul of the Firm

Weill was a paradox during this time. He is described as nervous, quiet and shy, eager to please the domineering Carter. He mainly kept to himself and didn't form intimate friendships with his partners. He would remain at his desk all day watching stock prices and trading on behalf of customers. Yet because he could be warm, open, and accessible to his clients, he was also an excellent "producer" (as stockbrokers who generate a lot of money for the firm in commissions are called). "At night he would go out and get the accounts of waiters and maître d's and come back and trade them," former colleague Asher Edelman remembers.[13]

Weill was especially effective with athletes and would become the broker for a variety of well-known sports personalities, including Sonny Werblin, owner of the New York Jets, Joe Namath, Wilt Chamberlain, and Howard Cosell. His sports connections even resulted in some hires for the firm. For example, Bill Mathis, a halfback for the Jets, joined Carter, Berlind & Weill when he retired from football in 1969. (He had to leave the firm and return to the team for the next season when injuries forced Jets coach Weeb Ewbank to ask him back.)

Ironically, Weill's success with his clients somehow limited him in the eyes of some for years to come, since handling individual brokerage accounts wasn't respected by the kingpins of Wall Street. "Even later when Weill was trying to do the Bank of America deal, he had to deal with this image that he was some scruffy little stockbroker from lower Manhattan," says Roy Smith.

But these retail accounts were helping the firm grow. As the bull market picked up momentum in 1966, the firm earned $1.4 million from retail brokerage commissions, compared with just $90,000 in institutional sales.

Despite this success at selling securities to individual investors, the partners at Carter, Berlind & Weill—especially Carter and Cogan—hoped to build the business by doing more investment banking. To generate this business, the firm continued to turn out top-notch research on which industry sectors were strongest, which companies were ripe for acquisition, and how firms could organize to best mitigate tax exposure. Providing advice to companies in any of these areas was a highly lucrative business.

One of the firm's research reports from this time seems to have provided Weill with a few ideas that he incorporated into his own thinking. It was called "The Financial Services Holding Company" and was written over two years by Edward Netter, a senior vice president at Carter, Berlind & Weill, and released in August 1967. Netter analyzed the property and casualty insurance sector and showed how the acquisition of a company in that line of business could provide extraordinary economic benefits to a large conglomerate. Netter wrote:

The day is ending when one company can write only property and casualty insurance and another company sell life insurance, a third offer premium financing, the fourth mutual and fund investments, and all compete effectively for the consumer dollar. The broadest possible range of financial services will be combined in an integrated marketing effort by the successful company of the future. The holding company's structure will become the dominant corporate organization of financial services institutions.[14]

It is striking how prescient Netter's research findings proved to be. Just as he foresaw (and Weill apparently agreed), the future indeed belonged to big, all-encompassing financial services powerhouses like today's Citigroup.

Walter Wriston Becomes Citibank President

That same year, 1967, Walter Wriston, one of the most visionary executives in twentieth century financial history, became president of Citibank (later gaining the CEO spot in 1970). Wriston, who, like Weill, recognized the changes coming to financial services, devoted much of his career to railing against the Glass-Steagall Act, which prevented Citibank from selling the range of products that other types of financial companies could. He felt that banks were, in fact, the institutions best suited for selling financial services. NYU Stern School professor David Rogers, in his book *The Future of American Banking*, quoted a Citicorp manager from the Wriston days:

He used to come around the bank with his list of top financial service institutions like Merrill Lynch, American Express, and Sears, and talk about all the products and services they provided which we could not. And he was furious that we would have been denied by legislation from competing in those fields. He was the one who then pushed so hard for deregulation.[15]

Thanks to The Bank Holding Company Act of 1956, banks were able to merge with banks in other states, which allowed Citibank to expand geographically. But it couldn't get into other lines of business as long as the Glass-Steagall Act was in force.

Era of Conglomerates

While Netter accurately predicted the changes coming to financial services, his advice at the time wasn't that broad in scope. He advocated that businesses acquire insurance companies because the premiums would serve as a steady source of cash for the parent company.

The mid-1960s was the era of conglomerates. CEOs combined unrelated businesses creating rapid sales and earnings growth and soaring stock prices. Figgie International, for example, completed four mergers in just 25 days in the middle of 1967. The stock went from $8 a share in 1963 to $74 in 1967. Litton Industries, Teledyne, and Textron are other examples of sprawling conglomerates formed at that time.

Hoping to get in on the lucrative action of helping companies find other companies to acquire or merge with, Carter, Berlind & Weill produced about 2,000 copies of Netter's report and urged the firm's brokers to hand them out to clients. The goal was to interest a client in purchasing an insurance company. If a prospect materialized, Netter himself would often swoop in to make a presentation, hammering home the message that an acquisition could result in major economic benefits for the parent company.

Then, Carter, Berlind & Weill would try to find an appropriate insurance company for the company to acquire. If the deal went through, the firm could charge a hefty fee for brokering the deal, as well as position itself for a role in future stock deals. In essence, the research arm produced reports that the brokers used as sales documents, a core Wall Street practice that continues to this day. This was very convenient for the brokers who wanted to drum up a deal, and quite lucrative for Carter, Berlind & Weill if some of the clients took the bait.

One did in 1968, and the deal changed the way Weill looked at investment banking forever. Netter showed his report to Saul Steinberg and Michael Gibbs, two executives at a growing Long Island computer leasing company, Leasco Data Processing Corp. Steinberg, just 29, had started Leasco in 1961, and in 1968 was intent on growing the company. After seeing Netter's report, Steinberg became interested in the idea of owning a property and casualty insurer. For some time, Carter, Berlind & Weill had been pitching Reliance Insurance as just the kind of insurance company a conglomerate should buy. Even though Reliance wasn't for sale, talks concerning a deal began.

On January 11, 1968, Steinberg and Gibbs met Carter, Levitt, and Netter at the offices of Carter, Berlind & Weill to discuss a potential takeover of Reliance. The partners of Carter, Berlind & Weill went into the meeting with guns blazing on every count. They immediately passed around a memo, signed by Carter, demanding an immediate seat on the Leasco board, a future role in any securities offerings or private placements, and a fee of $750,000.

Steinberg and Gibbs, who had expected a casual, friendly meeting, were stunned by the aggressiveness of the firm and stormed out after less than five minutes. One of Steinberg's associates arrived at the offices of Carter, Berlind & Weill a few minutes late to find that his associates had already left. They had walked down the street to the offices of their attorney, Wilkie Farr & Gallagher, ostensibly to examine Carter's "proposal." Steinberg later described the scene for an SEC hearing called to investigate the Leasco-Reliance deal, as well as Carter, Berlind & Weill's activities related to it:

> We left. We laughed. . . . First of all, we were not that far along in our thinking. It really jolted us and we didn't expect that the future would be edicted to us. . . . We met with [our] investment banker, and we showed him the list of demands and he said in his 40 years or 30 years on Wall Street he had not encountered such a thing.[16]

That Steinberg, who went on to become one of the iconic corporate raiders of the 1980s, was taken aback by the hunger and aggressiveness of Carter, Berlind & Weill speaks volumes about the firm at that time.

The incident reveals not only the collective scrappiness of Carter, Berlind & Weill, but contains a clue to discord within the firm that would surface just a few months later. It's hard to imagine Weill blindsiding a client with a list of demands at one of the first "get-to-know-you" meetings. Carter and Weill were both determined to succeed, but where Carter issued memos and demands, Weill preferred sharing a cigar or a night on the town.

It's also clear from the public records how little Weill had to do with the Reliance deal. Even though Weill says that he became interested in investment banking as a sort of third step in his business evolution (after retail brokerage and research), Weill attended none of the scores of meetings on the Reliance deal, according to testimony before a Congressional Subcommittee hearing on conglomerates given by Levitt. Even if Weill was completely uninterested in investment banking and the research that led to such deals, you might expect that as one of three founders of the firm, he would have attended one or two meetings about a deal worth at least $750,000. The fact that he didn't further points to a widening rift between Weill and Carter.

Leasco eventually did acquire Reliance. Exactly one of Carter's six demands were met: the $750,000 fee. The firm was also paid $47,000 when it acted as broker for Leasco in connection with Leasco's purchase of 133,000 shares of Reliance. Steinberg went on to gain notoriety and vast riches at what became the Reliance Group, which went bankrupt in 2001.

By mid-1968, investors had become disenchanted with the conglomerate idea and their plummeting stock prices triggered the SEC and the accounting profession to overhaul the rules for accounting for mergers. Carter, Berlind & Weill was later hounded for several years by the SEC and a House of Representatives subcommittee to testify at various hearings and provide information about the operations of their firm that they undoubtedly would have preferred be kept private.

It would not be surprising if the various outcomes of the Leasco-Reliance deal went a long way toward tempering Weill's enthusiasm for investment banking. Sure, the big deals that came together were lucrative: The $750,000 that the firm collected for the Reliance deal was one of two such $750,000 fees Carter, Berlind & Weill collected in 1968.

But such deals were also risky and difficult to execute. To actually collect a hefty fee, the firm would need to convince a company that it should go forward with an acquisition, find a suitable target, set up innumerable meetings between the suitor and the target company, manage the negotiations, and then pray that the deal went through. It was a long, risky, and painful route to a payday. Weill's conservative business nature lent itself to recurring, steady revenues. Asset management fees charged on the account of a wealthy investor, for example, generated revenues 24 hours a day, seven days a week for Carter, Berlind & Weill.

Weill may have developed a distaste for using research as a sales tool during this period. "He didn't believe in research," says Peter Solomon, former vice chairman of Shearson Lehman, in an interview. "He always thought stock research was sort of worthless. He believed it is a loss leader. His thinking was, 'Why pay people to do research when you just give it away?' He wanted to sell products and get a fee."

In fact, rather than see merger and acquisition deals as a way for the firm to make a big fee, such transactions left him with an emptiness. In Roger Lowenstein's August 2000 profile of Weill in the *New York Times Magazine,* Weill was quoted as saying that even though the firm made $750,000 on the deal, "The next day Saul Steinberg had a business, and we had to start all over again."[17] In an interview with the authors, Weill said that after being in business for a while, he "broadened out into trying to build the company rather than just working on deals for other clients."

Weill got his chance to start building the company through acquisitions soon enough. Even as Carter and Cogan were building the investment banking business, the firm saw an opportunity to reduce its dependence on the cyclical business of trading stocks. On July 9, 1967, the firm acquired Bernstein-Macaulay, a money management firm with investment portfolios worth $175 million. Unlike the brokerage or investment banking business, where fees are based on transactions, money managers collect annual fees for managing portfolios. Weill had found a way to turn all that trading volume into a steady, 24-hour, Saturday and Sunday revenue stream that would still be there when the market turned south. Though small and ultimately a more or less break-even proposition for the partners, this was Weill's first acquisition and started the firm in an important new direction.

Comings and Goings

The year 1967 was also one in which Weill did a lot of packing and unpacking. He and Joan decided to move the family to a four-bedroom Colonial in Great Neck on Long Island Sound. Great Neck was a wealthier community than Brookville and closer to the city. The growing brokerage firm also moved, to 55 Broad Street, where it occupied the top floor of the building and another half of the floor below.

Meanwhile, the firm continued to be more progressive than most of its Wall Street contemporaries. For example, a June 27, 1967, story in the *New York Times* describes how Carter, Berlind & Weill hired Clarence B. Jones as a vice president making him the first black member of the New York Stock Exchange. Since 1962, Jones, a Columbia College and Boston University Law School graduate, had served as special counsel and adviser on legal and economic affairs to the Rev. Dr. Martin Luther King Jr. The 36-year-old's duties included investment banking and brokerage, with legal responsibilities in corporate finance, mergers, and acquisitions. Jones would leave the firm in the early 1970s to become publisher of the *Amsterdam News*, a leading black newspaper in New York.

Jones helped bring in some of the firm's best deals in 1968. Carter, Berlind & Weill was hired that year as investment bankers for the Government of Jamaica, retained as financial adviser for a hotel planned for 125th Street and Third Avenue in East Harlem, and appointed financial adviser to the Government of Zambia.

PMA Closes Its Doors

Ever since graduating from Peekskill Military Academy (PMA) in 1951, Weill had maintained ties with the military school.

He eventually became vice president of the school's board of trustees, the position he held when the school unexpectedly shut down in the summer of 1968. The school's closing was abrupt, confusing, and left some PMA alumni wondering what role Weill and his friend and client, the late Sonny Werblin, played in the drama.

In the mid-1960s, Werblin, a real estate developer as well as owner of the New York Jets, decided to base the football team's preseason training camp at PMA. "That's where I got to know him," Weill said in an interview with the authors. Weill recruited Werblin to join PMA's board, and Werblin also sent two sons to PMA.

Werblin, however, soon got more than he bargained for. The Vietnam War and the resulting antiwar movement had hit PMA's enrollment hard. Very few teenagers were enthusiastic about attending a military school in the climate of the mid-1960s. Without the annual tuition that made up most of the school's operating budget, PMA couldn't pay many of its creditors. The school also had no organized alumni association or endowment program that could have built a reserve fund. Werblin, according to one source, was soon bankrolling much of the school's operations to the tune of $30,000 to $35,000 a month. When Werblin pulled the plug on the payments in 1968, the school closed and the town of Peekskill bought the insolvent institution, razed most of the buildings in 1969, and built Peekskill High School.

According to PMA alumni association director Lorman A. Augustowski, PMA's board of directors, including Werblin and Weill, couldn't or didn't get the word out to alumni that the school was in trouble. Werblin did schedule one meeting in Florida to try to garner support from retired PMA alumni, but only five men showed up. Werblin threw in the towel after that. "The alumni of PMA at the time included some very prominent people, from Latin American presidents to national business leaders," Augustowski says. "I'm not saying PMA's liabilities and debts were pocket change, but any number of people could have written a check." Augustowski estimates the school's total debt was approximately $300,000.

"The alumni could have bought the school for a song," says Stuart Fendler, Weill's high school roommate and tennis teammate. "But everyone was so busy that we weren't really aware of what was going on."

While several alumni wonder if there was anything further Weill could have done, fellow alumnus Winston Kulok doesn't blame Weill for not attempting to prop up the institution with a deal of some sort. Kulok points out that attendance at the school had been dwindling for years and that school administrators had not dealt with that fact, allowing the number of teachers and staff to keep growing. When the school closed, there were 52 staff members at the school, which was more than the number of students. "I think Sandy would have tried to help the school if he believed it could have survived," Kulok says. "He's obviously a very shrewd judge of deals."

A Power Struggle

In early 1968, business was humming at Carter, Berlind & Weill. Around this time, Carter decided the firm should become more of an investment bank. In a May 27, 1968, story in the *New York Times*, Carter told the newspaper that "Ten years from now, I'd like our firm to be a major [sic] in the investment banking business."[18]

With the benefit of hindsight, it's clear that Carter's ambitions proved his undoing at the firm. In September, he tried to unilaterally change the direction of the firm to better tailor his vision, proposing to name himself CEO and drastically reduce

Weill's and Cogan's percentage of the partnership. Carter enlisted the assistance of Julian Robinson for the coup and used Levitt as his messenger to the other partners. Levitt, however, sided with Weill and Cogan. Carter was asked to resign and he did, leaving with a few associates in tow, including Robinson. One source termed Carter's departure as "a palace uprising. They threw him out."

The sanitized story in the *Wall Street Journal* that followed on September 11, 1968, made no mention of the power struggle. "It was an amicable parting," Levitt told the *Journal.* "This wasn't a shake-up." For his part, Carter told the newspaper that the departure was "friendly," and said, "I resigned because basically I wanted to do something else and that something else was to become involved in the operations of a publicly-owned concern." He wasted no time setting up The Carter Group, a public company, with Robinson and investors Steven J. Ross, president of Kinney National Service, and Edward R. Downe Jr., chairman and president of Downe Communications. Eventually, Carter would make tens of millions of dollars running his company.

The confrontation with Carter was extremely painful for Weill. They had been working at each other's side for more than seven years, even vacationing together with their families (a trademark of Weill's throughout his early career). Carter's betrayal was a blow, and having to, in essence, fire his partner was difficult. Nonetheless, it was also a valuable learning experience. He had played his cards right, and—along with the others—had come out on top in his first major boardroom showdown.

Lipper, who at Burnham & Company had a bird's eye view of the strong personalities at the firm and the high level of energy that was involved in building the business, thinks that a split may have been inevitable. "Given the intensity of the relationships, I'm not surprised that there may have been some bad feelings when Carter left," Lipper says.

Corned Beef With Lettuce

Carter's departure left four men on the firm's executive committee: Berlind, Weill, Cogan, and Levitt. With one dominant voice gone, a true egalitarianism settled in.

One story has it that the four drew straws to decide the order of the surnames when renaming the firm after Carter's departure. Cogan picked the long straw, so his name came first, followed by Berlind, Weill, and Levitt. Then they picked their titles in reverse order. Levitt chose president, Weill chose chairman, Berlind chose chief executive officer, and Cogan chose vice chairman. On February 19, 1969, the firm changed its name from Carter, Berlind & Weill to Cogan, Berlind, Weill & Levitt, or CBWL. They soon moved their offices, leasing space on the 34th floor of the newly opened General Motors Building, a fifty-story tower at Fifth Avenue and 59th Street near the southeast corner of Central Park. The new office certainly had a high-profile address, but the four partners continued to sit together in one large, open room.

Weill would seek to replicate, wherever he landed in the years to come, the informal camaraderie and competitiveness in that room. A Harvard Business School case study on Weill's management style later in his career at Primerica said that his leadership there reflected the culture at CBWL: "Weill was determined to run a company where executive interaction was frequent, informal, and face-to-face, not dependent on memos and staff meetings."[19]

Jeffrey Lane started working at the firm in 1969, joining the research division. He remembers leadership at the firm rotating among the top four partners. "It depended upon the day, the time, and the position of the moon and the stars," he says.

While the responsibilities and the power in the firm may have been equally divided, each partner had different roles. Berlind and Levitt were the public faces of the firm. Weill was more of the behind-the-scenes strategist and Cogan the rainmaker. Berlind could see the big picture better than the others. He played more the role of the statesman, but didn't get into the nitty-gritty details of the business. In contrast, Weill was the strategist and focused on the details of running the firm.

In fact, Weill, still uncomfortable in the limelight, allowed Berlind to receive the lion's share of the attention. A 1969 article in the *New York Times* with the headline "Cogan, Berlind, Long Unstructured, Gets Boss," extolled Berlind as the leader of the firm, making no mention that Berlind's title of CEO apparently resulted from drawing straws (and was the third pick, at that).

"One of the reasons that Roger acted as chief executive is that Sandy was so damn shy," recalls George Murray, who would join the firm in 1970 through an acquisition. Nonetheless, he insists, "Behind the scenes, the driving force, the engine, was Sandy."

The Quest for Capital

In the late 1960s, Weill may have been one step removed from the high-stakes investment banking deals and the newspaper headlines, but he was already laying the groundwork for the surge in growth at the firm that was around the corner.

As the partner who focused the most on running the business, Weill came to understand the critical nature of capital in building a financial business. Many of CBWL's moves, dating back to its 1965 incorporation, were designed to procure capital. CBWL, in fact, invited investments from all sorts of people and businesses tangentially related to the firm, from their landlord to suppliers like ADP (Automatic Data Processing). In 1969, the firm raised money in a private placement of convertible debentures.

"It was clear that Sandy was interested in the business as a business, which was relatively unusual," Lipper recalls of those early days. "Most people were just interested in the business as a way to make money."

When the bull market started to fizzle, CBWL had plenty of capital to withstand the downturn. Fittingly enough, the securities industry started its slide in mid-1968, a year that became infamous for the assassinations of Robert Kennedy and Martin Luther King, the riots at the Democratic National Convention in Chicago, the political meltdown of President Lyndon Johnson, and escalation of the Vietnam War. On Wall Street, the slump that began in 1968 soon created a crippling back-office crunch.

Back Office Bumbling on Wall Street

It's a basic fact of life on Wall Street that within the froth and speculation of a bull market are sown the seeds of later financial meltdowns. The new era of retail brokerage that firms like CBWL helped bring about in the 1960s was fueled by a raging bull market.

To ride the bull market wave, many firms rushed to hire brokers, open branches, and expand into new cities. But most firms lacked electronic transfer ability and securities had to be traded and delivered manually. All the bold expansion plans typically didn't consider the paperwork—endless mounds of orders, bills, receipts, customer confirmations, and securities certificates.

In 1968, orders zoomed to an all-time high. Before that year, the busiest trading day in history was October 29, 1929—Black Tuesday—when 16.4 million shares were traded, a record surpassed 25 times in 1968.

For a time, the outrageous profits of the bull market papered over the glaring processing problems of the older firms. But when the market hit a slump in mid-1968, these organizations were exposed as hopelessly inefficient. Often, the longer a firm had been in existence, the more disheveled its operations.

Brokers were literally doing *too* good a job of selling and their back offices couldn't keep up with the paperwork. In some instances, the more sales that brokers made, the worse shape their firm was in. Orders were lost and costly mistakes made.

CBWL didn't encounter these problems. The firm had cleared its trades through Burnham & Company from the beginning, and eventually produced too much volume for Tubby Burnham to handle. The partners made appeals to several prestigious brokerages with clearing operations big enough to absorb CBWL's business, but were turned away. The firm had little choice but to build its own clearing operation from scratch. This serendipitous decision largely protected it from the back office chaos experienced by other firms.

In what would prove one of the firm's smartest hires, CBWL recruited back-office guru Frank Zarb, who went on to become "energy czar" under President Ford and then Chairman of the Nasdaq stock exchange. Zarb grew up in Flatbush, Brooklyn, the son of a refrigerator repairman, and like Weill was known for his toughness and savvy. Before joining CBWL, he was second in command in the back office of the brokerage firm Goodbody, which after Zarb left suffered its own back-office troubles and had to be rescued by Merrill Lynch. At CBWL, Zarb set up a state-of-the-art clearing operation. The firm spent nearly $3 million to cover the salaries of 150 new employees and the costs of computer services.[20]

With his eye for detail and penchant for staying in the background—where the real work was getting done—Weill worked side by side with Zarb in building the new clearinghouse. "In those days, most people thought the back office was for people in green eyeshades," Roger Berlind told *Forbes* in 1993. "But Sandy was fearful of anything going wrong down there. He became familiar with it."[21]

The significance of the move was lost on the rest of the investment world. In a January 1970 article, the *New York Times* referred to the clearing operation with a note of condescension. "After 10 years in the razzle-dazzle side of Wall Street, the firm also is getting involved in more of the nitty-gritty part of the business, namely, back-office operations," the paper noted.[22]

The clearinghouse became Weill's baby for another reason: It could handle the gigantic volume of trades he anticipated coming from hundreds of thousands of investors, both institutional and individual traders. Despite the slump in the retail side of the business, Weill believed the future of the firm was in providing brokerage services, not the investment banking deals that Cogan was so enamored of. Toward this end, in 1969, the firm acquired its first branch outside of New York, taking over the Beverly Hills office of disintegrating brokerage McDonnell & Co.

Weill later recalled that acquisition as a learning experience:

> We made a ton of mistakes with that one branch that we wouldn't repeat with 30. We'd left them too much on their own as to how they ran their business. We learned about the need for controls, for audit, for discipline, for communicating your philosophy as well as your research and other products and yet how to still keep people motivated.[23]

Despite the problems with that branch, CBWL saw that one way to generate more profits was to open more branches. Berlind announced at the time that the long-range plan was to open offices in other major financial centers, such as Boston, Houston, Atlanta, Chicago, and Detroit. Besides the newly minted back-office operation, CBWL could also afford to think big because it had successfully diversified into investment management. At this point, it managed more than $500 million in investment funds, most of which came from Bernstein-Macaulay.

Suddenly, as old-line firms began to totter under their own weight, it didn't matter whom you knew, what club you belonged to, or who your ancestors were. No one cared if Weill put ketchup on his steak, wore rumpled suits off the rack, or wasn't the featured speaker at industry events. CBWL had its house in order, which was more than many Our Crowd firms could say.

Beating old entrenched Wall Street firms at their own game would soon be child's play for Weill. The opportunity to snatch up ailing firms at a bargain price was about to emerge, and CBWL was ready.

Hayden Stone: The Prototype Deal

O f all the unofficial titles Sandy Weill has earned in his long career, "Master of the Deal" would probably come at the top of the list. But it is not just any deal that Weill has mastered. He has built his empire, fortune, and personal reputation by perfecting one very particular type of deal—and doing it over and over again.

Most dealmakers operate in a similar manner, specializing in a particular transaction—Donald Trump develops luxury real estate, Don King arranges boxing matches, Sandy Weill buys financial services companies—most often ones that are struggling in a tough market and available at a cheap price. "I wouldn't *exactly* call him a one-trick pony," says Roy Smith, the former Goldman Sachs partner. "But he doesn't need many notes to his piano."

A year after he left Citigroup, John Reed described a fundamental difference between him and Weill: "I'm a builder. He's an acquirer. Just totally different."[1] Reed, even if unwittingly, was paying Weill a huge compliment. Many top CEOs slip up on the rocky shoals of mergers: Jack Welch failed in his 2001 bid for

Honeywell; Hewlett Packard's Carly Fiorina waged a bitter struggle with her board and the founders' families over her proposal to merge with Compaq; and DaimlerChrysler's 1999 "merger of equals" eventually sent Chrysler CEO Robert Eaton packing and, ultimately, proved a bad match. In fact, almost every historical study shows that most large mergers destroy more shareholder value than they create.

Yet, nearly every acquisition Weill executed has increased value for his company's shareholders. The process is neither pretty nor pleasant—involving long hours, bitter negotiations, bruised egos, and, ultimately, firing "redundant" workers and executives who don't fit in. Weill's laserlike focus on the make-or-break transaction details is the main skill that accounts for his success at the merger game. But a look at his long career shows other skills he used to successfully orchestrate a deal.

Weill keeps a lean, smooth-running operation so he is prepared to take advantage of opportunities that come his way. At CBWL, that meant having a back office that functioned well enough to integrate other firms without disrupting business. Weill is also a consummate opportunist. For example, he gained control of both Commercial Credit (1986) and Salomon Brothers (1997) when each was struggling to a degree.

Not surprisingly, Weill negotiates favorable prices. But perhaps even more important, he is always careful to eliminate as much risk as possible from the transaction. For example, he typically demands that a company settle any outstanding liabilities. "One of Sandy's strengths is that he is very insecure," says Jeff Lane, who worked on deals with Weill throughout the 1970s and early 1980s. "He questions everybody, he questions himself. In this business that really is an enormous strength."

Once a deal goes through, Weill often takes the more prestigious name for the new company. Through this strategy, Weill turned what was Commercial Credit into Primerica, then Travelers, then Citigroup.

When integrating two companies, Weill homes in on details others might find niggling, but he recognizes them as vital to the success of the merger. If that means staying up all night to make sure accounts were transferred successfully to the new firm, he'll do it. Weill then moves quickly to cut costs and consolidate operations. If an acquired company has divisions that don't fit in with the core business, he'll sell quickly. A benefit plan too generous? He'll look at scaling it back. And, of course, any overlapping staff are shown the door.

Weill's serial acquisition of companies—at Citigroup, he started a new business group just to look at prospective deals—has led many to ask, "How much is enough?" It's the wrong question. Weill's knowledge of how to acquire and integrate a company to increase shareholder value is his greatest competitive advantage, and there is every reason for him to keep exploiting this advantage now that he is on the biggest financial services stage there is.

He has instilled this deal-making ethos at Citigroup where growth through acquisition remained a core strategy into 2002, a time when opaque accounting practices of conglomerates such as Tyco International called into question this concept. Weill has groomed a staff to keep the deal-mill running, even after he is gone. "If we stopped doing deals, a large part of what got us here would be taken off the table," says Charles Prince, Citigroup's operations chief. "I think one of the unique characteristics that we bring to the party is our ability to do big deals, to do them fast and do them effectively."

The first big deal for Weill—the one that really put him on the Wall Street map—was CBWL's 1970 acquisition of the once-great retail firm Hayden Stone. Tiny by today's standards, the complex deal was a watershed at the time—not only for Weill and his firm, but for a foundering Wall Street. Hayden Stone would prove Weill's signature deal in the 1970s. By repeating the same successful formula over and over, he would create first Shearson and later today's Citigroup.

Scrappy CBWL—The Strongest of a Weak Bunch on Wall Street

In the spring and early summer of 1970, the stock market was in retreat and individual investors had gone into hiding. But CBWL was holding its own. The partners could have lain low, ridden out the slump, and made a nice living with their boutique firm.

There was just one serendipitous wrinkle: Current conditions rendered CBWL, just barely 10 years old, one of the most financially healthy brokerages on Wall Street. The end of the bull market had caught Wall Street disastrously unprepared.

From mid-1968 through mid-1970, statistics tell a sorry tale of one of the worst periods on Wall Street since the 1930s. More than 100 New York Stock Exchange member firms were liquidated or acquired. An estimated 16,500 workers in the New York Stock Exchange lost their jobs. Hundreds of brokerages in the United States were shut down or merged with others and hundreds of millions in capital was either lost or pulled out of the markets. Wall Street struggles beset CBWL, to be sure, as the firm's earnings dropped from a peak of $2.7 million in 1969 to roughly $500,000 in 1970. Still, the firm had an excellent capital base and maintained much surer footing than other Wall Street brokerages.

The most spectacular collapse was that of McDonnell & Company, which in 1968 had $33 million in revenues, a net worth of $15 million, 26 branch offices in the United States and France,

1,500 employees and close to 100,000 customers. According to one account, Scotsman Thomas McKay, a McDonnell executive, had run the back office with enthusiasm characteristic of the time:

> Like many Wall Street executives of this era, he regarded the back office as a rather dirty, smelly warren, a realm in which a man of his abilities and attainments should not involve himself unduly . . . He maintained his office several floors above the back office and preferred to transmit orders through subordinates.[2]

The firm attempted to dig itself out of the mess by selling off some branches. That's when CBWL acquired its Beverly Hills operation in 1969. But by March 1970, McDonnell was in ruins.

In contrast, by early 1970, thanks to Frank Zarb's modern, efficient back-office system, CBWL's operations were running smoothly. The firm, with nearly 400 employees, had plenty of excess capacity to absorb the business of other firms. Soon, that extra capacity would be put to good use.

The Big Board Calvary

By 1970, the carnage in the securities industry was so great that Congress, in conjunction with the industry, created the Securities Investor Protection Corporation (SIPC) to insure losses caused by brokerage-house failures. Also that year, the governors of the New York Stock Exchange commissioned a panel to monitor the finances of member firms, dubbed the Crisis Committee. It was led by Felix Rohatyn of Lazard Freres, who became known as "Felix the Fixer." Later Rohatyn would become best known for his role as chairman of the Municipal Assistance Corporation, the agency that bailed New York City out of its fiscal crisis in the 1970s. He also served as the U.S. Ambassador to France for three years during the Clinton Administration.

Rohatyn's Crisis Committee established the Big Board Special Trust Fund to provide capital to firms in danger of toppling over. There were some firms that everyone wanted to see stay afloat, fearing their demise would start a chain reaction and bring down all of Wall Street with it. One of those firms was Hayden Stone. Like many of Wall Street's once-great firms, 78-year-old Hayden Stone—where Joseph Kennedy got his start in business—had expanded too quickly and become an unwieldy behemoth. It had gambled on a major expansion in the mid-1960s, growing to more than 80 branches, establishing 16 foreign offices, and hiring hundreds of brokers at One Wall Street and throughout the country. But like everyone else, Hayden Stone got into trouble trying to push too much business through its back office.

"The lack of credibility had the potential to engulf the whole industry," recalls George Murray, who was promoted to president of Hayden Stone in a 1970 management shake-up resulting from the firm's troubles. "It was a very, very precarious time." The stock exchange was not propping up failing firms "out of the goodness of their hearts," says Murray. "It was Holy Jerusalem, let's stop this thing before it gets out of control."

"Business was just overwhelmingly good," recalls Robert James, who at that time managed Hayden Stone's One Wall Street office. "We couldn't handle it." James remembers walking into the room where the paperwork was handled and seeing disorganized stacks of securities piled everywhere—on radiators and windowsills. "It was a nightmare," he says. The firm tried to hire more people to handle the work, but there was a labor shortage and many of the workers hired in desperation weren't up to the job.

Hayden Stone, like many troubled firms, decided that comput-erizing its back office was the only solution. This well-intentioned embrace of new technology turned out to be hugely disruptive and sent Hayden Stone into a further tailspin. For example, for several days the system inadvertently doubled all orders for mu-nicipal bonds—so clients received twice the amount of bonds as they were supposed to, remembers James. "Most of the clients, when we told them what happened, brought the bonds back," he says. "There were some who didn't." Lawsuits ensued.

To make matters worse, Hayden Stone was also seriously un-dercapitalized. Exchange rules required all firms to be privately held, and most operated as partnerships. When partners re-tired—and when the bear market struck, many did just that—they wanted to cash out their share of the firm's capital. "The elderly, long-term partners were drawing down their capital," Murray says. "But the younger people coming along, of which I was one, didn't have the money to buy out these people and re-plenish the capital required to run the business."

This dynamic meant that many big Wall Street firms with im-peccable reputations were chronically undercapitalized. A firm hit with a rash of retirements or resignations in a period of a few short years could find itself on the precipice of insolvency. Hay-den Stone was one of those. By 1970, Murray recalls, "Frankly, we had run out of gas."

To boost capital, in March 1970, the firm convinced some of its investment banking clients—including a number of Okla-homa City businessmen—to loan stock worth a total $12.4 mil-lion to Hayden Stone, which would count toward the firm's capital. Things failed to improve. Shortly after the Oklahoma City investors came on the scene, in fact, the firm announced it had lost $700,000 in March alone.[3] Meantime, the continuing bear market drove down the value of the borrowed stock, and

Hayden Stone's capital fell below required levels. The Exchange threatened to liquidate Hayden Stone and sell the borrowed stock.

That would have spelled disaster for Hayden Stone's employees and clients, and also for the Oklahoma City contingent. Not only would they lose all the shares they had lent to Hayden Stone, but they would have to pay heavy capital gains taxes on the liquidated stock. The value of all their remaining company stock would also sink due to the huge volume of shares flooding the market. The Oklahoma City investors hired local attorney Larry Hartzog to try to get them out of the mess.

Hartzog made a deal with the Exchange that if the Oklahoma crew put up cash, they could get their stock back. "That was basically the only equity that existed in Hayden Stone. So at that point, we were really in the driver's seat as far as what happened," says Hartzog.

Rumors of an impending liquidation circulated all spring and summer in 1970. Stories about Hayden Stone's inability to fulfill commodities contracts convinced the New York Stock Exchange and the Chicago Board of Trade to issue highly unusual, formal statements saying that they considered the firm to be sound.

In May 1970, the Oklahoma City investors and other members of the so-called Hayden Stone "rescue team" decided to make a management change. They demoted CEO Alfred J. Coyle to chairman of Hayden Stone's executive committee and promoted Murray to president and Donald Stroben from executive vice president to CEO. Stroben's mission was to find an acquirer for the firm. He talked to all the major firms on Wall Street, including Merrill Lynch, Bache, and CBWL—all of which passed on what they considered too risky a deal. Walston, one of the top-five retail houses on Wall Street, agreed to negotiate. A deal was struck and if it had been left solely up to the Crisis Committee, Walston would have merged with Hayden Stone.

With firms failing all over Wall Street, however, the Oklahoma City bankers believed that Walston wasn't in much better shape than the other big brokerage firms. Particularly suspect was Walston's plan to use the value of its pension fund to purchase Hayden Stone. Recalls Hartzog:

> When our guys found out, they said, "Go see if there is a way out of that trap." They told me, "Go up there to New York City, spend a weekend. We'll get you a suite in the Regency." I ended up living in that place.

Hartzog's first stop in New York City was to meet with an official at the New York Stock Exchange, an imposing institution to the Oklahoma lawyer, and tell him his concerns about the Walston deal. "He looked at me and said, 'Hartzog, you can do anything you are big enough to do.' I think what he meant was, 'get out of my hair.'" Hartzog took that as his cue to find a different sort of an acquirer, one with clean books, an exemplary back-office operation, and sound management.

CBWL Enters the Hayden Stone Sweepstakes

There were not many firms on Wall Street that fit Hartzog's profile. One was CBWL, and Hartzog approached Berlind to see if the firm would reconsider doing a deal. For CBWL, acquiring Hayden Stone would be far from a clear-cut decision. On the plus side, adding a firm the size of Hayden Stone would mean adding a large network of retail branches and a respected investment banking operation. Despite the strength of its back office, CBWL was still a relatively small company that mainly served institutions. It had only two offices and about 5,000 accounts. A deal with Hayden Stone would also raise the profile and prestige of the firm. As Weill would later say in an interview with *Institutional Investor:* "CBWL, at the time we took over Hayden Stone, an old WASPy firm, obviously wasn't their first choice."[4]

To Weill, Hayden Stone's financial problems appeared too daunting to take on. In fact, it's fair to say that if Weill had represented CBWL at the outset of the talks with Hayden Stone, there is little chance that CBWL would have ever acquired the bigger firm. "I was the cautious one," Weill later recalled. "Roger was a great risk taker."[5] Weill was initially against the deal, worrying about all the problems at Hayden Stone and the general contraction of business on Wall Street. Up to this point, CBWL had been involved in just one acquisition of a firm: the relatively pain-free and low-profile Bernstein-Macaulay deal.

"Weill was very suspect of doing the transaction," Stroben recalls. "He perceived that there was a lot of risk. He became the person that had to be convinced, which gave him a lot of power in determining how it would be done. He was also the most detailed and analytical person of the four of them." The CBWL partners declined to buy the firm and Stroben went back to negotiating with Walston.

But Rohatyn's Crisis Committee desperately wanted Hayden Stone saved. It sweetened the deal for CBWL, promising $7.6 million in incentives. Negotiations started up again. Berlind, seeing the big picture, understood that hooking up with Hayden Stone would establish CBWL as a serious player on Wall Street. But Weill was still not ready to go forward. The part of him that years before would have been happy if he and Joan saved enough to buy a deep fryer was still holding him back.

Even as he opposed the deal, Weill immersed himself in the details, studying documents to discover which Hayden Stone departments generated revenues, who the best individual brokers at the firm were, and which offices were the most profitable. In the end, perhaps because he understood Hayden Stone's operations so well, Weill agreed that CBWL should seriously negotiate with Hartzog. And because he knew the particular details of Hayden Stone better than any of his three partners, he was chosen to do the negotiating.

Hartzog experienced first-hand Weill's informal, yet hard-driving negotiating style. One sunny day, he found himself having a hot dog with Weill outside the Plaza Hotel discussing the details of combining Hayden Stone with CBWL. "Two things attracted me to Sandy at that point in time. He had his expenses absolutely under control. And he had Frank Zarb running his back office like a Swiss watch. When I latched onto Sandy down there having a hot dog, I said, 'This is my man. This is the guy,'" recalls Hartzog.

Weill drove a hard bargain. In the deal he struck, CBWL would acquire 28 Hayden Stone branches staffed by 500 brokers and the 50,000 customers those brokers served. In a multilayered financial transaction, CBWL received $6 million in cash and was not forced to assume Hayden Stone's substantial liabilities. For their part, the Oklahoma City investors and the trust fund received shares in the new CBWL-Hayden Stone. Walston would get what CBWL didn't want—18 various other Hayden Stone branches.

News of CBWL's deal with Hartzog took many by surprise, including Stroben and Murray, who were still negotiating with Walston. But Murray maintains that he and Stroben were all for the deal with CBWL when they learned about it. Walston already had a network of branch offices and was likely to cut out overlapping brokers. CBWL didn't have a large branch office system and would need the Hayden Stone brokers to service the accounts. "We both instantly recognized the potential for things to work out better for our people," says Murray. Furthermore, he also thought the mix of two companies with very different cultures would work well:

> My recollection was that it was an instant blend of what really were opposites. Hayden Stone was the grand old lady on poor times. Some would refer to it as very WASPy—which I'm not—but that was its aura, its reputation. Whereas CBWL was viewed as a super-aggressive, small, opportunistic boutique.

Once management at the two firms had aligned in late August, the challenge became to convince the Exchange to approve the deal. Rohatyn told Hartzog that the merger with CBWL could go forward only if all its many creditors were on board by a September 10 deadline.

Convincing the outraged Okalhoma City businessmen to accept the deal was no small feat. Many felt burned by their involvement with Wall Street. They weren't swayed by arguments that Hayden Stone had to be saved or all of Wall Street might fall like dominos. "They said, let the whole damn thing go down," recalls Hartzog. But because they all had millions in Hayden Stone stock, most could be convinced to go along. The investors buckled one-by-one until just one was left, Jack Golsen of LSB Industries. Recalls Hartzog:

> Golsen was so mad and upset we didn't even bother with him until we got everyone else. He thought the firm deserved to fail and shouldn't be able to scrape through the situation. He was willing to sacrifice all the money he had for principle. Nobody in New York understood that.

Years later, some observers believed that Golsen's perspective had merit, that Wall Street had brought the calamity on itself and shouldn't have been bailed out. Chris Welles wrote in *The*

Last Days of the Club that the rescues by the Crisis Committee were done mostly in self-interest:

> The rescues were really desperate attempts by NYSE leaders, not to preserve order in the financial community, but to preserve the Club. Although Exchange leaders predicted that the failure of Hayden Stone would precipitate a selling panic, chaos in the money markets, and the bankrupting of corporations and banks, most Club members knew better.[6]

On September 10, Golsen still hadn't given his consent and Rohatyn extended the deadline one more day. The partners had until the trading bell rang at 10 A.M. on September 11 to change Golsen's mind. For CBWL, these next 24 hours were the most important they would ever face. If the deal went through, the firm would be a force to reckon with—one of the few on Wall Street with positive momentum. If the deal fell apart, Weill and his partners would be back running Corned Beef With Lettuce indefinitely.

Weill ensconced himself at the Plaza Hotel, across Fifth Avenue from CBWL's office. That way, he could easily get to the office to transfer Hayden Stone's accounts to CBWL if Golsen capitulated. Cogan and Berlind flew out to Oklahoma with Hartzog and David Stone, grandson of one of the firm's two founding members, to act as the front men and try to persuade the recalcitrant Golsen. Stroben drove them out to the airport. He recalls:

> It was a very dramatic thing. The Exchange said if we didn't have the deal done by opening bell on that day, they were going to, in effect, foreclose. So the night before we went out to Teterboro Airport in New Jersey in the middle of a tremendous rainstorm. We got there and the pilot said, "No way. I'm not taking off." Time was passing. And we were all thinking

about how the next morning the Exchange was going to close the door. All of a sudden, a little hole in the sky appeared. The pilot said, "Let's get in." and these guys all took off.

By the time they arrived in Oklahoma City it was early morning and they had to roust Golsen out of bed and convince him to go to his office.

In the early morning hours of September 11, they all made their pleas to Golsen, who also fielded calls from Rohatyn and other Exchange officials including Exchange Chairman Bernard (Bunny) Lasker, a friend of President Nixon. They all asked him to go along with the deal for the good of everyone else involved. Nixon himself was even ready to call Golsen on the Exchange's behalf, but Hartzog quashed that idea, believing a call from the President would only make Golsen more intractable. The tenseness of the situation is described in *The New Crowd:*

> Cogan tried one more tactic. Drawing Golsen aside, he said: "If Hayden Stone goes under, there's something like $500 million to $750 million of stocks that won't clear, and there's a possibility of an enormous panic. You're a Jew. I'm a Jew. You'll do more harm than Eichmann has done to Jews in this culture. Jack, you sign the document and I'll see that you're okay.[7]

Another Oklahoma businessman, Bill Swisher, may have had the most influence over Golsen. He made an appeal on a personal level, asking Golsen, as a friend, to consent so he wouldn't lose his own stake in the firm. Golsen, believing Swisher was just caving in to the intense pressure of that conference room, told him, "Bill, if you can get up and walk around that table and still feel the same way after, then I'll do it," recalls Hartzog.

Swisher got up, and when he was half-way around the conference room table, a person unrelated to the situation wandered into the room, disrupting the meeting and ratcheting up the tension even higher. Then Swisher completed his circumnavigation and Golsen finally agreed, with 11 minutes to spare. Hartzog made the call to Rohatyn that the merger could go through. When news reached traders, a cheer went up from the floor.

A Done Deal

The new firm was named CBWL-Hayden Stone. It had a net worth of about $20 million, including $9 million in CBWL capital. Suddenly, Weill and his partners were running a company with hundreds of brokers and support staff. Soon, the cost-cutting began in earnest. Rumors flew about who was going to lose their jobs, and most people on the Hayden Stone side prepared to be fired.

There would be some controversial moves after the acquisition. Several Hayden Stone veterans were encouraged to leave. But it didn't take long for the employees who remained to realize that the new firm was much more sound financially and operationally. One branch manager from that time says once he knew he would be able to keep his job, he felt comfortable with the CBWL team. "Sandy had a reputation for being tough, which was true," says the manager, who remained with the firm for 30 years. "He was tough but fair."

CBWL encountered few problems integrating the operations of the larger firm. Zarb eliminated Hayden Stone's enormous and inefficient back office and shifted all of the processing over to CBWL's operation. "That's what made the whole acquisition work," says Stroben. "It also helped matters that, thanks to the cuts in branches, the volume of business slowed way down."

The success of the new firm was reflected in classified ads placed by the firm to find entry-level brokers, typists, and general office workers. These marketing efforts revealed a different kind of organization than the employees of the old Hayden Stone were used to: unpolished, collegial, and open to new ideas. Consider this jovial CBWL advertisement in the *New York Times* in late 1970:

Something for Everyone?

Maybe not. We know we won't please everybody. But we think we stand a pretty good chance! We are looking for people Period. Typists with clerical attitude. Clericals who can type. They will work at our handsome new downtown office in the center of the action called "Wall Street." And, even though we are a prominent member of the financial community, brokerage experience is not necessary. But if you have some. . . . Great! Wherever your goals may be, you will probably find a position just suited to your unique tastes.[8]

Perot, DuPont Glore Forgan, and Walston

The success of the CBWL-Hayden Stone merger is even more apparent when looked at in context of other attempts to save ailing firms by combining them with other enterprises. One of the many dramatic disasters that epitomized the brokerage business in the 1970s was Ross Perot's entry into the securities business. It's a story that Weill has pointed to a few times throughout his career with some satisfaction as evidence of how difficult it is to succeed on Wall Street. Perot's misadventures would eventually affect Walston, the runner-up to CBWL in the Hayden Stone sweepstakes.

In many ways, Perot, who later achieved national recognition when he ran for president in 1992, has much in common with

Weill. Each worked for a large company after college and experienced early success as a salesman, Weill selling stocks at Bear Stearns and Perot selling computers at IBM. Each started his own business in 1960, and each made it big about the same time by taking his respective company public, Perot in 1968 and Weill in 1970. Each ran a big business like it was a small business. For example, neither had any qualms about picking up the phone and calling anyone at any level in the organization to ask a question or resolve a dispute.

Unlike Weill, however, Perot made some of the same mistakes on Wall Street that doomed many of the big brokerage firms. He dumped good money after bad and then embarked on an ill-advised merger.

Perot's Wall Street debacle, ironically enough, started with a major triumph for his firm, EDS. On July 3, 1970, EDS won a $43 million contract to computerize the back office of DuPont Glore Forgan. That firm had been founded by the wealthy DuPont family of Wilmington, Delaware, but by 1970 had one of the most hopelessly muddled back offices of any of the big firms. When the Exchange required the firm to obtain another $10 million of capital in December, Perot stepped up with a short-term loan, partly to keep the company afloat long enough to fulfill the contract with EDS. Perot also viewed himself as a business savior.

In the spring of 1971, President Nixon encouraged Perot to provide more loans to the struggling firm, using some of the same logic that had been used in CBWL's acquisition of Hayden Stone: if DuPont Glore Forgan failed, the Exchange itself might actually fail. The diminutive Texan significantly increased his investment over the next year, making a $50 million loan and obtaining a 51 percent stake in the firm.

Perot sent his right-hand man at EDS, Mort Meyerson, to run the brokerage firm, but in 1971 and 1972 the firm lost $3 million a month. Weill recalled, years later, that part of Perot's problem was that he attempted to retool the salesforce in the EDS model:

> When Ross Perot took over DuPont [Glore Forgan] and applied a concept a little like the Marines to the salesforce, it didn't work. He lost a lot of money. . . . It showed how hard it was for someone outside the industry to come in, and that cooled a lot of people on the business.[9]

It also appears Perot didn't spend enough time pouring over the books. After EDS acquired DuPont Glore Forgan, Perot's accountants found $80 million in liabilities when they finally did their belated due diligence.[10]

In the meantime, EDS won another contract on Wall Street, this time for Walston, which seemed healthier than DuPont Glore Forgan. Perot decided to suggest an alliance between the two firms and Walston's board approved the deal, thinking that Perot could always bail them out with his deep pockets. But both firms soon tanked and in January 1974, Perot shut Dupont Glore Forgan and lost $60 million (not counting the millions EDS made on the two computer contracts). Perot's dream of big-time success on Wall Street was over almost before it started.

Running CBWL-Hayden Stone after the Merger

In some ways, CBWL was completely changed by merging with a firm more than twice its size. "Hayden Stone was the transforming transaction," recalls Jeff Lane. "It took us from being an institutional shop to giving us a presence on the high net worth side of the business. In addition, it was also transforming for Wall Street."

Nonetheless, after the acquisition, life at the firm didn't change much for the partners in terms of their surroundings, how they dealt with each other, or their daily routine. The firm's headquarters was still in the GM Building, and the four partners still shared one large room. Don Stroben and George Murray had offices on either side of the partners.

Weill later recalled, with humor, what it was like to work in such close quarters:

> When wives hung up angry, we had to make believe the conversation was still going on, saying into a dead phone, "Okay honey, I'll see you later." Because you'd get killed by the other guys.[11]

But Stroben says the office set up had a more important role.

"They all sat in an open room, so they could hear everything that the others had to say. All four of them could then keep tabs on each other," Stroben says. Even though the firm's executive committee broadened to include former Hayden Stone partners, the CBWL group retained the power. "The executive committee would meet, review issues, talk and argue and no decision would come forth," recalls Stroben. "Then the four of them would go meet at someone's apartment and they would decide."

Although they were equal partners, Stroben guesses that Weill was the most forceful of the four and got his way most of the time. "It was clear the four of them needed to be in agreement. But Sandy seemed to have the strongest personality in terms of making a decision."

The Hunt for Capital

With firms failing right and left and the market languishing, there were plenty of tough decisions to be made. Weill had to be aggressive about controlling costs and making money anyway he could. According to J. Michael King, a big producer at

Hayden Stone in the early 1970s, no investment banking business was too small or obscure for Weill and his partners at that time. "He did whatever he had to do for the firm to survive, regardless of the customer that put money in," King says. "He was pretty ruthless."

The Hayden Stone deal also gave Weill a significant amount of capital to use as a building block. But it was not clear that it would be enough to fuel the growth that the partners now envisioned. Weill and his partners had incorporated in 1965 and obtained capital from private investors, but the partners knew that the best way to raise capital was by selling shares to the public. At the time, however, New York Stock Exchange member firms could not be publicly held—or could they?

Going Public

There were many reasons that member firms of the New York Stock Exchange wanted to avoid going public. For one, they would then have to follow public company disclosure rules, which entitled shareholders to information in the form of annual reports, 10-ks, shareholder meetings, and opened up the firms to media scrutiny. For another, management would have to worry not just about profits and losses, but also shareholder value and the stock price. Tim Carrington wrote in *The Year They Sold Wall Street* about another big objection that Wall Street had to the notion of Exchange firms going public:

> Access to the public capital markets would open the way for the new breed on Wall Street to assume positions that had considerable clout. The old private firms had spent most of the century building up their capital. It disturbed officers at these houses to realize that others could rake in comparable

amounts simply by filing prospectuses with the SEC and issuing shares to the public.[12]

But eventually Exchange rules had to give way to the new realities of the securities business. In May 1969, Donaldson, Lufkin & Jenrette (DLJ) CEO Dan Lufkin shocked Wall Street by filing a registration statement with the SEC to hold a public offering, in clear violation of Exchange policy. As Weill would with the Citigroup-Travelers merger over 30 years later, DLJ openly challenged the regulators to disallow his action. DLJ stated, in fact, that it would quit the Exchange if the rules were not changed to allow its public offering. In April 1970, the rules prohibiting public ownership were struck down and DLJ could proceed.

Merrill Lynch was next, filing in mid-June 1971 to sell four million shares. Then came CBWL-Hayden Stone. On June 28, 1971, the firm filed its own SEC registration statement, saying it planned to sell one million shares. From the initial prospectus, CBWL-Hayden Stone hoped to price the stock as high as $17 a share. Before CBWL-Hayden Stone had its public offering in October, two other firms beat them to the punch, Bache and Minneapolis-based Piper, Jaffray & Hopwood.

The morning of the offering, October 4, 1971, there were plenty of skeptics. Even one of CBWL-Hayden Stone's own analysts was decidedly bearish about both his firm's offering and the market in general. Dan Dorfman of the *Wall Street Journal* wrote in his market column:

> It's anybody's guess how the shares of CBWL-Hayden Stone will fare when they probably begin trading today. But if you buy the view of its director of technical market studies, David Bostian, the near-term outlook for this stock, or any stock for that matter, is pretty poor. Mr. Bostian, who had called bullish moves in the market three times in the past year, early last

month predicted a sharp decline in the Dow Jones industrial average to about the 790 or 800 level by year-end.[13]

Luckily for Weill and his partners—who each held 284,000 shares, or 12 percent of the total—the pessimism proved unfounded. The offering was a sellout even though it wasn't priced as high as hoped. One million shares sold for $12.50 each. Weill, Cogan, Berlind, and Levitt became millionaires and the firm raised nearly $7 million in additional capital.

Soon other brokerage firms went public, trying to capture the capital necessary to stay in business. Some of the old-line firms resisted the trend, considering the notion appalling. Many of those couldn't keep up with the demands of a sped-up economy and were bought out by larger partnerships. But some, like Goldman Sachs and Lehman Brothers, stayed private until the 1990s and thrived nonetheless.

For Sandy Weill, going public was another right move at the right time. "The public offering was what really ultimately gave Sandy Weill the ability to do what he did," says Stroben, who recalls that Weill initially was against the idea of going public in 1971. The $13 million raised may not seem like much by today's standards, but with Wall Street flat on its back, it was a fortune. "From then on, he had the good fortune to have something that was rare on Wall Street at that time: capital, as well as a position of control and an ability to execute. That momentum carried him on and on."

Building Shearson

nherent in managing a business is managing people. And while Sandy Weill is best known as a deal maker, his tremendous success has just as much to do with his unusual management style as it does his ability to construct deals. Harvard Business School has written case studies about Weill's management techniques, crediting him for maintaining a small, hands-on executive staff of "corporate renegades" who shun bureaucracy. But that doesn't make him easy to work for.

Weill the boss is an amalgamation of Weill the small businessman's son, Weill the military school plebe, and Weill the fraternity brother. Like his father and grandfather, Weill manages his staff as if he were running a small, family-owned business. Like the reward system that gave him so much confidence at Peekskill Military Academy, Weill sets strict financial goals for managers, rewarding success and punishing failure. And in the same way Weill thrived in the collegial atmosphere of Alpha Epsilon Pi at Cornell, he tries to make work fun for his staff, managing with an exuberance that manifests itself in teasing and inside jokes with colleagues that can also sometimes boil over into fits of temper.

Throughout his career, Weill has treated his management team as an extended family. He knows his staff both personally and professionally, often playing the role of patriarch. As Weill once explained:

> I have always tried to build a family kind of environment. Part of my philosophy as CEO is to be responsive to the people— not just about what's happening in the company but about any other problem they have. . . . In my career, the things of which I'm proudest are the family environment at Shearson and that a lot of people are owners.[1]

Associates from various times in Weill's career say that he and Joan become very involved in the personal lives of the people Weill works with. The Weills vacation with key executives, attend bar mitzvahs and weddings, and hold important business meetings at their Greenwich, Connecticut, home.

This intimate management style is not without its downside. Weill's executive team can resemble at times a dysfunctional family, with screaming matches, hurt feelings, and surprising exits. In recent years, Heidi Miller, Bob Lipp, and Jay Fishman—all members of Citigroup's management committee and Weill favorites— have left the company of their own accord. Of course, like the prodigal son, the possibility of an executive returning to the Weill fold is always quite good. Lipp resurfaced in late December 2001, to head Travelers Property Casualty after Weill decided to spin off that business. Weill has demonstrated a talent for doing deals and making alliances with many of his ex-lieutenants.

Many of these former Weill lieutenants have been snapped up to head other companies. Fishman, for example, went on to become CEO of The St. Paul Companies. "I called Sandy and asked him why Jay Fishman left," says Jeff Lane, who helped Weill build Shearson. "And he told me, 'For a reason you are very familiar with: He wanted to be a CEO.'" (Lane left Travelers in July 1998 to head the investment firm Neuberger Berman.) Indeed, much like Bobby Knight, the controversial college basketball coach, Weill is famous for molding underlings who go out and take the world by storm. "I think it's flattering to Sandy that Jamie is running Bank One," Lane says, referring to Jamie Dimon, Weill's long-time right-hand man. "I am running Neuberger Berman, Joe Plumeri heads up Willis & Co., Jay Fishman is running St. Paul companies, and Bob Greenhill has his own investment bank."

But over the years Weill has bristled when his lieutenants have, in his view, overstepped their bounds, pursued private agendas or made clear their ambitions to assume a larger role. Most famously, he and Reed forced Weill protégé Dimon out of Citigroup in 1999 after their long and intense relationship soured. "Sandy is known for being very loyal to those who are loyal to him, but if he perceives you slipping away, watch out," says Howard Clark Jr., who worked with Weill at American Express.

The "Spaghetti School" of Management

Clearly, not every executive is cut out for Weill's intensely personal style of management. But Weill, who shuns executive recruiters, hasn't had a problem finding talent. One of the striking aspects of his management style, in fact, is how many people he has personally hired over the years. Says Peter J. Solomon, former vice president of Lehman Brothers, "He seems to hire in droves. Some are awful and some work out terrifically."

In Weill's early career, he was noted for identifying young financial whiz kids and giving them enormous responsibility for their age. "Sandy was able to grab people who could do his bidding," says Stroben. "He would give them the ego gratification of being associated with the success that Sandy could bring about. If they did well, he brought them along." As Weill's career progressed, he increasingly hired more seasoned executives, sometimes ones with blotches on their resumes who he knew would be fiercely loyal to him given a second chance. "He doesn't worry about whether they haven't succeeded recently," Solomon says.

Lane calls Weill's human resources philosophy the "spaghetti school of management." He explains:

> You ever see a young kid take a bowl of spaghetti and throw it up against the wall? Some of the spaghetti sticks and some of the spaghetti falls down on the ground. That is the way Sandy operates. He hires a bunch of people, a lot of people who are names in the industry, and some of them stick to the wall and some of them fall on the ground.

Why do they leave? Some fail to perform and others simply tire of the famous Weill pace and his incessant demands. "There are a lot of reasons that people have left working relationships with Sandy," Lane says. "Some people make it, and some people Sandy decides haven't made it."

The fact is, Weill is a notoriously tough boss. "Whatever the task," says Howard Clark Jr., "he wants it done yesterday." Lane, who over the years was a target of Weill's outbursts at Shearson, both on the trading floor and in the board room, admits that he hated the shouting. But he concedes that Weill produced excellent results.

Many people who work for Weill say that, unlike some temperamental bosses, he does listen. If he didn't like an idea on first hearing, he would let you know. But if you were right, he would eventually come around, although says one Citigroup executive, "You never hear later that you were right."

"Sure, he's a tough manager," says Stephen Schoenfeld, who worked as a trader at Shearson. "But you want a tough manager. He is also fair. He expects that if you're a manager, you are going to do your job efficiently, and I think that's wonderful. I respect him for that."

Overall, Lane says, it's tough to argue against Weill's management style. "You can tell me he yells and he shouldn't yell, you can tell me he hires people that don't work out. You can say whatever you want," he says. "But the fact is, whatever he does works."

A Blueprint Is Born

As Weill was developing his singular management style in the late 1960s and early 1970s, his credentials as a deal maker were established. The Hayden Stone acquisition was an epiphany for Weill—with a cool head, good timing, and an eye for a bargain, he could turn a small business into a big business in no time. Over the next decade, Weill would repeat his Hayden Stone triumph again and again, each time on a bigger stage and with a more discerning and hard-to-please audience.

"It's possible to grow in the brokerage business by acquiring firms and layering them on top of each other," Weill noted in a 1992 case study by Harvard Business School. "You can fold in the new firms, consolidate their operations, and expand market reach. . . . We dropped the new firm on the existing one."[2]

The next few years after the acquisition of Hayden Stone would see Weill evolve tremendously as a manager. During the 1960s, associates who knew him remarked that he was extremely intense, but also quiet and reserved. They noted he mainly stayed in the office, dealing with his retail accounts and operating mostly behind the scenes when it came to running the firm.

That's because Weill was profoundly shy at that time. Murray remembers a dinner with the Weill family one night in the early 1970s, just before Weill was to leave for Germany to deliver a speech at a conference. Weill was consumed with stage fright and everyone there, including Joan and the kids, spent the entire meal reassuring him that he would do a great job. "He was beside himself he was so nervous," recalls Murray. "I thought he was going to pass out at the table."

Throughout those early years, Weill willed himself to get up in front of various audiences to deliver speeches and presentations. Weill, by this time, had a vision for growing the brokerage through acquisition, and knew that he had to get used to explaining his goals to brokers. "It was painful but he made himself do it," says Murray. Murray compares Weill's work ethic on improving his presentation style to the hours baseball Hall of Famer Ted Williams put in perfecting his majestic, looping swing. Sportswriters invariably referred to Williams as a "natural" hitter, but as Murray explains, "Williams always said that his success was the product of lots of hard work and practice."

After completing the Hayden Stone deal, Weill made a point of visiting branches, attending sales conferences, and getting to know as many employees by name as he could. To retain employees at firms he acquired, he would not only share his vision for growth at the firm, but also give them stock options or a chance to buy the stock at a discount. "We really had to sell ourselves and show how we were going to build a great company and that it was going to be very good for them," Weill later recalled.[3]

Weill's casual, accessible manner also helped to win over employees of acquired firms. "He was remarkable," says Murray, who was in charge of the retail salesforce after the Hayden Stone acquisition. "For decades, these Wall Street firms were dominated by investment bankers who could be cold and aloof. Sandy made people feel important. He made people feel, and it was genuine, that he was interested in them, that theirs was a very important function of the firm."

At sales meetings, Weill was open and friendly and would reach out to the brokers. After hours, he would lead the late-night festivities. "Your evening would end at 10 P.M. and then he would say, 'Everyone, come on over to my place for a nightcap,' and it would run until 2 or 3 in the morning. That was unheard of," says Murray.

Most important, Weill made it clear that he not only understood the broker's job, but respected and appreciated it. He knew it was the high-volume salesmen—not his fellow executives—whom he needed to lavish attention on to make the brokerage firm prosper. "He focused on the people who deliver customers," observes Roy Smith. "Virtually everyone else is dispensable."

Over the years, Weill has emerged as a sort of folk hero for brokers and traders, who still see him as one of their own—straightforward, self-made, and street-smart. Schoenfeld to this day recalls Weill as one of his heroes, saying, "I would follow him into battle anywhere."

Tough Times on Wall Street

In the early 1970s, Weill had good reason for cozying up to the firm's brokers. CBWL-Hayden Stone had made a huge investment in its back-office clearinghouse, and needed to generate sales. Around the firm, the brokers used to joke that Weill had built a massive salami slicer and it was their job to provide the salami.

It wasn't an easy job. In 1972, the year after the firm went public, Wall Street suffered through another grim year. Worrying that the "Corned Beef With Lettuce" moniker was not helping business, the partners dropped "CBWL" for the more prestigious

Hayden Stone name, though only two of the firm's 12 directors came from the older firm. The four newly minted millionaires—each of whom owned just over 12 percent of the firm's stock with annual salaries of $140,000—now had the branches, the brokers, the management, and the back-office clearinghouse to handle tremendous volume. But there was little business to be done.

Market conditions meant that almost everyone was losing money, and earnings were stagnant even for a brokerage as well managed as CBWL-Hayden Stone. For its 1972 fiscal year (ended in June), the firm earned just $1.9 million, down from $3 million the year earlier. In his letter to shareholders in the annual report, Weill didn't mince his words, calling earnings, "unquestionably a disappointment."[4]

Weill would later term the early 1970s the toughest economic climate in his career. "The securities business was really nonexistent and it was a very, very difficult environment going into high inflation and very low growth," he said in a late 2001 television appearance.[5]

To stay in business, Hayden Stone had to take whatever deals it could, including underwriting a lot of small companies that wouldn't survive in the tough economic climate alone. "[Weill] would take anything that paid a commission," says J. Michael King, who claims to be one of Hayden Stone's biggest producers in the early 1970s. "A lot of other firms wanted the big deal. He took a lot of little deals. The firm wouldn't have survived it he hadn't done them."

Stroben, who headed investment banking at the time, remembers feeling strong-armed into doing deals with companies that were not high quality. "The standards were less than what they might have been," says Stroben, who left the firm in 1973. "I wasn't comfortable being coerced."

As the firm busily chased down every possible opportunity, it's not surprising that an underwriting done during this time would come back to haunt the firm. A transaction in which Hayden Stone underwrote securities for a toy company called Topper, and then sold the notes to the firm's clients, landed it in hot water with regulators several years later and cost Weill much of his personal fortune.

Management Shake Up

The relative success of the firm's "little deal" strategy quickly showed up in the firm's bottom line. For the first nine months of 1971, Hayden Stone reaped profits of $1.37 million, more than double its earnings of the year before. That was fine compared with the other floundering firms on Wall Street. But bringing mom-and-pop companies public wasn't the most satisfying work.

Cogan was particularly vexed with the way the business was going. For years, the demarcation between Cogan and Weill had become more and more defined. Cogan was the champion of the firm's institutional clients. Weill, on the other hand, continued to push to build the retail business. The firm rechristened the branch offices as "investment centers," in which customers could stop in to ask advice, place trades, inquire about tax help, and even buy the firm's research. This was an innovative new concept at the time, and it had Weill's imprimatur all over it.

Cogan began to openly criticize the direction of the firm, which looked even worse in the bear market climate. He was clearly despondent when he wrote a memo to the company's board of directors on October 25, 1972, saying: "The firm is progressing toward a mediocre and banal existence—that euphoric involvement we were once able to generate is getting harder to create."[6]

The *esprit de corps* among Cogan, Berlind, Weill, and Levitt was fading fast. Besides complaining about the schizophrenic activities of the firm, Cogan pointed out that Berlind's hands-off management style as CEO was not helping anything. Cogan believed, as he told the board, that "the growing company needed one strong general" and he wanted to be it. Cogan's vision of Hayden Stone had drifted closer to that of Arthur Carter's years before, that the firm should be doing more lucrative deals for big clients.

Weill, too, believed the company needed a stronger leader. He said in a 1986 interview, "It had become obvious that this was a big business and it was time to run it like a big business. We needed somebody who was going to be an active CEO, and I didn't think Roger was suited for it. Not everybody is."[7]

Even Berlind as much agreed in the same article, "I found it increasingly difficult to be chief executive to such an extraordinary, ambitious group of people."[8] By then, Weill had consolidated his power. When it came down to a choice between Cogan and Weill, the board sided with Weill. In August 1973, Hayden Stone announced that Weill was adding the CEO title to his chairman status. Levitt was re-elected president, Berlind became vice chairman of the board, and Cogan prepared to depart.

Other critical personnel changes occurred in 1973 as well. Most notably, Frank Zarb, the key to the firm's back-office success, left to become assistant director of the Office of Management and Budget. In 1974, he was named head of the Federal Energy Administration, the so-called "energy czar."

It was a good time to get out of Hayden Stone for those not at the company for the long haul. Throughout 1973, a major cost-saving and profit improvement plan introduced by Weill mandated that department heads turn a profit, even if trading volume kept dropping.

H. Hentz Acquisition: Following the Hayden Stone Model

Despite the management shake-up, the firm was already in the midst of another deal that would again double its size. The Hayden Stone acquisition had given all of the partners— especially Weill—both the template and the confidence to aggressively pursue more distressed firms.

H. Hentz & Co. was a firm that had been around even longer than Hayden Stone. Predominantly Jewish, the 117-year-old brokerage got in trouble in the late 1960s and early 1970s in much the same way Hayden Stone had. Hentz was in the process of being "rescued" in 1973 by a Virginia-based investment management company called the Fidelity Corporation. Then, the day before the deal was going to close, news broke of a scandal in which one of Fidelity Corporation's largest investments, the insurance company Equity Funding, had fabricated hundreds of insurance policies. Fidelity was left with a worthless investment and could not fulfill its obligation to Hentz.

That opened the door for Weill, who would later call the Hentz acquisition a watershed event in his career. This was the first deal in which he was clearly running the show. "It was the turning point of my career. I was 40 years old, and it was time for me to see if I could do it," Weill told *Business Week* in 1989. "People had been urging me for years, but I didn't have the guts."[9]

As it had during its signature acquisition in 1970, Hayden Stone added capital to its coffers with the Hentz deal. Hentz' lenders had sunk $11 million into the firm, and that became part of the overall firm's capital holdings. Hayden Stone had become one of the larger, and one of the financially healthiest, brokerage and investment banking companies on Wall Street. It's total capital was $41 million, up from $30 million the year before.

The fledgling firm had clearly arrived, but as 1974 dawned, the Wall Street slump continued. For Weill and his partners, it was as if they were the only ones at the party. In October 1974, two months after the Watergate scandal culminated with President Richard Nixon's resignation, the Dow dropped to 585 in October 1974, a 12-year low. The firm's stock hit a low of 1⅞ a share. Interest rates were high, inflation strong, and unemployment rising. Quoted in the *New York Times,* Weill described the mood on Wall Street as "total pessimism." Ever the broker, however, his advice was to buy high-quality stocks as they fell.[10]

Along with the market slump, the brokerage industry was thrown another curve ball in 1975. On May 1, the Big Board officially shifted to competitive, rather than fixed commissions, a development that forced firms to cut prices to compete and ultimately put many institutionally oriented brokerage houses out of business.

The move to competitive rates had been anticipated since August 1972, when a U.S. House subcommittee first proposed abolishing fixed-rate commissions. Hayden Stone, like almost every other brokerage house, opposed the shift. Only Merrill Lynch, secure in its standing as the largest and most innovative brokerage on Wall Street, initially came out in favor of competitive rates.[11]

The new regulations only strengthened Weill's hand. He had already been shrewd enough to remake his firm to face changing conditions in the securities business. By the time the new rules went into effect, Hayden Stone was firmly established as a predominantly retail shop. It had the size, scale, and efficiency to be one of the low-cost producers in the brokerage business. As the business got tougher, Weill's firm just became a fiercer competitor.

Doubling Up Again with Shearson Hamill

Weill soon had an opportunity to double his business again when Shearson Hamill, another venerable firm unable to survive tough times, suddenly became available. Cincinnati financier Carl Lindner had proposed bailing out the firm, but when he backed out, Weill's acquisition machine stepped in. Hayden Stone, with 49 domestic offices, acquired Shearson, with 65 domestic offices. The new firm would have 1,500 salespeople and join the ranks of true heavyweights like Merrill Lynch, Bache, and E.F. Hutton. It was renamed Shearson Hayden Stone, and became the tenth largest brokerage firm on Wall Street.

Weill wasn't after girth, however. He announced that both firms would lay off a "substantial" number of employees before their proposed merger came to a vote at Hayden's annual meeting in August. Not surprisingly, most of the cuts came from Shearson Hamill's staff. Ultimately, almost half of Shearson Hamill's 2,400 employees were let go, with most of the cuts coming in the back office.

The management deck was reshuffled again. Weill became CEO of the new firm and Arthur Levitt retained his title as president. Alger B. "Duke" Chapman Jr., president and CEO of Shearson, became the firm's co-chairman and chief operating officer. During the integration of the two firms, Chapman played the role of hatchet man, traveling to branch offices to break the news. In justifying the large number of layoffs, Weill was unabashed in his comments to the press. "Obviously, there are a lot of areas of duplication," he told the *New York Times*. "You don't need as many people as you start with."[12] On September 25, 1974, the boards approved the merger.

On Wall Street, Weill was gaining a reputation for ruthlessness. But according to George Murray, this characterization was unjustified. His observation after years spent working close to Weill is that he understands what needs to be done to make an otherwise unwieldy acquisition work, and then moves very quickly. While others order up reports or deliberate options, Weill simply makes the cuts—laying people off, closing branches, or eliminating divisions.

"That bruised some people," recalls Murray. "They'd say, 'Wait a minute, you haven't given it enough thought.'" But even if they were right, they couldn't prove their point because Weill moved so much faster than most people. Besides, Murray observed, "Usually, Sandy was right. Not always, but very often."

Pushing the Envelope

The Topper episode proved a thorn in Weill's side throughout the mid-1970s. Weill and Berlind gained seats on the company's board after Hayden Stone helped Topper bring an offering of $5.25 million in debenture notes. When Topper collapsed in 1972, investors who purchased those notes sued the brokerage firm.

The SEC filed a complaint in federal court charging Topper and Hayden Stone with violating antifraud sections of the Federal Securities Law. Hayden Stone settled the SEC charges without admitting guilt. But in November 1973, Hayden Stone was censured by the American Stock Exchange for conduct "inconsistent with just and equitable principles of trade," and fined $20,000, a reprimand that received wide publicity.

And it wasn't over yet. Six jilted investors sued Hayden Stone, saying that Weill and Berlind, sitting on the company's board, either did know or should have known of various problems in Topper's operations, including massive disorganization in inventory. Investors were incensed that while CBWL-Hayden Stone's investment arm underwrote the notes, the firm's money management arm, Bernstein Macauley, counseled investors to buy the Topper notes.

In a settlement reported on February 25, 1976, in the *Wall Street Journal*, Weill's firm paid $1.7 million to three of the biggest investors in Topper: the U.S. Steel Corporation pension fund,

Connecticut Mutual Life Insurance, and Omega Alpha Pooled Trust. Ironically enough, Citibank was also sued by the same three plaintiffs in the Topper scandal. According to the *Journal,* the suit said that "Topper used the proceeds from the note to help pay down a loan to Citibank."[13]

Weill seemed nonplussed when he told the *Journal* at the time, "We felt really that we did nothing wrong. But you never know how the jury is going to react."[14] Later he would admit that the Topper episode affected him deeply. "That whole thing knocked me out of business for a year," Weill said years later. "Personally, I was a basket case. Here was something I believed in and told my friends about. I had 34,000 Topper shares myself. That just about represented my net worth."[15]

Weill may have lost a lot of money in the Topper deal, but by 1977 he had clearly bounced back. That year the Weills purchased an eight-acre estate in Greenwich, Connecticut, one of the country's wealthiest old-money enclaves. The new home for the leader of Wall Street's new guard was a stately Tudor on a hill in the lush Greenwich "back country."

The Greenwich branch of Shearson was where Jessica Weill's business career started. While an undergraduate at Cornell, Jessica had a number of summer internships at the branch. Recalls Murray, "Of course, everyone knew this was Sandy Weill's daughter, but boy did she hustle. Everyone liked her." Murray says her talent for the business was clear at an early age. "Jessica looks like her mother and thinks like her father," he says.

Business Starts to Improve

The Shearson acquisition pushed the firm, now called Shearson Hayden Stone, into profitability. From a loss of $1.2 million in its 1974 fiscal year, the firm managed to be profitable in each quarter of the year ending June 1975, posting net income of $4.4 million, or $1.42 a share for the full year. Weill declared the Shearson deal, "the most successful merger of two large firms in our industry's history" and credited the back office with handling the additional accounts "with accuracy and efficiency."[16]

In 1976, Weill moved to fill some gaping holes in Shearson Hayden Stone's geographic coverage, both in the United States and abroad. That March, Shearson opened an office in Hong Kong, and then in May, Shearson acquired Chicago-based Lamson Brothers. This deal was somewhat unusual in that Weill paid a premium price of $4.5 million for the century-old firm.

It seemed a good fit, however, especially given that the firm never had a losing year in its 102-year history. More important, Lamson Brothers had offices in small cities in Iowa, Indiana, Illinois, Nebraska, and Minnesota where Shearson had no presence.

An Attempted Foray into Insurance

Not every company Weill pursued fell into his waiting arms. At the beginning of 1977, Weill started an intriguing courtship with a reluctant partner that marked his first interest in an insurance company, one of his first statements regarding the advantages of cross-selling, and his first public brush with Glass-Steagall regulations.

On January 13, 1977, Weill proposed merging with Orion Capital, a Parsippany, New Jersey, insurer, of which Shearson owned 7 percent. Orion was the reincarnation of Equity Funding, the scandal-ridden insurer that forced Fidelity to abandon its bid for Hentz, making way for Weill. After Fidelity, Orion's second-largest shareholder was BancOhio.

Weill's basic idea was that Shearson's brokers could sell Orion's insurance products—in essence the same cross-selling idea he was heavily pushing almost 25 years later at Citigroup. He was quoted in the January 14, 1977, edition of the *Wall Street Journal* as saying that "the expertise and products of Orion's insurance subsidiaries, coupled with Shearson's products and expertise, when distributed by Shearson's 1,700-man selling force, offer significant potential advantages to both companies."[17]

But like today, Weill's cross-selling theories drew some skeptics. One of them, unfortunately for Weill, was Orion's chairman and president, Alan R. Gruber. Gruber and Orion's board of directors rejected Weill's proposal, believing the firm would do better remaining independent.

Also troubled by the potential deal was Robert M. Edwards, a BancOhio vice president, who told the *Journal* that if Orion were acquired by Shearson, BancOhio's stock ownership of Orion violated Glass-Steagall regulations separating banks and securities companies. Edwards added that his company would either have to vote against any merger or sell its stock in Orion.

The deal derailed, and Shearson made over $500,000 when it sold its small Orion stake on March 6. That wasn't the end of Weill's interest, however. Shearson repurchased 350,000 Orion shares in May 1980, and on May 15, 1980, Weill met Gruber in secret at a restaurant on the top floor of a Columbia University dormitory in northern Manhattan so they wouldn't be spotted together. Again, Gruber declined Weill's offer, while dismissing Weill's idea of using Shearson's brokers to sell insurance. In a widely reported letter to Weill, Gruber wrote that "the benefits which you suggest would flow from a merger are, in my judgment, inconsequential."[18]

For Orion, cross selling was clearly an idea whose time had not come. Weill, who does his best to amicably end even failed merger negotiations, apparently succeeded with Gruber, who remained CEO of Orion until his death. His widow, Harriet

Gruber, says that her husband later became friends with Weill and had no bad feelings about the failed bids.

Wriston Leads Innovation at Citibank

Even as Weill was attempting to diversify into insurance and other areas of financial services, Walter Wriston, who became Citibank's CEO in 1970, was railing against the confines of the Glass-Steagall Act and changing the shape of the banking world with a remarkable record of innovation.

In many ways, Wriston was a precursor to Weill. Along with deregulating financial services, he believed cross-selling financial products was a key to higher profits. He, like Weill, also recognized the growing appetite of individual consumers for financial products and believed that a big business could be built around fulfilling those needs. Also akin to Weill, he could be tough and acerbic as a boss, but deserved credit for creating an entrepreneurial management team. So even though John Reed was the literal successor to Wriston in 1984, it was Weill who much later picked up Wriston's mantle.

Despite their similar goals, history may view Wriston and Weill quite differently. Today, academics and analysts regard Wriston as one of the true visionaries of financial services, while Weill has not yet attained this reputation. Wriston created a record of innovation that continually retooled Citibank to the befuddlement of competitors. Like Merrill Lynch in the brokerage business and Price Waterhouse in accounting, Citibank under Wriston became a bastion of best practices and new industry standards. His initiatives included developing a revolutionary new security called "floating rate notes," embracing technology throughout the bank, and interpreting the Bank Holding Act of 1956 in a new way that allowed Citibank to continue its expansion.

Both Weill and Wriston fully appreciated the dramatic emergence of the individual consumer, and both would revolutionize their respective businesses. While Weill dedicated himself to retail brokerage and the individual investor, Wriston understood that future growth for his company was in personal consumer products like credit cards and CDs. Wriston emphasized technological innovation that would enable Citibank to become the industry leader in providing these products. He pushed for more efficient mass marketing, better evaluation of customer creditworthiness, and seamless integration of customer checking and savings accounts.

Wriston is also noteworthy, as is Weill, for his ability to recruit and promote good people. The depth of Citicorp's talent was legendary, says NYU professor David Rogers in *The Future of American Banking*. In his book, Rogers quotes a bank analyst describing a meeting with a team brought together by Larry Small, Citibank's head of institutional banking around this time:

> The presentations of the senior managers and staff he brought with him were so good, one of us asked him how dependent the bank was on them and what it would do if they ever left. He replied that the bank was 14-deep in their positions, and we have found out since then that there was much to that.[19]

At the highest levels, however, Wriston and Weill had very different relationships with their top executives. Weill took trips with the families of his trusted lieutenants. Wriston pitted his lieutenants against one another, needling them and promoting them in tandem to keep them on edge.

During the 1970s, John Reed was zooming up Citicorp's notoriously treacherous corporate ladder on the strength of his technocrat credentials. In one of his few similarities to Weill, Reed revamped many of Citicorp's back-office operations, including its check-processing capability, before being promoted to head of the consumer banking division in 1974. Clearly, Reed was on his way.

Back on the Acquisition Trail

In August 1977, Weill acquired Faulkner, Dawkins & Sullivan, considered one of Wall Street's top research houses. The Faulkner acquisition proved to be one of Weill's few missteps in the 1970s, although an instructive one. Up until this point, Weill had been integrating distressed and battered brands into Shearson. Total absorption meant that the more prestigious Shearson brand dominated. Following suit, Shearson dropped the Faulkner identity.

Faulkner's 60 salespeople, however, had built strong customer loyalty in the Boston, Hartford, northern New Jersey, and Fort Lauderdale, Florida, areas. As Weill later reflected, "A lot of their people had gone there to get away from those big, faceless, boring, dumb firms, so a large percentage of them bolted over the next year."[20] The subsidiary badly foundered. But Weill wouldn't make the same mistake again. In 1981 when he acquired a similar money management firm, Robinson-Humphrey, he agreed to let it retain its existing name and identity.

Weill was still just as obsessive about the back office as he was in the days of CBWL. In an anecdote repeated in many articles through the years, Weill was so obsessed with back-office efficiency that, according to a colleague, after a merger in the late 1970s he showed up at the office on a Saturday night in his pajama top to double check that customers' accounts were being transferred without error.

Weill nearly had another chance to acquire an Our Crowd firm when it was announced in November 1977 that Shearson would acquire Kuhn Loeb, a century-old firm with an impressive list of corporate clients. The deal fell through, however, when the Our Crowd socialites with a controlling interest in the firm nixed the deal. As Tim Carrington wrote in *The Year They Sold Wall Street:*

> The wealthy Schiff family, which owned a sizable chunk of Kuhn Loeb and had long called the shots at the firm, viewed a merger with Shearson Hayden Stone as a clash of cultures. Its executives moved in different circles from those of "our crowd" financiers at Kuhn Loeb, who quickly put together a more compatible merger with Lehman Brothers.[21]

Weill, while humbled by being left at the altar, was now wise enough to know there would be plenty more Kuhn Loebs to be acquired. In 1979, Weill made a new string of acquisitions: He acquired parts of Reinholdt & Gardner, another firm with back-office problems, in January. In February, Shearson acquired the mortgage bank Western Pacific Financial Corp. for nearly $17 million in cash. The acquisition was the first for Shearson outside the securities and commodities industry.

Working with Weill

As Weill was leading deals and consolidating control, he was developing a new coterie of trusted confidantes. Peter Cohen, a hire of Marshall Cogan's, became Weill's chief lieutenant after Cogan left, crunching the numbers for various deals to figure out the best way to structure them. Even as Cohen ascended, Weill's remaining original partners were leaving the firm.

Midway through 1975, Berlind became the second member of the original four members of CBWL to leave the firm after suffering a devastating personal tragedy. On June 24, 1975, Berlind's wife and three of his four children were flying home from New Orleans on Eastern Airlines Flight 73. As the Boeing 727 approached JFK in an electrical storm, lightning struck the tail of the plane and it crashed into a marshy area east of Rockaway Boulevard. The four members of Berlind's family were among the 109 people who died in the crash, which 14 people survived. Emotionally shattered, Berlind left the firm within weeks. He told a reporter years later, "I wasn't in any shape to do anything useful at the firm, and I didn't want to be there."[22]

Cogan was gone. Berlind was gone. And Levitt, with the title of president, was now merely one of several executives Weill would consult with about the firm's direction. Levitt was also viewed as more of a rainmaker, making speeches, meeting with clients, and going to charity events and other functions to represent the firm.

Weill, whose take-no-prisoners mentality and gregariousness still connected with most brokers, didn't charm everyone. He brought his emotion and aggressiveness into encounters with everyone at the firm, including his favored young proteges. Often, it wasn't welcome. Particularly offensive to many was his penchant for blowing the smoke of his Te-Amo cigars in people's faces and shouting at colleagues and subordinates when angry.

George Murray stayed on for years at Shearson. While acknowledging that Weill was a tough boss, Murray said that Weill was as hard on himself as he was on everyone else. "He was extraordinarily demanding. In his interpretation, you either performed or you were gone," Murray says. Some high performers, however, felt as if they weren't being treated any better, and they left, too. "A lot of people went rather quickly by either one of those two processes," says Murray. "The people that stayed said, 'he's a demanding son of a bitch, but I like the direction he's going.' I'm in that camp."

Levitt, apparently in that camp for some time as well, decided to leave in November 1977 to succeed Paul Kolton as chairman of the American Stock Exchange, taking a pay cut from his salary of $195,000 at Shearson (Weill was making $220,000 at the time). Levitt was 46 when he left the firm, nearly 14 years to the day he joined. With Levitt's departure, Weill added the title of president to those of chairman and CEO. If it hadn't been clear already who was boss, it certainly was now.

CBWL's Legacy

Today, CBWL is remembered more for what it became—Shearson Loeb Rhoades—than for what it was, which is an oversight. In a few short years, CBWL, despite its relatively small size, became a player in every important specialization on Wall Street: retail brokerage, investment banking, venture capital, and money management.

CBWL also served as workplace, laboratory, proving ground, and locker room for five of the most maverick and accomplished business personalities anyone will ever come across. Weill is head of Citigroup. Levitt became one of the SEC's most respected chairmen and a champion of the individual investor. Berlind is one of Broadway's top theatrical producers. Carter made over $100 million with Carter Group and now sinks his money into the *New York Observer* newspaper, and Cogan ran a textile manufacturer called United Felt as well as an auto dealership consolidator United Auto Group. Weill was once asked by *Directors and Boards* about the divergent career paths of his former partners and why he was the only one who stayed in the securities industry. His response? "I guess I'm not as diverse or interesting."[23]

Perhaps not, but he forged a lifelong bond with his original partners. The inevitable slights and resentments and even major rifts that have come and gone have not stopped Weill, Cogan, Berlind, Carter, and Levitt from staying in touch.

Asked about the relationship among the partners in 2001, Levitt commented "that's a subject for an interesting book" and admitted they weren't close. "There are some strong animosities within the group, really strong, for different reasons," he said. "I've been the object of animus on the part of different partners through the years, but at this present time, I have at least a relationship with all of them." When the interviewer asked who got along with everyone the best, Levitt chose Roger Berlind.[24]

Most Wall Street partnerships end with some sort of animus between partners, so their respective relationships today are not really important. What *is* notable is that they got together in the first place. "Put all of them together and it was a remarkable group of people," Murray says. "Most notably, Sandy and Arthur Levitt have each in their own way left an indelible impression on the financial community."

The Acquisition of Loeb Rhoades: The New Crowd Overtakes Our Crowd

In 1978, the hard work that created the firm over the years—not just Weill's, but all of the partners' contributions—finally produced dividends as the long-lived slump in the equity markets ended.

In July 1978, Shearson Hayden Stone announced that profits more than tripled during the fourth quarter of the fiscal year, to a record $6.45 million, or $1.44 per share. Weill attributed the growth to a surge in equities trading volume and the increased diversification of Shearson.

Soon, Weill would be ready for another big deal. But first, in April 1979, he convinced Peter Cohen, who had left his side for a year to work with Edmund Safra at Republic Bank of New York, to come back to Shearson Hayden Stone as chief administrative officer and senior executive vice president. Apparently, Safra's bank couldn't match the excitement of life with Weill. Cohen returned just in time for one of the biggest victories of Weill's career.

In May of that year, rumors surfaced that Weill was planning to acquire one of New York's most venerable firms: Loeb Rhoades. The firm was founded in 1931 by John Loeb, son of Carl Loeb, a German-Jewish immigrant who grew wealthy working for the American Metal Company. John Loeb had convinced his father to buy a seat on the New York Stock Exchange in 1931, and the new firm Carl M. Loeb was born. A few years later, it acquired Rhoades & Co. and the firm grew apace. In 1955, Carl Loeb died, and John Loeb ran Loeb Rhoades & Co. on his own. Loeb was one of the most well-respected players on the national finance scene, and took his proper place in the upper strata of New York City social circles.

In January 1978, the 75-year-old Loeb had approved a merger with the struggling brokerage Hornblower, which turned out to be one of the worst moves he could have made. Though Loeb Rhoades had incurred losses due to continued back-office problems prior to the merger, Hornblower's back office, in fact, was in further chaos than Loeb Rhoades'.

As it tried to consolidate the operations of both firms, administrative and clerical costs soared. Loeb Rhoades earned only a small profit through the first three quarters of the fiscal year and lost about $7 million in the final three months of 1978. As a private partnership, the family stood to lose a lot of money if the firm went under. Again, the key to the merger was capital. The Loeb family wanted to preserve theirs; Weill wanted to acquire more.

Thomas Kempner, John Loeb's nephew, recalled that the firm needed to stop the bleeding after the Hornblower debacle. Kempner was one of three men Loeb had appointed to run the firm during the period directly prior to the deal with Shearson, so he had a front-row seat to the firm's woes. Today Kempner runs Loeb Partners, an arbitrage fund. "We, Loeb Rhoades, got to the point in the late 1970s when it seemed logical to sell the business," Kempner says. "We certainly weren't doing well. The acquisition of Hornblower was not successful. We were not terribly compatible. And frankly, we were having mechanical problems with our back office and the Hornblower merger really exacerbated those problems."

Kempner attended the negotiations for the Shearson merger at Weill's Greenwich house over Mother's Day weekend. Cohen handled the final details of the merger, allowing Weill to bask in the glow of adding this crown jewel to his empire. Kempner remembers the Shearson negotiating team as tough, but fair. "Was it a tough negotiation? All successful people are tough, or they aren't successful," Kempner says. "I think Sandy was a tough [negotiator]. He made the best deal he could for Shearson and I made the best deal I could for Loeb. And I think it worked out pretty well."

When John Loeb insisted that the press release announcing the deal describe it as a "combination," Weill didn't object. Weill himself said that the merger was not a "bailout," justifying this position to the *Times* by saying, "The proof is that all the Loeb Rhoades Hornblower capital is staying in the combined firm and that Mr. Loeb himself will become the largest single shareholder."[25]

Partly, Weill wanted to appease Loeb. He had taken over the old patriarch's firm; there was no sense in rubbing it in. George Murray says Weill seemed in awe of the older man. "Mr. Loeb had an aura about him," says Murray. "In the world of the Street, also in Jewish circles, this man was almost God-like." Kempner agrees that Weill was in awe of Loeb. "I'm sure that's true," Kempner says. "John could intimidate anybody he wished to. He also, by the way, could charm the birds out of the trees if he wished to do that. John liked Sandy, though. John always admired people who were successful. I don't think there was any culture clash there at all."

Weill would become head of the new firm, Loeb its honorary board chairman, and Sherman R. Lewis, 42, vice chair and co-CEO of Loeb Rhoades, would become president, overseeing all investment banking for the new firm. Kempner stayed on the board of directors for a short time and then left, feeling the firm was in good hands. "Sandy and his group, but I think it was largely Sandy, did an excellent job running it," he says. "He was risk averse and that was a time to be risk averse."

Shearson had doubled in size again. Shearson employed 5,000 and Loeb Rhoades 5,800. The combined firm would have 3,500 brokers. Shearson had 130 domestic branches and 14 foreign branches; Loeb Rhoades had 150 domestic branches and 11 overseas. On May 12, 1979, the *Times* called it "a remarkable victory" for Weill, "the dynamic chief of Shearson."[26] The two firms had combined capital of $250 million, making this the largest merger in Wall Street history up to that point.

As in each of his deals, Weill saw savings to be made in various operational and clerical areas. After the merger, Weill flew to Los Angeles, Miami, and Bermuda on successive days to explain the deal to office managers. Eventually, about 2,000 of 10,800 employees were cut following the acquisition.

Wall Street's Second Biggest Brokerage

Shearson Loeb Rhoades had become the second largest brokerage after Merrill Lynch. Its financial results reflected the firm's new status. After acquiring Loeb Rhoades, Shearson's stock price rose from $10 a share in 1979 to $37 a share in 1980, an increase of 257 percent. In 1980 profits grew to $56 million, up from $20 million the year before.

With the Loeb Rhoades acquisition, Weill was clearly a major player on Wall Street, as signified by his entrance into Kappa Beta Phi, a sort of exclusive fraternity for financial leaders. New members were asked to entertain the members and Weill asked Berlind to write lyrics for his performance. The following lyrics, later published in a profile of Berlind by John Seabrook, was to be sung to the tune of "You Oughta Be in Pictures":

I want to be a major
I think it's only fair
I want to be a major
With my nose in the air

We're not a bunch of gadflies
First Boston might have sacked
Got rid of all the bad guys
And cleaned our act. That's a fact!

We've purchased respectability we never had before
Now I plead with all humility, please Mister Whittemore

You've given us a hose job
But now I'm on my knees
I'll even get a nose job
If you'll please . . .
Make us a major!
An alphabetical major
Then lock the bracket up and throw away the keys![27]

In 1980, Weill decided the firm should be in offices fitting its new stature. The firm leased the top six floors of the World

Trade Center's south tower, where Weill had the world's highest fireplace installed in his office. Although it was later cited as a symbol of corporate excess, Weill always maintained that the Port Authority threw the fireplace in for free as an enticement for the real estate deal.

Throughout the 1970s, Weill used the lessons of earlier deals to handle the challenges of the next one. This worked even when the acquired firm was bigger and employed more experienced executives. As Peter Solomon put it, Weill "has the audacity to merge up."[28] It was this same audacity that also led to Weill's next move, one that led to the loss of the power base he had worked so hard to build.

For much of his career, Weill has been driven by one idea—one that very few in the business world believe works: cross-selling financial services products. From CBWL to Hayden Stone to Shearson to American Express to Travelers and Citigroup, Weill has followed the cross-seller's siren song: if only the stock brokers could sell insurance; if only the insurance agents could sign up customers for brokerage accounts. If only . . .

The fuel behind cross-selling is reciprocity. Various divisions within a big company sell each other's products, generating more sales without incurring additional costs. "Sandy claims that if you have a wider product range for the salesforces to sell, and really focus on sales management, they will have more to sell and will sell more," says Roy Smith of NYU's Stern School. This is a very cost-effective way for a company to boost sales. In addition, studies have shown that with each additional product you sell, your ability to hold on to a customer grows exponentially.

There is only one problem: Cross-selling is very hard to do. In fact, many academics and analysts say it has never really worked—

at least in a way that really benefits a company's bottom line. Richard Bove, a securities analyst at the investment boutique Hoefer & Arnett, says that almost *everyone* has considered the idea and then rejected it after some initial clumsy attempts.

"The history is dismal," says Thomas Kempner, the former Loeb Rhoades executive. "Nobody has succeeded. And I have very real questions in my mind as to whether they ever will because I think that the skills to sell life insurance are quite different than the skills it takes to sell securities."

Some of Weill's own attempts at implementing cross-selling strategies have been clumsy as well. In December 2001, Weill announced he was spinning off Travelers Property Casualty to the public. One of the reasons he gave for unloading the business was that efforts to cross-sell had actually backfired when it came to financial results. He attributed that to adverse selection—that is, Citigroup customers who bought the insurance filed more claims than the average Travelers customer. "We were able to get customers, but they weren't the right customers," Weill said in an interview with the authors. "Most of them seemed to be accident prone."

Yet Weill insists cross-selling is working in Citigroup's other businesses. He cites success in selling Citibank mortgages to high-net worth clients of the private bank and Salomon Smith Barney. He says Citibank account holders throughout the world are buying Smith Barney mutual funds. And by the end of 2001, customers of three divisions of Citigroup—Salomon Smith Barney, Primerica Financial Services, and Citibank—had bought over one billion dollars worth of Travelers annuities.

"The one that you read about most, which has worked out really well, is the connectivity between our Citibank commercial banking business and the corporate investment bank," Weill said in an interview. This is the corporate side of cross-selling: Investment bankers and commercial bankers offer companies a kind of one-stop shopping for all their corporate finance needs. With Citigroup's help, a company can efficiently obtain loans and issue stocks and bonds. This gives Citigroup a major leg up in attracting underwriting business over firms like Merrill Lynch, that don't have a banking arm. Indeed, in Wall Street's 2001 rankings, Citigroup came in first for debt offerings and fourth in initial public offerings, ahead of Merrill, according to Thomson Financial.

"Cross-selling doesn't work in a lot of other cases but in Citi's case it actually works," says Jeff Lane, the long-time Weill lieutenant who now heads Neuberger Berman. "I'm not there and I'm telling you it works."

But Weill still has some convincing to do before the outside world will acknowledge that he has been able to make cross-selling work. Several articles in 2000 and 2001 chided Weill for not being quicker to show the benefits of cross-selling, since he cited that as a major reason for the merger of Citicorp and Travelers. But analysts and investors have never really held Weill accountable for his cross-selling goals, because Weill has created so much value in other ways that his devotion to the idea is simply chalked up as an idiosyncrasy. Their thinking goes something like this: "If cross-selling—crazy as the idea is—inspires Sandy to make another well-timed acquisition, then we'll let him believe in such fairy tales."

Weill's devotion to the idea of cross-selling represents his best opportunity to be remembered for something other than simply executing deals and then making the numbers work. It's a chance to do something that no one else has been able to do. And one thing is certain: No one is ready to declare cross-selling at Citigroup dead. Weill has proven his ability to learn from mistakes. Just because the world hasn't learned how to cross-sell yet, Kempner says, "that doesn't mean Sandy or someone like Sandy won't be able to come up with a formula for making it work."

Hopes for the potential of cross-selling provided a major impetus for Weill's 1981 decision to sell Shearson Loeb Rhoades to American Express—to create what was, using the buzzword of the day, a "financial supermarket." The experiment ultimately proved a personal and business failure for Weill at many levels (although a financial windfall), and for reasons other than American Express' inability to cross-sell.

Sandy Lewis and His Big Idea

The idea of a merger between American Express and Shearson Loeb Rhoades was dreamed up by Salim "Sandy" Lewis, who believed the combination would not only create the ultimate financial services powerhouse, but also establish his fledgling one-man investment bank, S.B. Lewis & Co. Lewis pitched the idea to his old friend, American Express CEO James Robinson III, at a breakfast meeting in late 1979. Robinson didn't take the bait. But he mulled over the idea through the early days of 1980.

Around the same time, American Express and Shearson began discussions on creating a cash management account similar to the one Donald Regan had devised, which had become a gold mine for Merrill Lynch. Merrill's Cash Management Account (CMA) functioned like a traditional bank account, but with higher interest rates than banks were allowed to offer. The account-holder could also invest the money in securities. Because brokerage, checking, and debit card services were integrated, the account offered the appeal of one-stop shopping. It became a huge hit with customers.

Both Shearson and American Express hoped to replicate that success with their own version. The firms discussed a plan by which customers could use an AmEx card to draw money from a Shearson margin account or a money market fund. As Merrill had been before them, AmEx was bound to get criticized for trying to act like a bank. Luckily for AmEx, though, with Donald Regan now heading the Treasury Department, the Reagan Administration was expected to be tolerant of other brokerage firms attempting similar innovations.

Robinson Weighs the Deal

Encouraged by the two companies' discussions regarding the potential cash management system, Robinson began to consider an American Express acquisition of Shearson. (In fact, he even authorized a four million-dollar investment in S.B. Lewis & Co.)

Given its profits, Shearson looked like a very good company to own. In 1980, Shearson earned $56 million on revenues of $5.5 billion. The bull market was roaring, and there was no reason to expect anything but strong double-digit growth going forward. Most important, Shearson had a salesforce of about 3,500 brokers who had the kind of face-to-face relationship with customers that American Express lacked. The AmEx brand was represented by its credit card, which had over 12 million customers. Robinson must have had visions of well-off cardholders snapping up stocks and bonds and money management services from those aggressive brokers at Shearson.

For Robinson himself, such a major deal would give him a much-needed victory as a deal maker. Since assuming the CEO position in 1977, he had been burned by a spate of ill-fated acquisition attempts. Discussions had fizzled with Walt Disney Productions, Philadelphia Life Insurance, and the Book-of-the-Month Club. Robinson was also humiliated when his well-publicized 1979 attempt to take over McGraw-Hill was beaten back by Harold McGraw.

With American Express aggressively pursuing a strategy of becoming a financial conglomerate, Robinson needed to score a key acquisition to retain the confidence of the board and share-holders. For Robinson, a merger with Shearson was both the big deal he'd been looking for and an opportunity to absolve him-self of his botched attempt to acquire the publishing giant.

Courting Sandy Weill

Before Lewis invited him to breakfast at the elegant Stock Ex-change Luncheon Club on August 29, 1980, Weill had very little acquaintance with him. It was a clever move on Lewis' part to suggest that particular spot. The self-reverential Stock Exchange Club draped itself in Wall Street nostalgia and played up the Street's prominence in the world of finance. As head of Shear-son, one of the new pillars of Wall Street, Weill was comfortable in this setting. This was his world, one that he had helped create. Weill accepted the invitation.

Well aware of Weill's deal making prowess and penchant for emerging on top, it took plenty of courage for Lewis to suggest a deal in which the Shearson CEO would come out second or even third. Weill recalled that when Lewis first brought it up, his re-action was, "Geez, I don't see how that's possible. I don't think that Jim is ready to retire, and if he's not, I don't see how we can do anything."[1]

After his own career of humbling other brokerage house exec-utives, Weill could have been forgiven for wanting to avoid sell-ing his firm. But Weill, by then highly confident in his own ability to stay on top when merging with a bigger firm, truly was interested.

Weill Weighs the Deal

The truth is that Weill would have been crazy not to jump at the deal. American Express had a reputation for quality that surpassed any other firm. As the financial world became more global and new kinds of complex derivative securities began to proliferate, Weill knew it was going to take a lot of capital and first-rate technology to stay on top.

Plus, it would undoubtedly be a great deal for Shearson's shareholders. As Wall Street's most profitable firm, and the second biggest behind Merrill Lynch, Shearson would command a steep premium (later on, some would say the deal was a little too good for the Shearson executives who were stockpiling options right until the time of the merger). Personally, it would mark a clear triumph for Weill. A deal with American Express, whose brand name was associated with class and quality, would signal to the world that the Brooklyn-born son of immigrants had made it to the very top of Wall Street's major leagues.

Many assumed Weill had another motivation: to become number one at American Express. Today, it seems axiomatic that Weill would want to head a sprawling, financial superpower like AmEx. In fact, the big question then wasn't whether he wanted the top job, but whether he would be able to grab it. In later interviews, Weill has made it clear that he thought he could manage the company better than Robinson, commenting that he thought he could build a stronger firm by combining the entrepreneurial nature of Shearson with the sophisticated brand savvy of AmEx.

Leaving aside Weill's personal ambitions, the combination also made strategic sense. There were cross-selling opportunities. As his interest in doing a CMA-like product showed, Weill clearly had his eye on the 12 million-strong American Express cardholders. At that time it was one of the largest international customer groups in the world (far surpassing Merrill Lynch's 2.5 million customers at the time). All of these AmEx customers represented potential Shearson clients.

Weill also had his eye on American Express's largest unit, Fireman's Fund insurance, the biggest and most consistent income producer at the company, with a 1980 profit of $210 million. His failed attempts at purchasing insurer Orion in 1977 and 1980 did not deter Weill's interest in the recurring income that the insurance business provided. With policies renewed yearly, you could make money 24 hours a day and on weekends, and that's how Weill has always liked to do business.

American Express also offered strength in data processing and technology, which Weill could appreciate. Then, there was Shearson's growing need for capital, which AmEx had plenty of. American Express' mammoth capital base would give Shearson the heft it needed to pursue ever-larger deals.

Still, Weill had doubts about merging with AmEx. He questioned what his initial role would be with the parent company. He fully expected to be named to the board of directors, but from where would he get his authority? For Weill, it wasn't enough just to have Shearson people answering to him; he had that already. He desperately wanted the title of president, a position at AmEx that was vacant at the time. Weill was also somewhat unsure about his potential working relationship with Robinson. At this point in his career, could he work for someone else?

Climate of Deregulation Pushes the Deal Along

The climate for the AmEx-Shearson deal was created by a financial services regulatory environment that stood at a crossroads. The lurch toward deregulation in general started with the airline industry in 1977, and the financial world was next on the list.

The late 1970s were years of steady inflation that left many Americans dissatisfied with traditional savings and checking accounts and their measly rates of return. American consumers wanted insurance against future inflation and demanded innovative investment products. The leaders of the big financial services companies—Robinson at American Express, Walter

Wriston at Citibank, and Sam Armacost at Bank of America, among others—scrambled to design new offerings and mix and match disparate financial businesses to meet both customer demands and regulatory guidelines.

Chase Bank, for example, established a securities arm that pushed the tenets of the Bank Holding Act to the limit. Merrill Lynch's Donald Regan, before heading off to join President Reagan's cabinet as Treasury Secretary in early 1981, pushed through the development of the lucrative Cash Management Account.

Wriston also pushed the regulatory envelope. He helped persuade the South Dakota legislature to relax regulations that prevented out-of-state banks from establishing beachheads in the state. Soon after, Citicorp moved its credit card processing operations there, which is why—to this day—millions of Citigroup cardholders call office parks in South Dakota to order new cards and dispute their charges.

Fears of lost market share, conflicts of interests, and various political entanglements created an air of confusion and distrust in the financial services sector in early 1981. Banks believed that brokerages faced much less regulatory restraint; brokerages suspected that big banks, if unleashed from Glass-Steagall, would dominate the securities industry. The Reagan Administration clearly was going to enact some type of financial deregulation, and no segment wanted to be the loser.

Citicorp's Wriston gave some perspective on the financial climate when he appeared before the Senate Finance Committee that year to discuss financial services reform. Wriston was asked about Merrill's CMA account and its effect on the banking industry. To peals of laughter, Wriston said, "To just give you an example, Merrill Lynch's money market fund now exceeds the domestic deposits of Citibank by $2 billion. We've been at it since 1812, and they've been at it almost 24 months." Ironically enough for the banking industry, legislation intended to partially free the industry from regulatory restraint—the Garn-St. Germain Act, enacted in December of 1982—sparked the disastrous speculation by thrifts that led to the mid-1980s savings and loan crisis.

Prudential-Bache Merger Primes the Pump

On March 20, 1981, while Weill was in Hong Kong visiting Shearson's Far East operations, accompanied by former President Ford, news broke about the imminent takeover by Prudential of Bache. Bache had lent the billionaire Hunt brothers, Nelson Bunker Hunt and William Herbert Hunt, millions of dollars in their ill-conceived attempt to corner the silver market. When the brothers weren't liquid enough to cover their trading losses, Bache was nearly de-listed from New York Stock Exchange for lack of capital. The Prudential-Bache deal was simple: Bache needed an infusion of capital, and Prudential, then the largest insurer in the United States, had it.

Fittingly, Weill had barred the Hunt brothers from trading at Shearson years before when they chafed at his insistence on collateral for their big market bets. It was just another instance of Weill showing how he was more fiscally responsible than many of his contemporaries. While he had little sympathy for Bache's recklessness, Weill thought seriously about the implications of Bache joining forces with Prudential. Their merger marked the first salvo in a battle sparked by the combined forces of consumer demand and deregulation: to become a financial services supermarket.

After the Prudential-Bache deal, the tenor of the negotiations between Shearson and American Express changed. In this environment, it was clear that the biggest, most diverse financial firms with the strongest capital bases would be the survivors. To stay on top, both American Express and Shearson knew they had to move and move fast.

"That's when everyone started thinking about the idea that maybe we ought to do more with Shearson, or someone, other than just have a CMA-type account," says Howard Clark Jr., an AmEx executive at the time and the son of Robinson's predecessor, Howard Clark Sr. Clark says that AmEx chose Shearson because it was the best run of the top retail brokerages. "It had strength in retail accounts, a good back office, and an excellent management team—and it was really a team. It wasn't just Sandy, but a team of people that were very, very good."

Merger Discussions Heat Up

The merger discussions between Weill and Robinson were marked by their contrasting personalities and backgrounds. Weill was a striver who had fired thousands and alienated some of his former partners and, doubtless, many others on his way to the top. Robinson had glided into power, it seemed, stepping on few, if any, toes. Weill was as emotional as Robinson was cool. Shearson was as loud and noisy as AmEx was buttoned-down and corporate. They knew there would be a culture clash, but they hoped the new firm would gain the best of both cultures.

Not only were Robinson's and Weill's personalities and backgrounds different, so were their management styles. At the time of his merger negotiations with Robinson, Weill still ran Shearson as he had run CBWL-Hayden Stone, smoking cigars, getting in subordinates' faces, making snap decisions, and continuing to combine personal and professional lives. For example, he and Joan would go on vacations with key executives and their wives after weeks of all-nighters working on a deal.

Robinson, known as "Jimmy Three Sticks," ran American Express like the *Fortune 500* company it was. Son of a banker from a prominent Atlanta family, he spoke with polish. Thoughtful and considerate, Robinson embodied the image of a courtly Southern gentleman. In his frequent speeches and public appearances around the world, he came across as a strong, hard-charging CEO, yet inside the firm, his leadership style could be described as conservative. He eschewed risk, preferring a bureaucratic, committee approach to decision making. A formal process was in place to vet new ideas. Things moved slowly and inefficiently to avoid mistakes.

Importantly for Weill's later showdowns with John Reed, Robinson shared some similarities with the deep-thinking Citicorp banker. Both took the reins of power in their early 40s. Both were firm believers in the transforming power of technology. Both were happy to delegate authority, preferring to conceive of grand plans and let others perform the at-times mundane efforts to carry them out. Weill, of course, shared none of these characteristics with the two biggest adversaries of his career. Luckily for him, he had to face only one at a time.

Negotiating the Deal

As the talks heated up, Weill invited Robinson and his wife, Bettye, out to his home in Greenwich, a large Tudor bookended by an apple orchard and a three-car garage. Weill's home, at least, was of a manner that Robinson could identify with. Greenwich was—and still is—a town any CEO can relate to, with its country clubs and four-acre zoning. Weill later reflected on those discussions, "We did the financial part of it in two minutes. Who did what to whom personally took a lot more time."[2]

The foursome ate lunch before Joan led Bettye on a tour of their orchard and garden. Sandy took Jim into his study to talk. As soon as they sat down, Weill peppered him with questions. According to authors Jon Friedman and John Meehan in *House of Cards,* Weill wanted to know how he would fit in at AmEx:

"What would my role be? Who would report to me? What about my responsibilities?"

"You'll have to prove yourself," Robinson replied.

Weill's face reddened. Over the past twenty years, Weill had personally negotiated the acquisitions of a dozen or more firms. He had been a CEO for a decade. And here was Robinson treating him like some corporate virgin straight out of business school.[3]

Weill kept his anger in check. Then he got in his own subtle dig. Knowing that large Shearson shareholders, like himself, would make a fortune in the deal, he wanted to know whether it would be a problem if he ended up wealthier than Robinson. Robinson told him it was of no concern.

The next challenge was quelling the respective fears of American Express and Shearson employees. Louis Gerstner, later to become IBM's CEO, was then a rising star at AmEx and head of its Travel Related Services division. Gerstner believed in growing the company from within. Knowing Weill's reputation for acquisitions that grabbed headlines, he feared being overshadowed. Howard Clark Sr., the retired CEO who still carried considerable influence, also had serious concerns about the deal, mainly because American Express' earlier deal with Donaldson, Lufkin & Jenrette didn't work out. Robinson asked Clark's son, Howard Clark Jr., and Alva Way, a top executive at AmEx, to fly to Florida to visit several outside directors in the Palm Beach area, including Howard Clark Sr., to sell the deal.

Over at Shearson, many of Weill's top executives saw little need to risk their huge success. They questioned Weill's motives, some of them surmising that his real goal was to make a personal fortune. With well over 400,000 shares of Shearson stock, Weill stood to gain over $30 million in the deal.

Peter Cohen, especially, harbored doubts. Weill's clear number two at Shearson and a genius when it came to operations, Cohen's approval was critical for the deal's completion. He would be needed to help convince the rank-and-file brokers of its wisdom. Also, he did most of the detailed structuring of deals, and Weill needed Cohen's heart to be in it when it came down to negotiating with AmEx.

Cohen's concern was, understandably, remaining a player in the newly merged company. Weill promised to ask Robinson to give Cohen a seat on the AmEx board. At first, Robinson consented, only to have the AmEx board quash the notion of another Shearson board seat late in the negotiations. When Weill informed Cohen of the AmEx board's decision, Cohen felt that Weill had been cavalier and offhand in breaking what, to Cohen, was upsetting news.

Cohen appealed directly to Robinson and was reinstated onto the board, leaving Weill upset that he went over his head. Many associates believe the drama over the board seat fostered a mutual distrust between Weill and Cohen that endured for the rest of their time together at American Express.

A Done Deal

Wall Street and corporate America were shocked as the rumors of an impending American Express/Shearson merger surfaced in the spring of 1981. Even though the Pru-Bache deal was expected to trigger more such mergers, Shearson was no Bache; Weill's company was in great shape.

On April 20, 1981, the AmEx board approved the deal in principle and all that remained was for Weill to sign on the dotted line. During some late-night negotiations, Joan Weill had to convince her husband to trust Robinson. At one point, Weill even looked at Joan with Robinson sitting right there and asked her: "Do you believe him?" Joan said she did.[4]

The agreement was finally signed. Weill hadn't gotten everything he wanted. He didn't get the position of president; that went to Al Way. But Weill did extract a promise from Robinson: There would be no obstacles to his advancement at the company. It was undoubtedly one of the most emotional days of Weill's life. His voice cracked with emotion as he announced the deal the next morning to Shearson's nationwide corps of brokers in a 9 A.M. conference call. According to George Murray, the brokers were excited to be part of American Express, and eager to begin selling securities to AmEx cardholders.

Despite any misgivings he might have had about reporting to Robinson, Weill could feel very good about one thing: The deal made him very wealthy and provided a big payday for other Shearson shareholders as well. From a price of $34 shortly before the merger was announced, Shearson's stock climbed to $49 when news of the deal broke and kept rising to $65. Shearson executives (including Cohen) were still receiving options while merger talks were under way, which only bolstered speculation that the deal was motivated by the self interests of various executives. Weill maintained, with some credibility, that options had always been his preferred method of compensation, for himself, his managers, and board members. Lewis, the architect of the deal, earned a $3.5 million fee for the realization of his long-shot dream of joining AmEx and Shearson.

American Express purchased Shearson for about $900 million in stock, a price equal to roughly three times the book value of the firm. Weill himself held $30 million worth of stock as his shares of Shearson converted into nearly 600,000 shares of AmEx, making him the company's biggest shareholder. In fact, Weill ended up with 40 times more AmEx stock than Robinson did.

The deal was approved by Shearson shareholders on June 19, 1981. From the initial breakfast with Sandy Lewis to the board approval, 10 months had gone by. At one point during the bittersweet shareholders meeting, Weill was asked whether the whole company, not just the securities unit, would be called Shearson/American Express. "Not yet," he said. When the meeting ended, Weill drew a standing ovation.

In a 1989 retrospective article, *Business Week* called the deal a "spectacular coup" for Weill. Besides becoming AmEx' biggest shareholder, the magazine noted, "It seemed that he had stepped into a dream job. Symbolically, the acceptance by AmEx validated him. Big business no longer viewed him as an upstart from Brooklyn. He had the cachet of the corporate American elite."[5]

Strange Bedfellows

Now that the deal was complete and the transition under way, everyone could see just how different the cultures of the two firms were. As George Sheinberg, former CFO of Shearson, put it somewhat jokingly in February 1982, "You're combining Jewish guilt with Southern aristocracy."[6]

The executives at AmEx were forced to make room for various Shearson executives in the company's power structure. Sherman Lewis (no relation to Sandy Lewis), who had been Shearson's president, became an AmEx vice chairman and ran investment banking activities at the company. George Sheinberg, formerly Shearson's CFO, was named treasurer of AmEx. Duke Chapman, originally chairman of Shearson Hamill all those years before, joined the AmEx international banking division, and Gustave Hauser became the chief executive of AmEx' joint venture in interactive cable television, Warner AmEx.

With Shearson, Fireman's Fund, an AmEx subsidiary since 1969, and AmEx' card business all under one roof, AmEx now issued credit cards, sold securities, and sold insurance. And with Weill now on board, it was widely assumed that there would soon be several more blockbuster acquisitions.

Weill, in fact, didn't do much to mask any of his ambitions in those heady early days, when it seemed everything was on the table for discussion: potential acquisitions, his own role at AmEx, the nature of the relationship between his brokerage house and the parent company. But as time went on and Weill settled into the job, few of these discussions would go his way.

An Auspicious Beginning

In its 1981 fiscal year, Shearson American Express recorded a 25 percent increase in earnings. Full-year profits reached $107 million, up from $86 million the year before.

Unlike other deals Weill had been a part of, this one was not about cutting costs and consolidating operations. In fact, little effort was put into integrating Shearson with American Express, and the brokerage largely operated as it had before the deal, albeit with a far larger capital base.

And what of cross-selling? It never got off the ground. As Clark recalls:

> There were attempts at cross-selling. But at the end of the day the credit card people were not going to open their business to thousands of salespeople. They just weren't about to do it. The credit card list was called the "crown jewel of American Express" and the thought of having a couple of thousand salespeople calling credit card holders to try and sell them

common stocks, unit trusts, annuities, and partnership interests just never worked.

It was clear nonetheless that Robinson was pleased with his prized acquisition. In a speech to the American Bankers Association on October 5, he touted the Shearson acquisition as a development that would ease regulatory oversight:

> There's no need to tell you that banks have been stifled in responding to consumer needs, in part by regulatory impediments. The result, as you know, is that to meet customer needs, nonbanks have created such new products as money market funds and cash management type accounts. . . . Our acquisition of Shearson may serve as one catalyst that helps bring about some constructive change in these regulatory patterns—perhaps in McFadden, perhaps in Douglas, perhaps in Glass-Steagall.[7]

The Quest for Deals

Given the changing environment for financial services in the 1980s and Robinson's hunger for more acquisitions, Weill was ideally suited for his role of dipping into AmEx' deep coffers and making some timely acquisitions for the greater glory of the company. Yet Weill struggled to make significant deals for AmEx. In his new bureaucratic environment, he couldn't move as fast. And, as number three behind Robinson and Way, he couldn't call the shots.

Weill did his best to cut through layers of bureaucracy at AmEx. For example, when a major customer reached Weill with a problem with his margin account, instead of handing the problem off to the next rung down on the corporate ladder,

Weill went directly to the margin clerk to fix the problem. "He didn't need an organizational chart," says Clark. "He went to where the source of the problem was."

Clark says Weill brought energy and a sense of urgency to the corporate suite at American Express. "What American Express brought to Shearson was some strategic and long-range planning," he says. "I think the two organizations were good for each other."

Maybe so, but Weill was clearly hamstrung in his new environment. In his first two years, he managed to acquire only The Boston Company, a small money management concern, and two regional brokerages. His attempt to take over Foster & Marshall, a brokerage based in Seattle, failed when hundreds of its brokers, afraid their commissions would drop if they became part of AmEx, abandoned the company. In fact, many of Weill's ideas for acquisition languished in dead-end meetings, like unpopular legislation stuck in committee.

He was, however, reaping the benefits of his increasing wealth. In 1982, the Weills, who maintained an apartment in the city after they bought their Greenwich home, purchased a seven-room penthouse on the Upper East Side, with views of Central Park.

He was also in a position to do favors for old friends. Winston Kulok, a friend from PMA, hadn't heard from Weill for several years in the early 1980s. "I was sort of in a Bohemian period. I needed an AmEx Card," says Kulok. "I called American Express and asked for Sandy." Weill took his call and made sure he got a card. "I got one in the mail the next day," says Kulok. "Now it's a Platinum card."

Weill Loses His Power Base

Weill had less and less to do with Shearson. While Robinson was off giving speeches about how great Shearson was, Weill removed himself from Shearson's daily operations and looked for major initiatives to lead within the parent company, leaving day-to-day management to Peter Cohen. With many of his deals going nowhere and with little input in Shearson, Weill felt as if he had very little to do.

Nonetheless, in January 1983, at 49, Weill was named president of American Express, replacing Alva Way in a management reshuffle. Gerstner became chairman of the executive committee, succeeding Weill. The day of his promotion to president turned out to be the high point of Weill's time at American Express. For one day, at least, Weill received a little bit of attention after being virtually invisible for over a year.

Still, Robinson felt it necessary to dismiss suggestions that Weill would soon make a play for the number one spot. "Sandy and I make a terrific combination," Robinson told the *Wall Street Journal*.[8] "I'm not the least bit concerned about his ambitions. He's a fantastic working partner." The article noted that, in addition to overseeing financial and investment services, Weill, as president, would negotiate the construction of a new American Express office tower on the southern tip of Manhattan, the company's future headquarters.

Weill's promotion to the coveted role of president proved to be the worst thing that could have happened to him. With it, Weill chose to give up his power base to the 36-year-old Cohen, who became the youngest head of a major Wall Street brokerage. Explains Murray, "Sandy had great confidence in Peter Cohen and Peter had done some very remarkable work in making order out of the chaos of merger time after time. . . . Therefore, he was rewarded." Cohen was officially named CEO of Shearson, with Weill staying on as chairman.

Cohen moved into Weill's former office on the 106th floor of the World Trade Center, complete with working fireplace. As awkward as Weill felt in his new situation, Cohen quickly made himself at home and added an oversized pair of shoes behind his desk. "This was a present to myself," Cohen told the *Journal,* "a reminder that I had big shoes to fill." Corporate politesse aside, Cohen was even bold enough to slight Weill in the *Journal.* Cohen told the newspaper that he wouldn't be able to visit Shearson branches as often as Weill did. "One of the reasons Sandy was able to go off was that I was back here at the company," he said.[9]

After years of supporting Weill—crunching the numbers, dotting the i's and crossing the t's—Cohen, understandably, felt ready to make his own mark. Yet Cohen had a distinctly different management style than Weill. His slightly aloof demeanor was more similar to that of a traditional Wall Street manager. Cohen was even-tempered and visibly noncommittal during meetings and conference calls. Cohen was also considered to be less focused on Shearson's 3,800-strong retail salesforce and more interested in investment banking and real estate deals. He made a point, however, of continuing Weill's policy of taking a call from any broker from Shearson.

Still, there was a marked difference in Cohen's and Weill's styles, observed Murray. "Sandy would walk onto the elevator and start asking people, 'What do you do?' He wanted to know everyone on the elevator. Now, Peter would get on the same elevator and he just stared straight ahead, hoping no one would talk to him."

Seeing Cohen run the company he built in a completely different style was painful enough for Weill. Even worse, at that point Cohen was faring better than his old boss, even at the acquisition game. Cohen conceived of and orchestrated AmEx's purchase of Edmond Safra's Trade Development Bank, which Cohen had become familiar with during his year spent at Safra's

First Republic Bank. Capitalizing on his close ties to Safra, Cohen negotiated a reasonable price and convinced Safra to join AmEx as head of the private European banking division, which catered to very wealthy clientele.

Thanks to a generous bonus system he had created at Shearson, Cohen made more money than either Weill or Robinson in 1983: $1.3 million, compared with Robinson's $902,000 and Weill's $806,000. Unlike Weill, Robinson grew up wealthy and was unconcerned with Cohen's salary, just as he wasn't troubled about Weill's enormous windfall at the time of the merger. Robinson wanted to reward Cohen both for Shearson's record profits and for coping with meddling from Weill. "Sandy still has a network of moles inside Shearson keeping him up to date on what's happening," one source told the *Journal*. "Shearson was Sandy's baby, and it's been hard for him to let go."[10]

Case in point: In the mid-1980s, Larry Hartzog, the attorney who negotiated on behalf of the Oklahoma businessmen when Weill's firm purchased Hayden Stone in 1970, was working on a deal with some Shearson bankers in Oklahoma. Before the meeting, one of the Shearson men called him aside and said, "Sandy Weill sends his best regards." Hartzog later reflected, "How would he know that these guys were meeting with me? He clearly stays on top of things with people. And I remember thinking that if that guy hadn't delivered the message, he would really have been in trouble."

As Weill's relationship with Cohen frayed, he found a new protégé. In 1983, Weill hired Jamie Dimon, a Harvard Business School graduate and son of a Shearson broker. It was the beginning of an even more intense relationship than the one Weill and Cohen had shared. Dimon was soon indispensable to Weill, taking care of many of the same details that Cohen had handled. Cohen's journey with Weill—he had started at CBWL-Hayden Stone in 1971 as a 24-year-old analyst—would soon culminate with estrangement.

Weill's IDS Purchase Goes Unappreciated

While Cohen was basking in praise for the Trade Development Bank (TDB) deal, Weill scouted out a deal of his own that seemed pedestrian by comparison. He proposed that American Express buy Investors Diversified Services (IDS), a Minneapolis-based firm that sold mutual funds and insurance products door-to-door. Not surprisingly, the deal did little to improve Weill's status at AmEx, striking most as a hum-drum initiative, particularly in light of Cohen's prestigious TDB deal.

Getting the IDS deal through AmEx's bureaucracy would prove torturous to Weill, who saw great potential in the company's grass-roots approach. He negotiated with management and proposed a one billion dollar stock trade, which seemed, to him, a fair price given the company's growth potential. But other Shearson and AmEx executives, including Cohen, balked at the price. Although they agreed it looked like a decent business, they thought Weill had offered too much.

Cohen's unenthusiastic response to the deal enraged Weill, particularly during the trip out to Minnesota to look at IDS. Cohen, upon leaving IDS headquarters, said he planned on telling Robinson that the company was worth acquiring, but not at Weill's price. At that point, Weill lost his composure, screaming obscenities at Cohen. Robinson, as it turned out, agreed with Cohen's assessment. He sought the counsel of Sandy Lewis, who, after all, had sewn together the AmEx/Shearson deal. Lewis told Robinson that $750 million would be a more suitable price. Finally, in December 1983, Robinson agreed to the deal, at a price of $773 million.

IDS would eventually prove to be AmEx's best acquisition, more profitable by far than either Shearson or TDB, both of which would eventually be shed at a loss for the parent company. But at the time, AmEx's top brass believed that Weill had miscalculated the price. That perceived stumble would pave the way for Gerstner's ascendancy as Robinson's most trusted and influential lieutenant.

As would happen with some frequency in Weill's long career, he ultimately got the last laugh. Weill hired his old Brooklyn friend Harvey Golub from the consulting firm McKinsey & Company to run IDS after the acquisition was finally approved. Golub would prove such a star, and IDS such a success, that after the AmEx board asked for Robinson's resignation in 1993, when the company's sprawling financial services empire was unraveling, they decided to name Golub CEO.

Saving Fireman's Fund

Weill, still smarting from the IDS pricing debacle, would soon have his hands full with a key role in resuscitating American Express' ailing insurance subsidiary, Fireman's Fund. But it was far from a plum assignment.

In late 1983, serious problems at Fireman's Fund emerged. Like many commercial insurers, Fireman's Fund paid out much more in claims in 1983 than it had projected. Meanwhile, the property/casualty industry was suffering a major downturn, which Fireman's Fund CEO Edward Cutler had warned Robinson and Weill about. Without adequate reserves, American Express had to sink capital into the company. Worst of all, the sharp losses in the insurance subsidiary dragged down the parent company's results. American Express was forced to announce that its profits would fall about 10 percent for the year

Top: Weill was the captain (center) and best player on the Peekskill Military Academy tennis team.

Middle: A leader and top student at PMA, Weill (fourth from left) made the National Honor Society.

Bottom: Weill's senior photo at PMA. (Credit: 1951 Yearbook, Peekskill Military Academy)

Arthur Carter, Roger Berlind, and Sandy Weill (right) built one of the most aggressive brokerages on Wall Street in the mid-1960s. (Credit: E. Hausner/ *New York Times*)

Weill stopped smoking cigars after his grandson said he didn't like it. (Credit: Larry Barns)

Many years after the merger of American Express and Shearson, Weill (right) famously referred to himself as Jim Robinson's "Deputy Dog." (Credit: Thomas Victor/TimePix)

Left: When Weill left American Express in 1985, Jamie Dimon went with him and spent the next 13 years working at Weill's side. (Credit: Suzanne Opton)

Bottom: After Weill bought 27 percent of Travelers, it was only a matter of time before he was holding the umbrella. Shown here with former Travelers CEO Ed Budd. (Credit: John Abbott)

Top: In September 1997, Travelers announced the acquisition of Salomon Brothers, creating Salomon Smith Barney. From left are Deryck Maughan, co-CEO of Salomon; Weill; Robert Denham, co-CEO of Salomon; and Jamie Dimon, longtime Weill protégé and CEO of Smith Barney. (Credit: Reuters/Getty Images)

Right: For much of his career, Weill loved having a fireplace in his office. (Credit: Rob Kinmonth)

Top: Asked by the authors what his greatest achievement was, Weill answered "marrying my wife." He and Joan are shown here at their home in Greenwich, Connecticut. (Credit: Rob Kinmonth)

Right: Marc Weill and Jessica Bibliowicz both held high positions at companies run by their father. (Credit: Suzanne Opton)

Top: John Reed left Citigroup after a February 2000 boardroom showdown with Weill. (Credit: John Abbott)

Bottom: After the merger that formed Citigroup, Weill and his wife, Joan, rang the opening bell at the New York Stock Exchange. (Credit: Reuters/Getty Images)

Top: Citigroup's Robert Rubin, Banamex's Roberto Hernandez Ramirez, and Weill announce that Citigroup will buy Banamex for $12.5 billion on May 17, 2001. (Credit: Daniel Aguilar/TimePix)

Right: On top of the world. (Credit: Rob Kinmonth)

in December 1983—the first time in 35 years that the company didn't have an annual earnings gain.

For Robinson, this was a disaster. Along with Gerstner's card division, Fireman's Fund had been a cash cow for AmEx. But it was a high-cost producer in an industry that was getting increasingly competitive. After Cutler made a presentation at AmEx headquarters detailing Fireman's Fund's financial woes, he would soon be on his way out.

The writing on the wall became clear for Weill when Robinson decided to send him out to California in late 1983 to rescue Fireman's Fund. Weill was smart enough to know that he was being exiled. From *House of Cards:*

Weill: Your mind is made up, then?

Robinson: It's the best solution.

Weill: What about Shearson?

Robinson: Shearson can report to me. Don't worry about that, Sandy.

As Friedman and Meehan wrote, "It was a fatal blow to Weill. AmEx's president would be out of New York and out of mind. Even better, Weill would be completely severed from his remaining power base at Shearson."[11] For the next year, Weill could no longer complain of not having enough to do. Fireman's Fund was a mess.

Weill told colleagues he welcomed the challenge, despite more honest intimations to friends. To his credit, Weill attacked the job with his customary gusto. He rented a small apartment three miles from the Fireman's Fund offices in Novato, California, north of San Francisco, where instead of overlooking the Manhattan skyline his office had a view of a cow pasture. He worked full-time there, flying back to New York and his family on the red-eye Friday mornings and returning on Monday. Adopting his old Shearson ways, he set about turning around the insurance subsidiary.

Weill moved fast. He cut the staff by one-fifth, reduced costs by $65 million, and attempted to thin an entrenched bureaucracy. Many of his cuts came from within the executive ranks. Weill expected immediate changes to produce immediate results, as they typically did at the brokerage firms he had turned around. But it took about a year for Fireman's Fund to get back on firm footing—far longer than Weill had expected.

Predictably, Weill alienated some executives at Fireman's Fund who criticized him for moving too fast. The complaints were familiar: Weill was abrasive; he would shout; he would not take time to think things through. The staid insurance company had probably never seen the likes of Weill before. "Fireman's Fund was an old, low-key organization long on trust," a former Fireman's Fund employee said in an article from that period. In contrast, Weill was described as, "abrasive and insensitive."[12]

Weill and Cohen Clash Again

At the same time Weill was shaking things up at Fireman's Fund, Cohen came up with an even more high-powered acquisition idea. In the spring of 1984, news broke that the partners of Lehman Brothers, the venerable Wall Street investment bank, were warring and looking for a buyer. Lehman had merged with another ailing Our Crowd firm, Kuhn Loeb, six months earlier and attempts to integrate the two firms were failing miserably. As CEO of Shearson American Express, Cohen was eager to purchase an investment banking firm. Shearson was still known for its fleet of retail brokers. As Cohen saw it, Lehman could bolster

Shearson in the key areas of banking, fixed-income trading, and government securities.

Not surprisingly, Weill was against it at the start, arguing it was bad timing. The market was booming and he preferred to buy firms when the market was suffering and he could get a good price. But, his clout at the firm badly damaged by the IDS pricing debacle, Weill had no power with which to restrain Cohen.

Weill Looks for an Exit from American Express

Weill's stint running Fireman's Fund had rekindled his longing to be on top again, and it was abundantly clear to him that Robinson wasn't going anywhere soon. In August 1984, Weill started selling AmEx shares by the hundreds of thousands. As the months went by, he kept selling. For anyone who cared to look, Weill was clearly signaling his impending departure, as he had always viewed the willingness of employees to stockpile company shares a litmus test for their loyalty.

"American Express' Weill Sells 150,000 More Shares" ran a *Journal* headline on March 8, 1985. Weill sold those shares of common stock for about $6.1 million, leaving him with about 150,000 shares. In the prior six-month period, Weill had sold 450,000 shares of American Express, or about three-quarters of the 605,000 shares he owned. An American Express spokesman told the newspaper that Weill sold the stock merely as a result of "personal financial planning that includes diversification of his portfolio."[13]

It became even clearer that Weill would soon be leaving when another management reshuffle in December 1984 left Weill out of the loop and gave Gerstner a top role. Gerstner's mandate was broadened beyond the credit card and traveler's check area to include various corporate financial and planning duties. Weill was relegated to chairman of the finance committee of the board of directors, a role that had been fulfilled by Robinson. It was a swift kick upstairs for Weill.

Weill alighted on a potential exit strategy. Robinson and the board decided that, even with a turnaround under way, Fireman's Fund wouldn't be able to achieve benchmarks for growth and should be sold. Weill, who liked the insurance business, decided to buy Fireman's Fund himself.

The strategy he came up with for buying Fireman's Fund was a leveraged buyout, with assistance from Warren Buffett of Berkshire Hathaway. It called for Buffett to get 40 percent, AmEx to retain 40 percent, and Weill to take the remaining 20 percent. Robinson weighed Weill's proposal for nearly a month. But the board balked, so Robinson rejected Weill's offer. Instead, the AmEx board decided on a strategy of selling Fireman's Fund to the public over the next few years while the turnaround continued. As it turned out, one of Weill's big mistakes during his tenure at AmEx was not doing more to cultivate the board.

But Weill was not completely rebuffed. Robinson offered him the chance both to become the CEO of Fireman's Fund and to buy a significant stake of the public company. Though skeptical, Weill negotiated with Robinson. But when Robinson wouldn't grant him as big a stake as he wanted, Weill turned down the deal, which included a five-year, $80 million offer from Robinson to run Fireman's Fund full-time—a compensation package that would have been the richest in corporate history.

Clark believes that the deal, as it happened, was the right one for AmEx. He says that AmEx shareholders ultimately made out far better with the decision to fix the company over time while gradually selling shares to the public. "The way Sandy had structured a number of his purchase offers, there were a lot of contingencies that American Express would have kept. So American Express would have ended up putting in more money after selling it." In 1990, the company was sold to Allianz A.G. of Germany for $3 billion.

In June 1985, Weill resigned from American Express, effective August 1. His stated reason, as he would frequently tell the press, was that he was exhausted with the corporate grind. He said he was determined to take it easy for a while. Not surprisingly, Gerstner succeeded him as president. One thing Weill did, incidentally, before leaving was to give Cohen his blessing to go ahead with the Lehman deal—not that it was really needed.

AmEx after Weill

Cohen, whose first few years at American Express were a stunning success, floundered in the years after Weill's departure. Apparently caught up in the excesses of the day on Wall Street, Shearson was hurt by bad real estate deals, junk bonds, and bridge loans. "There was a lot of bad stuff going on and it affected a lot of companies, not just Shearson," says Clark. "It was clear that Peter was very smart, a terrific back-office person, and a great integrator of the acquisition strategy that Sandy Weill had. But he always had Sandy." Cohen resigned on January 30, 1990.

As for Robinson, he, too, would see his once sparkling reputation lose luster in the late 1980s and early 1990s. "Jim did a lot of very good things for American Express over a long period of time," says Clark, pointing to the firm's tremendous growth. But Robinson inevitably suffered at the hands of the press when many of the acquisitions, including Shearson, ran into problems. *Business Week* ran a punishing story "American Express: The Failed Vision," on March 19, 1990. Robinson eventually resigned from AmEx in January 1993.

Despite never quite hitting his stride at American Express, Weill has said many times in the business press that he would do the Shearson/American Express deal all over again. His AmEx years were a time of tremendous growth, if not great achievement. The lessons he learned—about cultivating the board of directors, keeping a power base in operations, and never accepting a number two spot—would all serve him well 17 years later when Travelers merged with Citicorp.

Starting Over

The ultimate measure of success for the super-rich—from John D. Rockefeller to Bill Gates—is just how much money they can comfortably give away. Sandy Weill, appropriately enough, has assumed his rightful place in the philanthropic major leagues, with two headline-grabbing $100 million donations to Cornell, first in 1998 and again in January 2002. Both donations were to the medical school, which now bears his name.

Cornell, Weill's alma mater, is just one of his many charities. Weill is the chairman of three organizations: the Weill Medical College, the National Academy Foundation, and Carnegie Hall. "And if I said that any was the favorite over the others, I'd be in big trouble," Weill joked in an interview.

What distinguishes Weill from other philanthropists—akin to what distinguishes him from other CEOs—is the hands-on role he plays. He doesn't just give money away, he donates his time and energy. This rule goes for Joan as well, chair of the board of the Alvin Ailey American Dance Theater. As Weill says, "we stay pretty active."

The Weills have become fixtures on the social pages not merely for attending charity balls, but for hosting various fund-raising events for their organizations all year-round. Philanthropy "is a very important part of my life and has been for a long time," says Weill. "I've devoted a lot of time to it."

Weill's first serious philanthropic pursuit was a career-oriented educational organization he founded himself, the National Academy Foundation. He used the same approach he employed in launching his first brokerage—start with clear goals and a willingness to work hard, and you really don't need a lot of money to get going. As his friend Michael Lipper sees it, "This was the classic example of using some capital, but more just intelligence and effort, to do something about a problem."

Weill founded the Academy of Finance (which grew to become the National Academy Foundation) in 1980 as a training program for high school students interested in careers in finance. Weill was disturbed that, while New York had survived its mid-1970s fiscal crisis, businesses were still threatening to move out of the city because they couldn't find enough qualified workers. Meanwhile, city kids were missing out on the opportunity for lucrative careers in finance. This may have been particularly galling to Weill, who knew from personal experience that even young people born well outside New York's elite could make it on Wall Street given hard work and determination.

Weill talked about his motivation for starting the Academy of Finance before a 1996 House Ways and Means Committee hearing on how to improve American education and produce a better workforce. It was his first testimony before a Congressional committee, and he admitted to being "a little bit nervous" as he began. He described how he came up with the idea for the Academy while driving around the five boroughs of New York City:

You saw young people playing in the street, young people without having a clue of what life was about, and how they can become part of the system. That was the beginning of the idea that maybe the private sector should get together with the public sector and see if we can create a high-school level program that can train young people for a career in the financial services industry.[1]

Weill brought his deal-making skills to the challenge of getting started. First, he worked behind the scenes to create a network of powerful people who would back him. He went to Frank Macchiarola, who was at that point chancellor of the New York City schools, and offered to contribute his experience and skills as long as Macchiarola would accept the help of someone from the private sector. Knowing the teachers union might oppose his plan to include courses designed by financial services practitioners, he included Sandra Feldman, head of the United Federation of Teachers, in his discussions about founding the Academy.

The Academy of Finance debuted in 1982 at John Dewey High School in Brooklyn as a two-year pilot program for 35 juniors and seniors. Weill insisted the program include paid internships at financial institutions, so that students could experience working in a thriving corporate environment, as opposed to toiling away at a Wendy's or a minimart. It was a hit with students and after three years, the program was expanded to another school. By the time of Weill's testimony before Congress in 1996, it was active in 200 schools in 25 states. That year, Weill started the first full four-year Academy of Finance program, at a high school near the American Stock Exchange in downtown New York City.

The program continued to grow and diversified into other fields. By September 2001, the National Academy Foundation operated nearly 500 programs in the United States—255 in finance, 148 in travel and tourism, and 57 in information technology. By then, Weill had also made Citigroup a key part of the program, launching the Citigroup Academy of Finance Scholars Program, which awards $20,000 college scholarships and provides internships to 20 graduating Academy of Finance seniors every year. More than 80 percent of the participating students, the majority of whom are minorities, go on to college. Weill has attributed the success of the program to the courses designed by financial industry professionals, the program's emphasis on technology, and the paid internships.

Big-Time Philanthropy

As Weill became a multimillionaire many times over, he expanded his philanthropic endeavors to many other organizations. Today, Weill is the chairman of the Weill Family Foundation in New York City (Joan is president, Marc treasurer, and Jessica secretary). In 2000, they contributed $52 million to the trust, bringing its total assets to more than $200 million. That year the trust dispensed $7 million to nonprofit organizations such as the Memorial Sloan-Kettering Cancer Center, the New York City Ballet Company, the Fund for Public Schools in Brooklyn, the Jewish Theological Seminary, and the Resident's Committee to Protect the Adirondacks (a conservation group).

Skeptics point to Weill's generosity as an effort to burnish his image and provide good public relations for Citigroup. To be sure, it does that. "Sometimes, socially responsible actions are just good business decisions," says Wayne Guay, assistant professor of accounting at the University of Pennsylvania's Wharton School. "For example, charitable activities, such as sponsoring a fund-raising event or providing goods and services to underprivileged groups, have publicity value that may outweigh the costs. Managers can feel good about taking the socially responsible action *and* maximizing shareholder value."

Weill's charitable endeavors are also a way for him to use his tremendous energy and drive for more than, as his chief of operations Chuck Prince joked, driving his top executives crazy. His passion for philanthropy may even reveal a glimpse of what Weill will do with his time once he steps down from Citigroup. Stock analyst Richard Bove of Hoefer & Arnett doubts that Weill will ever step down willingly from his top post at the company, but predicts that if he did, he would "take the Andrew Carnegie or John D. Rockefeller route." Weill first realized the rewards of philanthropy in the year after he left American Express. That was a rare point in his career when he had very little to do.

1985: No Deeds to Do, No Promises to Keep

As painful as the American Express years were for Weill, he grew immeasurably during that period. The cigar-smoking, bellowing boss had mellowed some while observing how the polished, board-savvy American Express executives operated. Even as his days at AmEx became numbered, Weill spoke and acted in a more distinguished manner. Weill may not have become CEO of AmEx, but he did take a giant step toward becoming a world-class executive, rather than simply a successful deal maker.

By the time he left American Express in August 1985, Weill's energy, drive, and talents for whipping troubled companies into shape were already legendary, so no one expected him to fade into the sunset. But many wondered if the famous momentum that propelled him to build Shearson had been broken.

Not Jamie Dimon. When Weill left American Express on August 1, 1985, Dimon, who could have had his choice of jobs at AmEx, willingly followed him into unemployment. It was a testimony to Weill's hold on the young executive that Dimon decided that anyone who couldn't find a place for Weill's talents couldn't—by association—find a place for his.

Weill's ability to hand-pick talented young executives and then encourage, motivate, plead, and—yes—bully them to achieve is legendary. While Weill's relationships with Cohen and Dimon were critical to his building of Shearson and Citigroup, respectively, he established and maintained relationships with numerous proteges, among them: back-office wizard Frank Zarb, Hayden Stone executive Hardwick Simmons, CEO of the Nasdaq Stock Market; and Jeff Lane of Neuberger Berman. These were people who saw, up close, the complete Weill—warts and all—and still decided to entrust their career to him. "These are among the smartest people you are going to find anywhere on the planet—people who are not just smart, but who can effectively execute," observes analyst Bove.

But, as it has turned out, the intensity of these relationships inevitably led to conflict. The same drive and commitment, for example, that impelled Dimon to walk out of AmEx with Weill defined a relationship that couldn't last forever. As Bove says, "After a period of time [people like Dimon] want to be running their own show. There is only a limited amount of time a guy like that is going to work in the shadow of someone else. Ultimately that builds up to a massive conflict between that person and Sandy."

"What Do You Mean You're Working?"

Initially, Dimon could have been forgiven if he regretted his decision to leave AmEx with Weill. They started out by renting an office in an American Express-owned building on Park Avenue and Fifty-third Street with the intention of hunting for deals. But the phone didn't ring as often as either of them would have liked. After maintaining a breakneck pace for 30 years, Weill literally had nothing to do.

Still, he went to the office every morning in a suit and tie, ready for business. When he got to his desk, he spent the time watching the day's stock prices. "It was a strange time for him,"

Dimon commented later. "He had been running nonstop his whole working life."[2]

Often, Weill would jog by himself around the reservoir in Central Park. But he drew the line at attending matinees with his wife, who would occasionally call him up and suggest they go to a film. According to a newspaper report, one day Joan had called him at the office:

"Let's go to a movie," she said.

"I can't. I'm working."

"What do you mean you are working?"[3]

During this time, Weill continued the image softening that had started at American Express. He didn't have much choice. After all, in the situation he was in then, he could no longer wander the halls, yelling at subordinates about details of deals. As he himself jokingly pointed out to a reporter later, " I had nobody to scream at."[4]

Although Weill is not an introspective person, he has made some of his most reflective comments about this period of his life. He said his relationships improved with his children, Marc and Jessica, ages 29 and 26 at the time. "With me not working and them doing well, they could see me as a little bit vulnerable, and that made things friendlier," he told a reporter.[5]

Eventually, Weill began to network again. When he was at AmEx, Weill had become involved in the effort to renovate Carnegie Hall, which had only recently escaped demolition by the city. Still, the drive to refurbish the historic recital hall had stalled. A new leader was needed. Looking for an outlet for his time and energy, Weill decided to throw himself into the project wholeheartedly. Weill became the chairman of the $50 million Campaign for Carnegie Hall, and he and Joan jumpstarted the fund-raising effort by donating $2.5 million to the fund themselves—Weill's first charitable contribution that made news.

Running the campaign was exactly the kind of management challenge Weill loved to tackle. As his friend Michael Lipper sees it, the city of New York was the beneficiary of this period of downtime in Weill's career:

> This was a classic Sandy operation. He called the people he knew. He organized. He was intense. He got into the details. Not only did he raise the money but he spent it well. As somebody who enjoys Carnegie Hall, I'm delighted he did it.

The renovation started in mid-1986, and Weill recruited additional donations even as the work went forward. Seven months of seven-day workweeks later, Carnegie Hall had its facelift, and Carnegie Hall President Isaac Stern and Chairman James Wolfensohn recognized Weill as a major force behind the project's success.

In tribute to Weill's efforts, Wolfensohn announced on November 5, 1986, that a 268-seat third-floor auditorium adjacent to the main performing space would be renamed the Sanford and Joan Weill Recital Hall at Carnegie Hall. On December 15, the main auditorium reopened with a gala concert televised by CBS. Two weeks later, at the formal unveiling of the Weill Recital Hall, a charmed Weill described the concert hall as looking "like a little jewel."[6]

For Weill, the entire experience was a revelation. He learned friends and colleagues would take his calls and meet with him, even though he was not at that point in a position of financial power. As he later reflected, "It was not unnerving being 'on the beach' for a while; on the contrary, it was rewarding. I found out that I had relationships with people because of *me*."[7]

Weill also got to know one of the most influential New Yorkers of the twentieth century through his work with Carnegie Hall. The late Isaac Stern was a legendary violinist and performer, as well as a champion of aspiring classical musicians. (Stern also had a legendary ability to motivate Carnegie Hall board members.) He made groundbreaking teaching expeditions to China in the late 1970s that illustrated how tremendous cultural and political divides could be bridged through music. Weill soaked up all he could from Stern, embracing Stern's broad worldview and emulating his skill at managing the Carnegie Hall board. After Stern's death in September 2001, Weill said that, "Isaac was somebody who developed an incredible relationship with all the board members. He was an inspiration in the way he talked about the world, government, economics, and how we can all contribute more."[8]

A Proposal to BankAmerica

Philanthropy, gala dinners, and Carnegie Hall concerts were winning Weill friends and respect, but they didn't do much to satisfy his desire to run a company. Some of his associates at the time expected he would start another brokerage. Others thought he might wind up as CEO of a big, well-known financial services company. Weill had his own idea.

Since late 1985, he had been thinking about going after one of the toughest financial services jobs in the country: turning around BankAmerica. The San Francisco-based bank, the nation's second-largest after Citibank, was in trouble. It had been founded by A. P. Giannini in 1904, but by the mid-1980s was bleeding red ink. In December 1985, BankAmerica (the holding company for Bank of America) reported that it had lost $337 million that year and eliminated its dividend payments for the first time since the Depression. Its nonperforming loans totaled more than $3.4 billion at yearend.

As the bad news kept pouring out of the bank, Weill developed an interest in taking a leadership role. He had met CEO Sam Armacost once before, when he solicited a donation for the Carnegie Hall Fund. To Weill, the situation seemed tailor-made for his brand of management. Like the many badly managed brokerages that Weill seized control of in the 1970s, BankAmerica had plenty of underutilized assets that Weill thought he could turn into real value. "During that year's sabbatical, BankAmerica appeared to be the largest troubled financial thing around," he later said to a reporter, explaining his interest. "It was a shame what was happening to a great old institution."[9]

Knowing that any kind of interest from him would seem to come from out of the blue to Armacost and the BankAmerica board, Weill decided that his manner and approach had to be open, friendly, and nonadversarial. He held meetings; consulted with lawyers, investment bankers, and board directors; doing his best to build a network of support before officially making a proposal to run the bank.

One of the people Weill reached out to was Warren Hellman, former president of Lehman Brothers, which by this time had been purchased by Shearson. Hellman came from an influential San Francisco family that had built Wells Fargo into a world-renowned institution. Hellman had moved back to San Francisco in 1981—several years before the Shearson/Lehman Brothers deal—to set up his own investment bank. When Weill called to tell him about his idea of running BankAmerica, Hellman was all for it. He felt that Weill could turn the institution around and, in the process, help revitalize San Francisco's business community.

Hellman recalled the call from Weill in an interview for this book:

Sandy said to me, "Wouldn't it be great if I became CEO?" I thought it was a fantastic idea. To say he had a record of success before was a huge understatement. He really has this unusual charisma; if he works at an organization he knows everybody. I knew he could take a demoralized large organization and really move it forward.

Despite support from people like Hellman, Weill needed more than that to gain the favor of the BankAmerica board. Before long, Weill secured exactly what he needed from Shearson Lehman: the promise of $1 billion in capital if Weill was named CEO of BankAmerica. On January 29, 1986, according to court documents, Weill received a letter from Shearson with the headline "Commitment to Place $1 Billion of Equity Capital for BankAmerica Corporation under Certain Circumstances."

Weill was able to drum up support from Shearson, despite his all-too-recent clashes, because he still had many loyalists there who would have done nearly anything for him. The deal would also have been good business for Shearson. It would have given the predominantly retail brokerage house a chance to show Wall Street that it could make a major deal. "Making bets on Sandy was always a good idea," says Lane, who was by then number two at Shearson. "He was a friend, but much more important, it was a good business decision." Even though Weill's relationship with Cohen at the time was "strained," Lane observes, "Cohen was just as much an economic animal as anyone," and willing to back Weill for the firm's benefit. Like a divorced couple staying civil because of the children, Cohen and Weill were held together by a bond of mutual self-interest—and Weill making a huge return for Shearson on an investment in BankAmerica would definitely be in both of their interests.

Still, American Express, a public company, couldn't just write a check for one billion dollars for Weill to wave in front of the

BankAmerica board of directors. There had to be parameters and conditions. A meeting was arranged to hammer out the details of Shearson's commitment at the very headquarters in the World Trade Center that Weill had moved the company into years before. Bove was one of the Shearson representatives. He recalls:

> Sandy had made presentations about what he would do at BankAmerica. He knew BankAmerica had valuable assets that were being mismanaged. He knew that if he put in reasonable management, he could turn it around. And American Express made the commitment to back him. The problem was that it was necessary for American Express to have an operating plan. Some others and I were asked to put together a program. They put us on the 102nd floor of the World Trade Center with instructions that no one was allowed to go home until the operating model was put together. In three days we put it together.

During negotiations, some lasting impressions were made on Bove concerning Weill's negotiating tactics and skills: "He has an enormous degree of intelligence and a staggering degree of self-confidence." Weill was starting to delegate more. In fact, despite Weill's legendary attention to detail, Bove insists, "He was not a detail guy at all. He would get a conceptual grasp of the issue, move on the concept, and leave the details to all sorts of other people. Ultimately, the details had to match his thinking."

With Shearson's support secured, Weill held more intimate strategy sessions at Hellman's investment bank in San Francisco with a group that included Hellman as well as other investment bankers and attorneys. Hellman remembers Weill as a persistent, hard-nosed businessman who, incidentally, almost smoked Hellman and others (none of whom smoked themselves) out of their own offices. "I finally decided I couldn't go home with all of my clothes smelling like smoke," says Hellman. "I told him I'd give him an office, and when he wanted to smoke cigars he could go in his office, close the door, and smoke. And he did, too."

Weill also reached out to bankers, including Walter Wriston, and a few sympathetic BankAmerica board members he knew were at cross-purposes with Armacost. One was Charles Schwab, founder of the discount brokerage. Schwab, whose company was owned by BankAmerica, supported Weill's bid in the belief that Weill would allow him to buy back his company, a move Armacost then opposed. Another was Robert McNamara, the former Secretary of Defense. According to *Breaking the Bank,* a history of BankAmerica, it was McNamara who finally convinced Weill to put his offer in writing in a letter to Armacost:

> Without a letter, McNamara had counseled, Weill's idea would never reach the board. If Weill sent a letter, McNamara assured him that the board would give his ideas a fair hearing.[10]

On January 31, 1986, Weill sent a letter to Armacost offering his services in a CEO or co-CEO position, with Shearson's promise of $1 billion in capital attached. According to *Breaking the Bank:*

> Armacost panicked. At first, he wouldn't open the letter. He seemed to believe that if he didn't open it, he could argue that he had never received it. But he immediately prepared to repel Weill, reaching out for assistance.[11]

Armacost hired a team of advisers that included merger and acquisition advisers First Boston and the law firm Morrison & Foerster. First Boston's chief mergers and acquisitions specialist, Joseph Perella (who would later found Wasserstein Perella, the leveraged buy-out firm, with Bruce Wasserstein), was particularly effective at discrediting Weill's offer. He termed it "nothing more than a job application from Sandy Weill and a solicitation for new business from Shearson Lehman."[12]

Armacost then used similar terms to characterize Weill's offer to the board, further describing it as half-serious and worthy of mocking. The board rejected the offer and Armacost phoned Hellman to tell him as much. "The letter was described by the investment bankers to the board of BankAmerica as a billion-dollar job offer," Hellman says. "They said, 'the guy wants the job so badly he's willing to offer $1 billion to have it.'"

A Second Try

After a two-week vacation in the Caribbean, Weill was ready to try again in late February. Having fought countless battles throughout his career to find capital, Weill had a hard time believing that a struggling institution such as BankAmerica would cavalierly dismiss his offer. This time he went to the board with a more formal letter of commitment from Shearson for one billion dollars, written by Lane, as well as some more specifics for running the bank.

His plan was that the one billion-dollar infusion of capital would be used to write off bad debts and make deals that would strengthen the bank's position. Weill's proposal also entailed deeper cuts at the bank than Armacost had ever considered, mostly by eliminating tiers of management and more branch offices. To increase revenue, he proposed channeling more products and services through the bank. He cited his success both in growing Shearson and resuscitating Fireman's Fund, and predicted that eventually he could increase BankAmerica's stock from $13 (its price before his takeover bid became public) to $20 or $22. Weill also promised to put in $10 million of his own money.

Before the BankAmerica board could formally evaluate his second offer, news leaked and the press starting reporting on the potential re-emergence of Weill as head of BankAmerica. The share price jumped. But on Thursday, February 20, 1986, *Reuters* carried a story that reported BankAmerica had denied any management changes were being discussed.

It became clear, however, how most investors felt about the idea of Weill leading BankAmerica. On February 27, 1986, one week after BankAmerica had denied the rumors, it announced the board would seriously review Weill's offer. The company's stock price jumped $2 on the news.

But Armacost was skilled at using the advantages of incumbency to protect his job. He drafted a five-year plan that promised great things for the bank. He made it known that Thomas Cooper, a well-respected member of the management team with a reputation as a cost-cutter, would be promoted to chief operating officer. BankAmerica spokesman John J. Keane told the *New York Times* that management, "is not interested in [Weill's] ideas and has had no further communication with him," and that the board would soon make a decision on his offer.[13]

On March 3, 1986, the 21-member board met and Armacost, largely on the strength of his five-year forecast, convinced them to spurn Weill's offer. Of the 21 board members, 17 voted to reject Weill's bid. "I think they got into sort of a bunker mentality," Hellman says. He described their thinking: " 'Nobody is going to tell us who the CEO of this bank is going to be. How dare this guy come to San Francisco and offer himself up to be the CEO of our most important local institution?' "

The Fallout

One option Weill didn't pursue was a hostile takeover of BankAmerica. Though early 1986 was prior to the boom time of hostile takeovers—1988 saw the most such deals, including the infamous Kohlberg Kravis Roberts takeover of RJR Nabisco—

Weill certainly had the muscle, with Shearson's one billion dollars behind him. But Weill has never wanted to do hostile deals. He has always preferred to go where he was wanted, notes Lane:

> This is a people business. You are not buying a widget factory. So if the people don't want to be with you they are going to go down the elevator the following night and they are not going to come back. You can't do a hostile deal in the world of financial services.

Years later, however, Weill still bristled at the BankAmerica snub. "I never got through the gate to make a proposal," Weill told *Business Week* in 1989.[14] Some Wall Street observers speculated that, as a Jew, Weill never stood a chance with BankAmerica. For his part, Weill told the magazine he hoped that had nothing to do with it.

In July 1986, BankAmerica reported that it had lost $640 million in the second quarter that year—the second largest loss for a bank in U.S. history. Like many banks at the time, including Citicorp, BankAmerica was suffering from bad loans to Latin American and other Third World countries. Later in 1986, First Interstate Bank, a bank so much smaller than BankAmerica that it was only the fourth biggest bank in California, attempted to buy the bank, which BankAmerica rebuffed. Armacost was replaced before the year was out by his predecessor, Tom Clausen.

Looking back, Hellman thinks that if Weill had gotten the job, he would have built the equivalent of Citigroup in San Francisco. "Bank of America has been as humiliating an experience for San Francisco as you can imagine," Hellman says. "The irony of this whole thing has never been spelled out. Supposing we had Citigroup here. If Sandy had come in here, Citigroup would have played out but it would have been Bank of America, not Citigroup. Bank of America is not even headquartered here, but in

North Carolina. The whole dynamic was backward. They should have been begging Sandy to come here."

The BankAmerica Deal and Insider Trading

A small-time, insider-trading scheme related to Weill's Bank-America bid, perpetrated by Joan Weill's psychiatrist and the psychiatrist's stockbroker friend, sheds light on just how much Weill discussed business matters with his wife.

From at least 1980 through 1987, Joan had sessions with a Manhattan therapist named Robert Willis. According to court documents, Weill told Joan of his interest in making overtures to become CEO of BankAmerica in the first days of January 1986. By late January, he told her that Shearson would commit capital if, in fact, Weill was named the CEO of the company.

According to court documents, "Mrs. Weill, as a patient, regularly confided to Dr. Willis the progress of Weill's plans concerning BankAmerica." Willis took that information and passed it on to a friend, Martin Sloate, president and part owner of Sloate, Weisman, Murray & Co., a small Manhattan brokerage. Both Willis and Sloate traded BankAmerica securities on the information, and Sloate recommended BankAmerica shares to his clients. According to court documents, Willis purchased 13,000 shares of BankAmerica common stock in accounts at Sloate Weisman in his name or under his control, from January 14 through February 6, 1986.

In fact, this was not the first time Willis had taken confidential information gleaned from Joan Weill's therapy sessions and supplied it to Sloate, or used it for his own account. Five years earlier, Joan had told Willis about Weill's plan to sell Shearson to American Express, and Willis and Sloate acted on that information as well, buying thousands of dollars worth of Shearson shares. The SEC brought a civil lawsuit related to both schemes against Sloate and Willis, and both were heavily fined.

Latin American Lessons at Citigroup

BankAmerica wasn't alone in its troubles in the mid-1980s. From the S&L crisis to Third World loan losses, the American banking system was struggling more than it had since the Great Depression.

Citicorp had its own troubles, as did other big banks like First National Bank and Trust Company and Manufacturers Hanover. The problems for the big banks were due to bad loans issued years earlier to Third World countries (Wriston, speaking of Citicorp's loans to Third World countries and municipalities, used to say that "Jakarta picks up the check around here") and businesses in domestic industries that had since fallen on hard times, including energy, commercial real estate, and agriculture. Bank competition had also become fierce, as Citicorp was granted at least part of its wish for financial deregulation and restrictions on interstate banking were eased.

Reed at the Helm

After officially becoming CEO on September 1, 1984, Reed led Citicorp to a banner year in 1985. Mainly through acquisitions, Reed increased Citicorp's assets from $23 billion to $174 billion. That year, the bank earned nearly $1 billion, with revenues of $998 million.

In 1986, though, Citicorp was hit hard by defaults on loans to Third World countries, including countries in Latin America, where Citicorp had been a pioneer for American banks. In May 1987, Reed took the unprecedented step of increasing its reserves for Latin American defaults to $3 billion, effectively covering a $2.5 billion loss for the second quarter of 1987, and a $1 billion loss on the year.

One executive at the bank called the Latin American crisis one of a series of "seven-year crises," as they are jokingly referred to by some employees at the bank. Every seven years, this executive says, Citigroup manages to land itself in hot water through bad luck or incompetence. But somehow the bank rebounds, and that was the case for Citicorp after the Latin American crisis. In 1988, the bank would earn higher revenues than any U.S. bank had ever made—$1.86 billion.

Back in the Game

It seemed that Weill, who had possessed a golden touch through the 1970s, could now do nothing right. Since 1981, Weill had experienced four frustrating years at American Express, been rejected by the AmEx board in his bid to buy the Fireman's Fund, and been publicly rejected by the BankAmerica board of directors. At that point, Weill "did something smart," according to Peter Solomon, who had worked with Weill at Shearson. "He sat around and bided his time."

He soon received a surreptitious phone call in mid-1986 from some executives at Commercial Credit, a subsidiary of Control Data Corp. of Minneapolis and one of the largest consumer finance companies in America. The executives knew their company was in deep trouble and wanted Weill to help them save it. Weill flew to Minneapolis and met with Bob Price, the CEO of Control Data, who urged him to take the helm of Commercial Credit and spin it off to the public.

Weill knew the company quite well. He had briefly considered buying it in 1984 for AmEx when Goldman Sachs was shopping Commercial Credit around. At that point, Commercial Credit was on its last legs and clearly a candidate for Weill's trademark prescription for unhealthy companies. For Weill, it was a case where his talents were appreciated and wanted.

Commercial Credit needed him. Control Data's credit rating had been downgraded to the point where none of its subsidiaries could borrow money. Subsequently, Commercial Credit launched a fire sale of its holdings, but still couldn't meet its debt. According to Chuck Prince, Commercial Credit's chief counsel at the time and now COO of Citigroup, the clock was running out. "We were down to where we had nothing left to sell and we would have run out of money and closed up shop by the end of 1986," Prince says. When news got around about the possibility of Weill leading the company, "it felt like Dunkirk," says Prince. "It felt like the boats had finally reached the shore because we were up against it."

Joseph Minutilli, CEO of Commercial Credit in 1986, was unaware that several of the company's executives had approached Weill. Minutilli, 59 at the time and a 35-year veteran of Commercial Credit, met with Weill at the request of the Control Data board and was favorably impressed. "Control Data wanted to know what I thought," Minutilli says, "so Sandy and I had a meeting in Baltimore and had dinner. I thought we hit it off pretty well; the chemistry was good. I, like most of us in the business world, knew who he was and what he had accomplished."

Confronted with the inevitable, Minutilli pitched in to help Weill, Dimon, and the rest of Weill's team. In September of 1986, Weill and Dimon scoured the company for information, doing their due diligence and peppering Minutilli and his staff with questions. At the end of September, it was announced that Control Data had agreed to spin off Commercial Capital and turn it over to Weill and his executives to run. Minutilli would stay on temporarily to help with the transition.

Control Data, the parent company, planned to retain 20 percent ownership and sell 80 percent of Commercial Credit in an initial public offering, which would occur in late October. According to the *Times,* Control Data's stock rose $1.75, to $27 a share, after reports of the deal.

Weill told the *Times* that legal restrictions about the offering prevented him from commenting, other than to say he was "very excited about the challenge." A soon-to-be competitor of Weill's, Martin S. Davis, chairman of Gulf and Western Industries, paid him a compliment in the *Times* article: "Sandy's one of the best executives, and they're lucky to have him. He's going to be a tremendous addition to what's obviously been a dormant asset for a very long time and he'll bring new life to it and be more than worthy competition."[15]

Today, Bove still expresses admiration of Weill's ability to look past the tarnished reputation of Commercial Credit. "He saw what had to be done. He saw the opportunity and, working with Jamie Dimon, had the methodology." It was clear to Bove that despite Weill's setbacks at AmEx and with BankAmerica, his confidence remained intact. "He had a great deal of pride in the successes he had historically," says Bove. "He felt he had the ability to take a look at a business and see where the true opportunity exists and did not exist and to move to capture the opportunity."

Commercial Credit's Initial Public Offering

Weill descended on Baltimore with a team of executives, determined to turn Commercial Credit around. They had only a few weeks before the critical IPO to improve the company and make it more attractive to the market. Weill stayed at the Harbor

Court Hotel in Baltimore five days a week and returned to New York on weekends, leading a dual-city existence, much as he had while running Fireman's Fund. "There was no social life," Robert B. Willumstad, who was part of the rescue squad Weill brought with him to Baltimore, told a reporter. "Everybody would come in at 7:30 or 8 and just work all day. There was so much to do."[16]

To position the company for the IPO, Weill began cutting costs at Commercial Credit right away. The company announced it was eliminating 2,000 jobs and selling almost $2 billion in assets, including the majority of its business financing. It trimmed itself to $5.2 billion in assets and fewer than 4,400 employees.

Initially, the all-important institutional investor community hesitated to back the IPO. The first strong interest in Commercial Credit's shares, not coincidentally, came from Shearson's retail brokers, who were unabashedly enthusiastic about the chance to sell issues of a company led by their hero. Shearson's push to get the word out about Commercial Credit's IPO eventually sparked interest from institutional investors.

Weill instituted various incentives for himself and his management team that would reward them if the value of Commercial Credit's stock price went up. Weill held options on about 6 percent of Commercial Credit's stock, which he could exercise after five years at roughly $19.50 a share. Weill had also stayed true to his conviction that executives should also be owners of the companies they work for. He invested $5 million of his money in the new Commercial Credit. In late October 1986—just days before the IPO—Weill, Minutilli, and various investment bankers met with investors in 18 cities, including six cities abroad, during a final 11-day push.

Minutilli later described the whirlwind tour of the United States, Canada, and Europe as "a period of great excitement." He also recalls that Weill knew how to enjoy himself on the trip.

"It was grueling morning, noon, and night. But Sandy knew he had to relax. He enjoyed good food and good wine. He didn't pay much attention to the 'No Smoking' light." Minutilli was particularly impressed with Weill the presenter and salesman. "Sandy told me that he was always nervous before he made speeches," Minutilli says. "I couldn't believe that because he did such a good job."

As part of his pitch to potential investors, Weill said Commercial Credit could get higher returns from its consumer finance, real estate, leasing, and insurance businesses by further reducing staff and gaining better access to capital markets. Weill thought it likely that as an independent company with capital from the IPO, Standard & Poor's and Moody's would improve their credit ratings on the company, which would make Commercial Credit more attractive to investors. Weill also promised that Commercial Credit's entire board would be paid in stock, which he believed would give board members more incentive to speak up if they disagreed with him.

Weill and Minutilli were in Edinburgh when they learned that the Commercial Credit stock issue was fully subscribed and the shares could soon open for trading. They were scheduled to go to London, but Weill suggested they go back to New York so they could be at the New York Stock Exchange on the morning the stock started trading and be the first to buy the new shares. Weill quickly procured the use of a Falcon Jet for the last-minute trip.

On the way home, while the plane refueled at an Air Force base in Newfoundland, Minutilli and Weill shared a cup of coffee out on the frozen tundra in the wee hours of October 29. It was Minutilli's last day as a CEO. He would officially transfer the reins to Weill as the shares started trading. It was a poignant moment for Minutilli as he pondered ending his tenure as active CEO.

But when the two men got back on the plane, they learned they couldn't take off because of a mechanical problem. They were stuck waiting on the tarmac. "I remember thinking, what a way to end a career," Minutilli says. But while he was anxious and exhausted, Weill seemed unperturbed by the delay and pitched in to try and find someone who could come fix the plane, flipping through a phone book. "He was helping them try to solve the problem. I had a cold and wasn't feeling too great. I was doing more complaining," Minutilli admits.

They finally got the plane fixed, flew on to New York, and had just enough time to check into a $300 hotel room and shower before heading down to the Exchange for the opening bell.

Commercial Credit was the most actively traded stock that day as investors paid $857 million for 80 percent of the company, making it then the third largest initial public offering in history. The IPO's success was largely thanks to Weill. Investors were betting on his track record, his aggressive management style, and his ability to increase shareholder value. In fact, Weill was emerging as one of the first chief executives whom people invested in, regardless of company, industry, or product. "There is a whole theory of investing that many people subscribe to: Don't buy an industry. Don't buy a company. Buy the CEO," says Howard Clark Jr. "Buy Jack Welch, buy Lou Gerstner, buy Warren Buffett, buy Sandy Weill, and you will make money."

Minutilli continued to serve on the board after Weill took over as CEO and said he respected Weill and the decisions he made to turn the company around. Just as he had on the road-trip, Minutilli says, "I admired his intensity and I admired his ability to relax."

Just a few years later, Weill would give up one of his trademark ways to relax: smoking cigars. Weill kicked the habit at the urging of his young grandson, Jessica's firstborn. Weill quit cold turkey, keeping lollipops on his desk for a week or two, but very quickly didn't need the crutch.

Managing Commercial Credit

At Commercial Credit, the hours were long and the perks were few. If Weill missed the rarefied atmosphere at American Express, he didn't let on. He and his team would take a 7:15 A.M. flight from LaGuardia to Baltimore every Monday morning, work all week, and return to Manhattan on Friday morning to share a small office in the city for the day. On Friday night, Weill would release his management team to their New York-area homes for the weekend. Often, even those respites would be interrupted by confabs at Weill's house in Greenwich or golf and tennis outings.

There was a lot of work to do to turn the company around. "Sandy will be sticking to basic blocking and tackling for awhile," Robert Greenhill, director of investment banking at Morgan Stanley, told reporters in November that year.[17] He predicted that down the road, Commercial Credit would make some major acquisitions and it was clear he would be on hand to help with those deals. (Six years later, in fact, Greenhill would be hired by Weill to run one of these acquisitions—Shearson Smith Barney).

Perhaps Weill's greatest initial success was the management culture he created at Commercial Credit. The small transition team that worked with Weill around the clock leading up to the Commercial Credit IPO wasn't deep enough or experienced enough to run an entire company. Weill brought in people who were interested in managing a financial services business in a new way and were willing to take substantial cuts in salary to join a new and risky venture. He sought both entrepreneurial types who wanted to return to their roots, as well as seasoned managers who had never had start-up experience but longed for it. He also wanted men and women who would demonstrate their belief in Commercial Credit and their confidence in Weill by seeking reward through stock ownership.

At least one member of Weill's Commercial Credit inner circle did not have to be brought in from outside the company. Weill had come across Chuck Prince, Commercial Credit's chief counsel, whom Weill would later describe to the *Harvard Business Review* as one of the best "talent discoveries" of his life.[18] Prince, who met Weill during his negotiations to take over Commercial Credit, remembers the first time Weill seemed to notice him:

> I was standing outside my office down in Baltimore and Sandy walked by and asked a question about something. I don't remember what it was, but he was holding a piece of paper. He said, "Are you sure this is right? This is important," in that kind of boring-in way. It was like facing a lie-detector test. And I said to him, "I know it's right because I did it myself." He stopped and said, "Well, that's good."

Another key hire for the management team was Robert Lipp, a former president of Chemical Bank, who was brought on to run the consumer finance operations. Not surprisingly, Weill reached out to former colleagues to fill other key roles on the Commercial Credit management team: he recruited a tax partner from his accounting firm, as well as John Fowler, a young executive he knew from AmEx with superior administrative skills. Soon Commercial Credit thrived. Earnings soared from $10.8 million in 1985 to $37.7 million in 1986, and then nearly tripled again in 1987 to $101.5 million.

A few years after taking control of Commercial Credit, Weill told a reporter that he already was glad that the BankAmerica deal had not worked out. "Baltimore is much closer than San Francisco Bay," Weill said. "And BankAmerica would have been fix-fix-fix, problem-problem-problem, whereas here at Commercial Credit it's been a little fix, and if there are any insurmountable problems, we haven't found them yet."[19]

Weill was back. And it really didn't surprise most people. Thanks to his tremendous success building Shearson in the 1970s and 1980s, Weill still had an enormous amount of credibility in the financial world, even though he had made a few missteps. Former Hayden Stone CEO Don Stroben explains:

> Once you have momentum in business, that power feeds on itself. You have to do something disastrously dumb to have that momentum break. Some people who have momentum do bad things and their momentum breaks, but most of the time the momentum carries on. I don't think everything Sandy did was perfect. But he had momentum and he had money. That carried on, enabling him to make those deals. That success and the ability to get people to follow him, lend him money, and back him, was there.

Back in the Big Leagues

In the late nineteenth and early twentieth centuries, many of America's corporate titans—including Our Crowd Wall Street leaders—built rambling, rustic hideaways deep in the Adirondack Mountains in northern New York State. These Adirondack "Great Camps," as they came to be known, numbered somewhere between 20 and 30, and were mostly spread around the high peaks region near Saranac Lake. Many of the corporate titans of the early 1900s staked their Adirondack claims. There, they would gather the whole family, mostly in the summer but sometimes even in the frigid, snowy winters.

John Pierpont Morgan, one of the most celebrated Adirondack residents, brought his own outsized élan to mountain living, furnishing his camp with two Steinway pianos and building an iron foundry and a sugarhouse on the grounds. Morgan and several other famous owners of Great Camps, such as William C. Whitney and W. W. Durant, even built their own 18-mile railroad line to connect their homes with the main train station in Clearwater. Morgan had his chartered Pullman Palace train coach steamed up 24 hours a day, ready to make the 250-mile journey back to New York if the mood struck him.[1]

Like these tycoons of an earlier age, Sandy Weill, too, relaxes at his own Adirondack camp. Joan had spent time in the Adirondacks as a girl and always had a fondness for the area. In the late 1980s, she convinced her husband that they should vacation at The Point, a former Great Camp recast as an Adirondack resort. The Point, so private that there are no published driving directions, is the kind of place where, if one wished aloud for, say, a cookie, there would appear minutes later a tray of freshly baked chocolate chip cookies on a nearby coffee table.

After their stay, Sandy and Joan decided to investigate purchasing property in the area. In 1990, they bought Green Bay Camp on Upper Saranac Lake, just a couple of miles from The Point. Green Bay Camp consists of a main lodge and surrounding guest cottages. The master bedroom has a hot tub with a picture window looking out on the lake. Hunting trophies of a previous owner hang from the walls of the main lodge (the city-reared Weill sticks to tennis and golf).

Given the care that went into the renovation of Green Bay Camp, it is clear that Weill's attention to detail extends beyond the corporate suite. He hired New York City architects and decorators to handle the renovation, which included installing a glassed-in swimming lane that looks out on the lake. During construction, Weill flew up to the camp on a moment's notice when a question arose about a particular aspect of the renovation.

He even got into a dispute with a local contractor over a $3,000 bill. "That may not be a lot of money to him, but it's a lot to me," says the contractor, who described working for Joan and Sandy much the way Weill's employees do. "They are very demanding," he says. "They want things done in a New York minute, which is a little bit unrealistic in the Adirondacks."

Yet even that contractor acknowledges that the Weills have been significant contributors to the local community. In 2001, Sandy and Joan made a $3 million contribution toward building a new library for Paul Smith's College, which will be known as the Joan Weill Adirondack Library. Joan was also named one of Paul Smith's trustees. In 2000, the Weill Family Foundation gave generously to a handful of other local charities in the Adirondacks. In that part of New York State, a gift of, say, $50,000 goes a long way.

Green Bay Camp, along with the Greenwich home and Park Avenue apartment, is one of three pieces of property owned by Sandy and Joan. For a couple worth nearly $1.4 billion, that reveals a certain admirable restraint. There is no Scottish castle, no personal island in the South Pacific. All three homes are often used for business meetings or work-related socializing. In the Adirondacks, for example, Joan and Sandy typically host New Year's gatherings for several close friends. None of the homes is particularly ostentatious, at least as far as billionaire residences go. But all the addresses—Greenwich, Park Avenue, and Upper Saranac Lake—show just how far Weill has come from his Brooklyn roots.

Commercial Credit Launches Weill Again

It took Weill 20 years to build Shearson. Although his accomplishments at American Express fell woefully short of his expectations, Weill gleaned something from his stint there: the realization that he wanted to run a diversified financial services company.

In building his second empire, Weill's focus was not simply on running Commercial Credit's core business—he could hire people to do that. And he wasn't setting out simply to build another big brokerage—he'd already done that with Shearson. His real goal was to acquire other companies and build a diversified financial services powerhouse. For him to accomplish this, Commercial Credit had to turn in strong financial results and Weill had to demonstrate that he still had a magic touch with turnarounds. After only 18 months at the helm of Commercial Credit, Weill had done so—the company had its expenses in order and was generating plenty of cash. Soon enough, Weill would be able to start building his dream company.

An Ailing Primerica

One lesson Weill had learned through the years was that many executives don't pay attention to the details. This always left plenty of opportunities for Weill to make good on their mistakes. Inevitably, whether the company was Hayden Stone, Loeb Rhoades, or Commercial Credit, all it took was a look at the balance sheet and Weill was able to identify underutilized assets that could be built up or overfunded divisions that could be cut back. Armed with this philosophy, Weill and his team of managers at the newly entrepreneurial Commercial Credit needed to find the perfect candidate to acquire and turn around.

One company that was experiencing difficulty at the time was Greenwich, Connecticut-based Primerica, formerly known as the American Can Company. As American Can, the company had once been America's greatest producer of the metal can. Retooled as a financial services company, Primerica was a good potential fit for Weill and Commercial Credit.

Primerica's mix of businesses included an underperforming brokerage, Smith Barney, that Weill was confident he could turn around. It also included a hugely profitable life insurance company, A. L. Williams, that had been started by charismatic ex-football coach Art Williams and had produced more than 35 percent of Primerica's revenues. The company also operated American Capital Management, which ran a group of about 40 mutual funds; RCM Capital, a money manager with $12 billion in assets under management; and Margaretten & Co., one of the nation's largest mortgage lenders.

Primerica was run by Gerald Tsai, a Wall Street acquaintance of Weill's of 25 years. Tsai, born in Shanghai, had more than a little "Sandy Weill" in him. He had been a star money manager in the 1960s, founding the Manhattan Fund and investing in Polaroid, Xerox, and other "glamour" stocks of the era. Tsai became a millionaire by the age of 30 when he sold the Manhattan Fund to CNA Financial Corporation in 1968. The bear market, however—the same one Weill took advantage of by acquiring floundering brokerages—wiped out the Manhattan Fund's assets. So Tsai started out again by founding a new company, Associated Madison, which he eventually sold to American Can in the late 1970s. Tsai joined the company as an executive vice president, and Chairman William Woodside put Tsai in charge of building a financial services component of American Can. In 1986, Tsai convinced the board to shed its packaging operations.

Tsai was soon named CEO, a promotion he took as a mandate, and went about completing the company's shift from manufacturing containers to providing financial services. Eventually he renamed the company Primerica. When all was said and done, Tsai had entirely divested Primerica of its manufacturing operations and recast the company as a financial services firm. But, like so many others, Tsai eventually made the kind of critical mistake with his company that would one day directly benefit Weill.

Caught in the Crash

In May 1987, Primerica purchased the investment bank Smith, Barney, Harris and Upham for $750 million, more than twice its book value. The timing couldn't have been worse for Tsai (although it would make the Smith Barney partners very rich). When the stock market crashed on Black Monday in October 1987, falling more than 500 points, or 23 percent in one day, the brokerage business fell apart. Like the Wall Street firms that expanded in the late 1960s to capitalize on a bull market, Tsai had badly overplayed his hand. Smith Barney lost more than $43 million after taxes in the fourth quarter of 1987. For the entire year, Smith Barney registered $93 million in pretax losses, followed by another $53 million in losses in 1988.

The premium price he paid for Smith Barney forced Tsai's hand. He had borrowed heavily to finance the acquisition and the debt, combined with aftereffects of the October crash, created major cash flow problems for Primerica. Adding to Tsai's problems was that his life insurance subsidiary, A.L. Williams & Co., although phenomenally successful, needed more capital to keep expanding.

Court documents related to a shareholder lawsuit surrounding the sale of Primerica provide a rare glimpse into a Weill negotiation, the elaborate rituals of a merger, and the many months of fruitless talks that may occur before anything is accomplished. In December 1987, Weill expressed an interest to Tsai in acquiring Smith Barney, not all of Primerica. In January 1988, those talks broke off, perhaps partly because Weill was angered that Tsai had also been talking to a Japanese trading company about making an investment in Primerica. Those negotiations also fizzled. In fact, Tsai was so eager to find a buyer for Smith Barney and Fingherhut, another division of Primerica, that during this period he held preliminary merger talks with Merrill Lynch, Xerox, and Elders, an Australian company.

In April 1988, Tsai decided he needed some high-powered investment banking help. He retained Lazard Freres to help him sell Smith Barney as well as additional parts of Primerica if necessary. This move may have been done with Weill in mind as a potential buyer, since one of the investment bankers at Lazard was Felix Rohatyn, who had helped deliver Hayden Stone to Weill almost 20 years earlier. In May, Rohatyn and J. Ira Harris, another top investment banker at Lazard, approached Weill about reconsidering the acquisition of all or part of Primerica. Weeks later, Rohatyn and Harris told Weill that a fair price would be to exchange one share of Commercial Credit stock plus $9 for each share of Primerica stock. Weill balked—for him that was a starting point.

Talks continued off and on over the next two months. Court documents characterize Weill during the negotiations as "often bitter and at arms' length." To represent him, Weill engaged Morgan Stanley and its star deal broker, Bob Greenhill, as well as the law firm Skadden Arps Slate Meagher & Flom. But much of the due diligence was done by Weill's Commercial Credit staff, who descended on Primerica to examine the financial health of its businesses and come up with an appropriate price. Weill came back to Lazard and said that if the cash price were reduced to somewhere between $4 and $5 a share, he would do a deal. Lazard rejected the offer and talks broke off once again.

Instead of this being the end of the deal, however, this was when negotiations began to really get serious. Talks continued into August and on the 24th, Weill and Tsai reached a deal. They would exchange one share of Commercial Credit stock plus $7 for each share of Primerica. Though initially interested in just Smith Barney, Weill had acquired all of Primerica. Rohatyn told the *Times*, "This is an old-fashioned merger done by old-fashioned people."[2]

On August 29, Tsai announced that he had agreed to sell Primerica to Weill for $1.7 billion. Besides making around $40 million on the deal, Tsai became a director of the company, head of the executive committee, and the largest shareholder in Primerica. But he had no day-to-day responsibilities.

Now, Weill was back on Wall Street with Smith Barney, and back in the big leagues as chairman and CEO of Primerica. Just as he had with his acquisitions of troubled brokerages in the 1970s, Weill had purchased Primerica when the company was under pressure. In another similarity, he had bought a company several times the size of the one he was running. Commercial Credit had 3,700 employees and assets of $4.4 billion at the time, compared with Primerica's 25,000 employees and $13.8 billion in assets. Also true to form, he took the name of the larger firm. And just like those acquisitions in the 1970s, the price Weill got for those assets would prove to be a bargain.

Citicorp: The Reed Era

In the late 1980s and 1990s, Citicorp continued to grow its consumer banking business and to expand internationally under Reed. Throughout his tenure, Reed made big bets on technology—he bought Quotron in 1986, the nation's leading supplier of securities information. Quotron terminals were early incarnations of the Bloomberg terminal, but didn't become nearly as successful. Reed found more success with automated teller machines (ATMs), which turned out to be his greatest triumph, as Citicorp ATM usage dwarfed the competition, starting in the early 1990s.

As far as management and leadership styles went, it would be hard to find a CEO more different from Sandy Weill than John Reed. While Weill has spent his career focusing on near-term financial results, Reed looked years ahead to try to anticipate consumer banking needs that Citicorp could plan for. Weill roamed the halls asking questions; Reed used memos and a few trusted aides to communicate his ideas. Weill viewed technology as a handy tool, if it applied to specific operational problems; Reed believed almost religiously in the transforming power of technology, and pushed ATM technology even when it looked like it would end in disaster for the bank. Reed, like his predecessor Walter Wriston, encouraged risk taking among his managers; Weill disdained risk, rewarding managers for hitting their quarterly targets.

More generally, while Weill maintained a financial approach to business success, Reed viewed business as an outlet of his intellect and creativity. In 1996, in fact, Reed even considered moving Citicorp's headquarters from New York to a university town like Berkeley or Palo Alto, where he thought his management team could better engage in long-term strategic thinking, far removed from operational issues. He ultimately decided against that move, but Reed did inaugurate other unusual initiatives.

For example, in 1994 Reed acted on a dream he had harbored for several years: To invite academics into Citicorp to do research. Reed created an academic council made up of leading scholars in management and business that would review proposals for academics to come into Citicorp and conduct studies about the bank. Reed felt the findings would benefit the bank, and he could indulge his lifelong affinity for intellectual pursuits at the same time. The project was slated to last 10 years, long enough for the research findings to be absorbed and acted upon by Citicorp management.

With Reed at the head of the council, academics from all over the country were given unprecedented access to Citicorp managers and employees to do their research. One of them was Sheena Iyengar, a management professor at the Columbia University Business School. She did her research on cross-cultural employee attitudes at Citicorp toward benefits and perks. "Reed said he was going to use this research as a window into his organization," Iyengar says. "Reed also liked hanging out with academics."

At one point, over 50 different research studies were in progress at Citicorp. Weill, not surprisingly, shut down the academic program as soon as he became the lone CEO of the bank. "Sandy Weill isn't the only CEO who wouldn't do something like this," said Iyengar. "Very few would commission such a project."

A former Citicorp marketing executive who was with the company in the mid-1990s says that Reed's strengths as well as his weaknesses were embodied in his love for both technology and intellectual stimulation. "He was always really curious," said the executive. "He would go to this futuristic think tank in New Mexico to think about ideas like retina scans for ATM machines. He was also a policy wonk. He would send managers to a banking boot camp at the University of Michigan to learn about issues."

Despite mixed reviews on some of his initiatives, Reed was successful in leading Citigroup through crisis after crisis, narrowly escaping with his job at one point. After the Latin American loan crisis in the late 1980s, the bank got into trouble during the real estate crash in the early 1990s, when again Citicorp was hit with billions in loan defaults. The bank loaned Donald Trump millions, for example, backed by little more than his reputation, and Trump eventually had to be bailed out by other lenders. The Federal Reserve had to step in in 1992 because of the real estate loan debacle and, essentially, declared Citicorp insolvent, embarrassing Reed (the business press speculated that the Citicorp board would replace him). The Fed monitored the bank's activities very closely from then until the economic upswing in 1994 turned Citicorp around.

One investment banker who worked with Reed for years described him as "one of the toughest men in the business." He told *Euromoney:*

He has always been bold: in the way he embraced technology in the 1970s and pushed Citicorp into consumer banking in the 1980s. At the time he was heavily criticized for both of those moves. And he was at his best during the crisis of the early 1990s. He thrives on chaos and danger.[3]

Weill's Corporate Renegades

When Commercial Credit bought Primerica in 1988, Weill was quick to employ his well-established formula for reinvigorating a newly acquired company: cut costs, replace dead wood on the management team with his own lieutenants, and get rid of unneeded operations. As Bob Lipp told the *Harvard Business Review* at the time:

> We're operations people. Our heroes have been those who cut costs, who increase margins, and who run a tight ship. For the most part, our talented people are not marketing people, not new product people, but operations people.[4]

Shortly after the merger, Weill promised to cut costs by $50 million at Primerica. That was a conservative estimate, as it turned out. Among other actions, Weill cut over 20 percent of the 250 jobs at Primerica's corporate headquarters, as well as another 120 people at Smith Barney.

Even while ordering the cost-cutting measures, Weill was working on building the Primerica management team. One of his first hires was Frank Zarb, who had been key in building Shearson in the early 1970s by revolutionizing back-office operations. Zarb, who had spent the last 10 years as a partner at Lazard Freres, agreed in late October 1988 to take on one of Primerica's biggest challenges: Smith Barney. Although best known for this famous brokerage unit, Primerica generated most of its income from insurance sales and consumer lending. At that time, Smith Barney provided Primerica with 27 percent of its revenues, but only 11 percent of its income. To Weill, this showed there must be costs to cut and more money to be made at Smith Barney.

Among those who joined Weill at Primerica in the next couple of years were Lew Glucksman, former CEO of Lehman Brothers, and Jeff Lane, who had worked with Weill for years at Shearson. In November 1989, Lane, president of Shearson, decided to leave the company, which had stumbled under the leadership of Peter Cohen. As Cohen's lieutenant, Lane was associated with the disastrous E.F. Hutton deal.

"I was getting progressively less happy at Shearson," Lane remembers. Flying to Germany for a one-day business trip that fall, Lane asked his wife to join him for company and told her that he was going to leave Shearson. When she asked what he would do next, he said, "I'm going to call Sandy." She replied, "That's a good idea." Cohen was pushed from the top spot of Shearson just two months after Lane left.

Advisers and friends warned Weill against bringing in Glucksman, who had developed a reputation as someone who couldn't control his temper. Despite the advice, Weill hired him as vice chairman and director of securities trading. The Lane and Glucksman hirings at Primerica were typical Weill personnel moves: He brought in talented but undervalued executives whom others had overlooked because of a stumble or two. Like so many other such hires, Lane and Glucksman worked extremely hard and were fiercely loyal to Weill.

"It was actually exciting to me," says Lane, "because I'd been in the brokerage business since the 1970s. To get involved with insurance and all the other businesses, that was fun." One reason Lane remembers it as fun is because all their efforts paid off.

Talented newcomers were recruited for Primerica as well. For example, Jay Fishman, who would become Citigroup's COO years later, was recruited as treasurer. As Weill would tell the

Harvard Business Review, "I had good fortune in finding partners who were also renegades, who came from environments that were bureaucracies and not meritocracies. So we had something special and exciting to offer them at Primerica."[5]

One executive who joined Weill as part of the Primerica acquisition—and at a very steep price—didn't work out quite as well as Glucksman, Lane, and Fishman. Art Williams, head of the company's A.L. Williams Insurance subsidiary, had a fascinating life story. As a young adult, Williams was a high school football coach with little knowledge of finance. When an acquaintance suggested that he buy a term life insurance policy, Williams became obsessed with the benefits of term insurance. He started his own insurance firm, which grew to over 150,000 agents, dwarfing every other insurance company in the country. The insurance industry loathed Williams because his mantra "buy term and invest the rest" made the pitch for more expensive whole-life insurance policies seem foolish. Williams' message resonated with consumers who wanted to pay cheaper premiums and didn't care about building up cash value in an insurance policy.

Weill recognized the value of Williams to Primerica, and paid a large premium to insure that Williams, the heart and soul of the division, stuck around to motivate his life insurance salespeople. When Weill acquired Primerica, the company owned 70 percent of A.L. Williams. Weill then paid $400 million for the rest of the company, and gave Williams a 20-year, incentive-laden contract worth up to $35 million a year.

Weill and other senior executives gave Williams plenty of leeway to run the company his way. But, Williams' unorthodox approach to sales extended to other areas of management, including hiring. For example, a high-level consultant, who earlier had been convicted of stock and land sales fraud, was paid an estimated $5 million a year for his work at A.L. Williams. The arrangement was an indication of the loose ship Williams ran, which would soon attract the attention of regulators.

In the summer of 1990, the Tennessee Department of Commerce and Insurance forced A.L. Williams to halt an "untruthful and misleading" advertising campaign that belittled the cash value aspect of whole-life insurance. In July, allegations surfaced that Williams' agents were spying on competitors. Williams went on a leave of absence during the investigation and never returned. Williams, however, remained a successful businessman.

Exercising Control, Weill Style

Within six months, Weill produced positive cash flow at Primerica through the deep job cuts, as well as more aggressive cash management. Many of the cuts were made at Smith Barney. In late December 1988, after management had already announced it was laying off 120 in New York, it eliminated nearly its entire fixed-income securities sales staff in London. There, 44 out of 50 jobs were cut.

Weill instituted other changes as well: Primerica's corporate headquarters were moved from leafy Greenwich to midtown Manhattan. The financial management for the entire company was centralized out of this headquarters, where Dimon closely monitored it. This early period at Primerica marked the ascendancy of Dimon, who took on a dual role. He became the parent company's CFO, as well as Smith Barney's senior executive vice president and chief administrative officer.

Exercising tight financial controls while giving division heads autonomy in running their businesses is a hallmark of Weill's management style. As one senior Citigroup executive explains, "He manages people and things based on economics. There are no unallocated expenses in any organization he runs. Every expense is charged to somebody." Each division is required to deliver a certain amount of profit to the corporate coffers, ensuring that the company meets earnings targets Weill has given Wall Street. Then the people running the division get what's left over. Make the company a lot of money, and bonuses are big. Experience a bad year or incur big expenses, compensation suffers. "Nobody gets paid on the basis of, 'you did a good job,'" says the executive. "There is no A for effort."

It may seem cold, but it works for shareholders and the executives who make the grade at Weill's companies. "People are highly motivated by the operating and economic and budgeting process he has set up," he says.

Though Weill had become an increasingly polished executive by the time he purchased Primerica, he still ran things in his singular way: roaming the halls among the corporate staff of about 200, ignoring reporting lines, asking questions of anyone he pleased, and, above all, avoiding memos and staff meetings as much as possible.

Weill, who could be quite pleasant, even joking in meetings, could also blow his stack. As he had at CBWL and later at Hayden Stone, Weill had members of the Primerica management team working together in very close quarters, which made it easier to reach more people with a single bellow. One of his subordinates said the office layout at times became "an echo chamber for Sandy's rage. We would all hide and wait 15 minutes until it blew over—it always did."[6]

Lane says Weill isn't mean or belittling, just very open about his feelings. "When it's on his mind, it's on his tongue. When it's on his tongue, it's out there. I'd be shocked if he ever had an ulcer because he lets everything out. He gives everyone else ulcers."

Despite Weill's disdain for formal staff meetings, Primerica's 12-member planning committee came together once a month for an off-site meeting. It was described in a Harvard Business School case study on Primerica:

> Once a month, the committee would go off-site to a large Connecticut house the company inherited along with the Primerica acquisition. Meetings usually began with dinner on a Tuesday evening, after which the members would work into the night, stay over, and work through dinner the next day. Although the agenda was flexible and permitted spontaneous additions, the dates for the meetings were set a year in advance and all members were expected to attend and participate.[7]

Once monthly plans and goals were outlined, Weill delegated much of the day-to-day operations of running the company to Dimon and Fowler. Fowler handled legal and administrative operations, while Dimon, as CFO, took care of anything related to the financial management, including the accounting and tax functions. Dimon was also was Primerica's public face to lenders.

Additions and Subtractions

In April 1989, Weill happened upon an opportunity he couldn't pass up. Primerica swallowed 16 Drexel Burnham branch offices in what Lane called a "great deal." Weill paid a reported $3 million for the offices, which many considered a steal. In fact, there was no premium on the purchase: the price was for the desks, equipment, and leases on the offices. Weill, coming full circle, had purchased some of the last remnants of his mentor Tubby Burnham's old firm.

What was driving Weill as he went about building this second empire? His denials notwithstanding, one line of thought was that he was spurred by competitiveness with American Express, eager to use talents that had gone unutilized at his former firm.

In a December 1989 article in *Business Week,* a brokerage analyst, Perrin Long, predicted, "Sandy wants to overtake American Express in revenues in the 1990s."[8] At that point, Weill had a long way to go. In the first three quarters of 1989, AmEx had revenues of $19 billion, while Primerica's revenues were $4 billion.

Weill denied any rivalry with American Express. "It's just not true," he said. But in the same article, he made it clear that comparisons to AmEx, while unfounded, were not going to stop him. Primerica was just the beginning. "I'm putting it all on the line again," Weill told the magazine.

Despite the purchases of the Drexel offices and progress in turning Smith Barney around (the brokerage was well on its way to a record $63 million in profit in 1989), Wall Street still didn't know what to make of Weill and his fledgling financial supermarket. The stock languished in the low 20s for much of 1989 as several of Weill's initiatives stalled. For example, his attempts at unloading Primerica's Fingerhut catalog business for $600 million failed because of a weak market for the sale. Investors also worried that, despite Primerica's pretax profit growth of 26 percent, the looming recession could cause customers to default on loans. In addition, analysts recognized that, while Weill hadn't made major stumbles to that point, running full-fledged financial services conglomerate was a lot different than running one big brokerage.

After a few years of smooth operations and steady results, Wall Street started to gain confidence in Weill's new company. It helped that in 1991, Weill finally sold some of Primerica's non-core assets. That year, Primerica divested PennCorp, American Credit Indemnity, and sold 58 percent of Fingerhut. In January 1992, Weill sold the mortgage company, Margaretten, at a premium price.

In early 1992, business at Primerica was humming. First quarter earnings set a company record, with profits from Smith Barney up

90 percent over the same quarter in the prior year. "I'm happy with all our businesses, but the one that really shot the lights out was Smith Barney," an exultant Weill told the *Times*.[9]

Acquiring a Piece of Travelers

Primerica wasn't the only financial services company that suffered when the stock market crashed and the real estate market soured in the late 1980s. Travelers Insurance, based in Hartford, Connecticut, had two units that were devastated by the recession, its home mortgage and relocation businesses. Even though the company divested of both, Travelers was still financially weak in the early 1990s. That weakness attracted the attention of Weill, who had learned first-hand how to run a property-casualty insurance company from his tenure at Fireman's Fund. Long before that, he had learned from the research of CBWL analyst Edward Netter that insurance companies could provide steady cash for a financial services conglomerate.

Travelers, the eighth-largest insurance company in the United States, had all of the characteristics of a typical Weill target. Primarily due to its soured real estate investments, the company's credit rating had been downgraded and it was having trouble finding capital. The company still maintained a strong brand, but needed an infusion of cash. Another good omen for a potential deal was that Weill maintained a cordial relationship with Travelers CEO Ed Budd. When Weill was at Fireman's Fund, the two had brought together a group of insurance industry executives to exchange ideas. Weill also believed the five-year downturn in property-casualty insurance was close to a turning point.

Bob Greenhill, Weill's outside merger strategist from Morgan Stanley who had helped him with the Primerica deal, suggested Weill make a minority investment in Travelers. In September

1992, Weill acquired a 27 percent stake, investing $723 million. He and Dimon joined the Travelers board and Weill became chairman of the board's finance committee.

It was around this time that Weill came under criticism for sharply reducing the health benefits of retirees of the American Can Company, Primerica's earlier incarnation. After years of subsidizing their benefits, Primerica in late 1992 forced the 1,600 American Can retirees to choose whether to pay the cost of continuing their health coverage or do without it. At least two dozen large companies made similar moves at the time, in response to a new federal accounting rule that required employers to deduct from their profits the future cost of providing retiree health benefits, but Primerica was singled out. The *New York Times* ran a front-page story on the subject on Christmas Eve 1992, in which Primerica figured prominently. The article pointed out that as CEO, Weill's compensation package in 1991—estimated at $12.4 million—exceeded the $8.7 million that Primerica spent that year on health benefits for all of the American Can retirees.

Managing a Financial Services Supermarket

With the stake in Travelers, Primerica now had consumer lending, brokerage, life insurance, and property/casualty insurance businesses under one roof. With every new acquisition, Weill made it clear that he wanted his new employees to be owners of the firm, in the form of taking some pay in stock options. On Wall Street, this was relatively rare at the time.

As he has stressed in repeated interviews over the years, Weill believes having company stock encourages employees who deal directly with customers—and thus have the best ideas about improving the business—to speak up and come forward with new ideas. As Weill later told *Investor's Business Daily:*

Ownership gets employees to think like owners, to think the company is really theirs. Really good ideas and innovative ideas come from the bottoms of organizations, where people are dealing directly with customers . . . People can see the silly things the chairman may be doing that is wasting a lot of money, and there might be a better way to do it. We encourage people to think that way.[10]

Five years had passed since Weill took the helm at Commercial Credit, and net profits had risen from $50 million to almost $500 million.[11] From 1988 through 1992, Weill increased earnings an average of more than 20 percent each year.

Weill's goal during this period was to create a large, diversified financial services firm. While many analysts at that point believed the idea of the financial supermarket was dead, Weill saw it as a way to reduce risk. With several different businesses under one umbrella, if one part of the financial services industry was going through a down cycle, he would have other businesses that could thrive.

Peter Solomon, a former vice chairman of Shearson Lehman Brothers, says Weill's basic psychology played a role. "He always wanted to be king of the world," Solomon says. "His goal has always been to be the biggest. It's what he is. He always wanted to go one level more."

Shearson Reclaimed

Meanwhile, Shearson Lehman was performing dismally for American Express. Shearson lost $116 million in 1992, mainly due to legal expenses and losses from the late-1980s deals struck under Peter Cohen's leadership. Shearson developed a number of liabilities in the form of products that went bad, such as tax-sheltered limited partnerships, property and oil-and-gas investments, and old E.F. Hutton insurance policies.

Weill was watching as the company he had built sank deeper into disrepair. As early as 1989, stories circulated that Weill was weighing a deal to reacquire his old firm. He obviously retained a major emotional connection. As of December 1989, according to a story in *Business Week,* his 86-year-old-father, Mac, worked in the firm's Miami office as a part-time clerk. His daughter, Jessica Bibliowicz (she took the last name of her husband, architect Natan Bibliowicz), had joined Shearson directly out of college in 1982 and still worked there, and his son, Marc, had just left Shearson for Smith Barney. But in 1990, Shearson lost $900 million, and Weill and Robinson were unable to agree on a deal.

Bibliowicz, 30 years old in 1990, was coming off eight solid years at Shearson. Joining the firm shortly after its sale to American Express proved excellent timing. With Weill removed from Shearson's day-to-day operations, Bibliowicz was left to succeed on her own merit, which by all accounts she did. She then joined Salomon Brothers, where she put in long hours, going home to spend time with her kids after school and then coming back to the office.

From Salomon, Bibliowicz was recruited to join Prudential Securities, where she eventually became the only woman on the firm's operating council. When Prudential's CEO, Wick Simmons (who had himself been one of Weill's lieutenants at Shearson), was recruiting Bibliowicz, Lane, then vice chairman at Smith Barney, was trying to do the same thing. After Bibliowicz chose Prudential, Lane asked Weill why he didn't help get her to join Smith Barney. Weill replied that Prudential offered "a better opportunity, and there was more money."[12]

Shearson's terrible performance throughout 1992—along with slowing growth in its core charge card business—helped ease Jim Robinson out the door at AmEx. Weill's friend Harvey Golub, who had been the head of IDS, the Minnesota-based financial planning company, replaced him. Once again, Weill's ability to maintain good relations with former colleagues won the day. Golub wanted desperately to jettison the Shearson operation, and Weill had first dibs on his old company.

In March 1993, Primerica bought Shearson's retail brokerage and asset-management businesses for $1.6 billion, a price that Lane now says was "fabulous, just fabulous." Primerica's stock price jumped 17 percent on the news. With the purchase, Primerica now had a retail brokerage operation on par with Merrill Lynch. AmEx retained Lehman Brothers, with its corporate finance and securities underwriting business, only to spin it off later in a public offering.

Weill, Lane, and the Primerica management team were greeted with wild cheering and applause when they met with the brokers from Shearson. "It was like the return of the conquering hero," Lane says. "They were standing up and screaming in the aisles. One broker, as I recall, stood up and waved the white flag. He said, 'I've left you several times and you keep buying me back. I give up. I'll stay!'"

Another reason the deal made so much sense was that it solved a major real estate headache for Weill. Smith Barney needed to relocate its headquarters because its lease on its Sixth Avenue office was expiring in 1995. "We knew that Shearson had excess space, so I told them that if this deal was ever going to make sense, now is the time," Weill told a reporter.[13] Smith Barney moved into Shearson's headquarters on Greenwich Street, just north of the World Trade Center. The Shearson space also had a superior computer and communications system in place.

When Weill bought back Shearson, it was a vindication on many levels. He had reclaimed Shearson from Robinson, Cohen, and all the others who had sent it into a downward spiral in the late 1980s and early 1990s. The *Economist* noted in March 1993, just before the deal became official, that "If Primerica now gets the broker [Shearson], then Mr. Weill will have proven himself mightier and richer than Mr. Robinson. It would be naïve to think the point was lost on either of them."[14]

The deal wasn't just a symbolic victory for Weill. Despite its problems, Shearson still had an excellent core brokerage business. With the deal, Primerica picked up 9,000 Shearson brokers (Smith Barney had 2,400 of its own), 394 Shearson offices, and 49 Shearson mutual funds with assets of $53 billion, as well as the company headquarters. The new firm of Smith Barney Shearson actually had more assets under management than Merrill Lynch at that point.

Right away, Weill and his management team set aggressive goals for Smith Barney Shearson, announcing that the brokerage's goal was to raise average broker production to $500,000 a year, from an average of $300,000 at Smith Barney and $260,000 at Shearson.

In June 1993, Weill lured Bob Greenhill away from Morgan Stanley and made him chairman and CEO of Smith Barney Shearson. A pioneer of the hostile leveraged buyout era of the 1980s, Greenhill had steadily earned Weill's confidence with his sage advice on big deals. Greenhill had advised Weill on Primerica and Travelers—considered by then superb investments—and advised him not to buy E.F. Hutton (the purchase of which had sent Shearson into a funk for years). The idea behind Greenhill's hiring was that he could boost the investment banking division and lure blue chip clients like General Motors and IBM away from Morgan Stanley. The *New York Times* noted that Weill "displayed Mr. Greenhill like a trophy" at a news conference announcing his hiring.[15]

The spot for Greenhill at Smith Barney Shearson had opened up when Zarb, along with Robert Lipp, were promoted to executive positions with Primerica. Zarb would run the money management and life insurance operations, while Lipp would

oversee consumer finance and Primerica's complicated investment relationship with Travelers, then six months under way
and clearly developing.

Weill opened up the purse strings for Greenhill, who was allowed to recruit high-priced bankers from his former firm and
other prestigious houses to bolster Smith Barney's investment
banking division. "A lot of money was spent on bringing in Morgan Stanley people," says a senior Citigroup executive. "Then
Sandy found out that the best people were still Smith Barney
people. The Morgan Stanley people were there for their own personal benefit more than the organization as a whole."

In mid-1995, two years after Greenhill and his dozens of
bankers with lucrative contracts had arrived, Smith Barney was
still a minor player in stock and bond underwriting. To make
matters worse, even as Smith Barney was doling out as much as
$50 million each year in guaranteed contracts to the former
Morgan Stanley bankers, the original Smith Barney team received smaller bonuses than before the new bankers had arrived. Throw in small, but telling episodes like the Morgan
Stanley veterans flying first class on the same flight as Smith
Barney bankers flying coach, and Smith Barney had a cultural
war on its hands.

The internal battle manifested itself in several ways, both large
and small. In early 1994, Smith Barney was hired to handle a $750
million RJR Nabisco stock offering, but could only sell $250 mil-
lion of the issue, a debacle that landed on the front page of the
Wall Street Journal. Greenhill staffed and then shut down Smith
Barney's Hong Kong operations, all within one year. Bankers with
Smith Barney roots were initially left out of Greenhill's Monday
morning strategy sessions.

On January 10, 1996, the Greenhill era came to an end at
Smith Barney. He resigned after it became clear that Weill
wanted Dimon to step up from his COO position and run Smith

Barney himself. Yet Weill and Greenhill remain friends today. "You would think that after going through all that, Sandy would be pissed off at Bob Greenhill, but that's not the case," says a senior Citigroup executive. "Bob has his own prestige."

Completing the Travelers Acquisition

As a board member at Travelers, Weill made it clear from the outset that he felt the insurance company was not using its assets as well as it could. He urged Travelers to cut costs, throwing his support behind a plan to save Travelers $100 million by eliminating 5,000 jobs by mid-1994. Ed Budd, then Travelers' CEO, says he welcomed Weill's input. "My impression was that here is a very astute, analytical businessman with good sense of risk and reward, who brings a fresh approach outside of the insurance industry," he says. "It was refreshing to hear questions from his perspective."

The thought of fully capturing Travelers was never far from Weill's mind, and he wanted the company to be in decent shape when it happened. With the support of Weill and the rest of the board, in 1992 and 1993 Travelers sold numerous real estate properties.

"We listened very carefully to everything he had to say," says Budd. "Once Sandy saw the company and its attributes from inside, he liked it even better. And the board felt that if we saw synergies that were valuable, we would do it."

In September 1993, just months after acquiring Shearson, Weill made his move and offered to buy the remaining portion of Travelers Primerica didn't already own for $4.2 billion. Weill became leader of the merged company, which assumed the Travelers name. The deal was largely aided by the rise in Primerica's stock, which had shot up in seven years from about $20 to $100 a share. The Travelers board approved the merger on September 23, 1993. Weill's insider status and presumed knowledge of

Travelers' operations had paid a huge dividend. On October 25, *Forbes* noted the "Sandy Weill premium," meaning that investors were willing to pay more for the stock, purely because Weill was at the helm.[16]

Budd became the next in the long line of executives who were nudged into retirement by a merger with a Weill-led company. Budd was 60 at the time and had been leaning toward retirement anyway, so he stepped aside, taking a board position. "It came at a good time in my life," he says.

From his experience working on the Travelers board for several years after the deal, Budd believes that Weill deserves credit for fostering a team-centered approach to leading a company. "Sandy's management style is to have an ecumenical, broad-based management team," Budd says. "His concept is that everybody is involved with the company. Everybody has a large equity stake and that makes us all better managers. This has been a very powerful idea. Nobody runs a big company alone. That is a myth. A team runs a big company. But you have to have a leader, and he is an excellent leader."

The deal more than doubled the company's assets to nearly $90 billion and reduced its reliance on Smith Barney Shearson, which at the time was contributing approximately 45 percent of its profits. Weill moved his office to the thirty-ninth floor of the Travelers building in lower Manhattan, which was emblazoned with the brightly lit Travelers umbrella.

More deals soon followed. In October 1995, Travelers sold its health-insurance operations to United HealthCare for $830 million. "That proved an ingenious decision," Lane says. "The business was lousy and we didn't like it, and it deteriorated substantially from there." In May 1996, the company acquired the property-casualty insurance operations of Aetna for $4 billion. Then, in 1996, Weill combined Aetna with Travelers' property-casualty business and spun it off in an IPO, headed by Bob Lipp. If that scenario sounds familiar, it's because Weill did much the same thing with Travelers Property Casualty, which had earlier been reintegrated into Citigroup, in March 2002. He brought back Bob Lipp from retirement to once again lead the spun-off company.

Trouble for Dimon and Bibliowicz

By 1997, Jessica Bibliowicz was running Smith Barney's mutual fund business. She had joined Smith Barney in 1994 following two years at Prudential. Bibliowicz and Smith Barney chairman Jamie Dimon had been friends—and rivals in a sense—outside of the office for years. Theodore Dimon, Jamie's father, had worked for years as a broker for Weill in the 1960s. Given Weill's style, the families got to know one another, and Jamie and Jessica spent time together on joint vacations.

Earlier in their careers, there had been plenty of room for Dimon and Bibliowicz to claim business success without stepping on each other's toes. But as Bibliowicz climbed the ranks within the Smith Barney division, she began to clash with Dimon, then her boss. In 1996, Bibliowicz and Dimon were at loggerheads over the issue of Smith Barney's entry into no-load, no-commission mutual funds. Bibliowicz wanted to stick to Smith Barney's traditional "load" funds, while Dimon pushed the no-load initiative, believing that Smith Barney had to match the product offerings of other leading brokerage firms. Dimon's vision won out and in June Smith Barney announced it would offer clients no-load funds.

The debate was part of a bigger issue: for several years, the growth rate of Smith Barney's stock and bond fund assets was 32 percent, far behind the overall fund industry's growth of 74 percent. Smith Barney's domestic stock funds had returned just under 50 percent during the bull market between January 1994 and May 1997. That sounds excellent, until compared with the 64 percent returns of similar funds.[17] Bibliowicz was under enormous pressure to improve the performance of the company's mutual funds, and apparently, Dimon was not impressed with her performance. Bibliowicz was passed over for the job of heading asset management in the summer of 1996 and was left off Smith Barney's executive committee in February 1997.

In the middle of June 1997, Bibliowicz, ready to start fresh somewhere else, decided to leave Smith Barney. She took a job as president of John Levin & Co., a money management firm with $7.6 billion in assets—tiny compared to the $73 billion operation she had been running at Smith Barney. Levin had courted Bibliowicz for months, and she hadn't made the decision lightly. Among others, she sought the advice of Greenhill, but did not discuss her decision with her father.

After it was announced that Bibliowicz was leaving, both Dimon and she described their clashes as typical business discussions about the best way to revive Smith Barney's mutual fund business—just two executives trying to do the best thing for the company. "A lot of the differences were on the tactical side, not on the philosophical," Bibliowicz said after she left the firm. "Sure, we disagreed, but we worked it through." Dimon of Bibliowicz: "She was a friend before she got here. She was a friend while she was here, and she's a friend now."[18]

Dimon shouldn't have been feeling too comfortable. He was left with an underperforming set of mutual funds and had just, unwittingly or not, pushed his boss' daughter out of the company. Weill's public comments about Bibliowicz' departure make it clear that he had not been kept in the loop about the deteriorating relationship by either Dimon or Bibliowicz. "Jessica spoke to me less than what somebody else might have in that position if they weren't related to me," Weill told a reporter. "In a lot of ways, I knew a lot less of what was in her mind. She bent over backward not to involve me, which bothered me a little."[19]

Going Global with Salomon

In July 1997, the Commercial Credit division of Travelers acquired BankAmerica's consumer finance business, known as Security Pacific Financial Services, for $1.6 billion. Also that summer, Travelers held merger talks with investment bank J.P. Morgan that failed to culminate in a deal. Even though the J.P. Morgan talks went nowhere, Weill was more convinced than ever that Travelers needed an international presence to obtain overseas deals.

He turned to Salomon Brothers. "Up until that time, he wanted to run the best financial services company in the United States," says Lane. "This was the first time he would start to say his goal was to be the best financial services company in the world."

Salomon Brothers had been immortalized in Michael Lewis' *Liar's Poker* as the brashest, most aggressive investment bank on Wall Street. There, according to Lewis, traders threw telephones at the heads of trainees, former CEO John Gutfreund once challenged the head trader to a $1 million hand of liar's poker, and the big earners on the trading desk were commonly referred to as "big swinging dicks."[20]

Partly because of that macho culture, Salomon suffered a major bond trading scandal in 1991. The debacle forced Warren Buffett—whose Berkshire Hathaway became a major shareholder in Salomon just weeks before the stock market crash of 1987—to serve a nine-month stint as interim chairman to restore investor confidence. Gutfreund, the embattled CEO, stepped down to make way for Buffett. When he felt Salomon was back on its feet, Buffett asked Deryck Maughan, Salomon's vice chairman responsible for global investment banking, to take over as CEO.

Not long after Maughan was installed as CEO of Salomon, Weill called him up and invited him to be on the Carnegie Hall board. Maughan recalls their conversation:

"Deryck, we haven't met but I hear all sort of things about you. Why don't you join me on the Carnegie Hall board?" Weill asked him.

"Well, Sandy, I've heard a lot about you, too, and I like music and I'd love to get to know you better, so sure," Maughan responded.

Maughan, who had only recently moved to New York, was pleased to make Weill's acquaintance. "Sandy, I think, is an extraordinary networker," says Maughan. "He knows an awful lot of people, and he's naturally gregarious. I had no idea that knowing Sandy would lead me one day to sell the place to him."

The idea of Weill acquiring Salomon at that point would have been unthinkable. The firm was still struggling to regain its footing after the bond trading scandal and Weill, who doesn't mind buying companies when they are down on their luck, nonetheless avoids ones mired in negative publicity and controversy. More important, his risk-averse nature usually keeps him away from volatile businesses. Salomon's risk arbitrage division was about as risky and volatile as they come on Wall Street.

By 1997, Salomon was back on its feet, but needed more capital. Maughan felt merging with a larger company made sense. He explains:

Salomon had restored its reputation and its earnings, but it had a number of very large strategic challenges. The economics of investment banking are that if you are not in the first tier of three or four firms, it's problematic to generate a satisfactory return on capital, and we were stuck just below that tier. And given that we were a somewhat smaller firm, with a somewhat smaller footprint, I didn't know what the chances were of us penetrating that first tier, occupied by Goldman, Morgan Stanley, and Merrill Lynch. They were larger, they were generating more profits. I thought it was a race I might not win.

Ironically enough, given the fact that Travelers announced its merger with Citicorp just months after acquiring Salomon, Maughan believed that Salomon should merge with one large institution because he wanted to avoid multiple mergers that consolidation in financial services was likely to bring about. That, he thought, "would be just too exhausting." Maughan made up a list of companies he thought would be interested in Salomon. Travelers was on that list.

Weill knew that even if he decided to explore a deal with Salomon, he would need the backing of Buffett, whose Berkshire Hathaway was Salomon's largest shareholder. Weill had previous business dealings with the Oracle of Omaha, dating back to his failed bid to purchase Fireman's Fund from American Express. "Sandy basically said, I don't want to waste my time unless there was a good chance it would be supported by Warren," says Bob Denham, who was co-CEO of Salomon with Maughan. "There were three or four discussions of price," Denham says. "Sandy wanted Warren to commit that Berkshire Hathaway would vote its shares in favor of the merger."

When negotiations began, the talks centered around Salomon's high-risk, high-profit risk arbitrage division. "The hitch was whether Sandy would take the proprietary trading book, which generated more than half the profits," Maughan says. After interviewing the head of trading at Salomon, "Travelers satisfied itself that this was a high-risk, high-return business, and that it wanted to keep it," says Maughan. The proprietary trading, or arbitrage group, would later become a major headache for Weill, but Maughan says that Weill knew what he had bought and never complained about losing money on it.

Amazingly, the complex negotiations were kept secret from the press. "I hated the idea of a leak," says Denham, "and it would have been hard to proceed with just about any buyer, other than Sandy, without the news leaking." Denham explains why:

> The great thing about talking to Sandy about a sale of a company is that he's done it so many times. He knows what is important and he understands the financial services business so well. We were able to go through a due diligence process that was a lot simpler than it would have been with a lot of buyers. He doesn't waste a lot of time; he moves quickly and makes decisions quickly. He knew what was important and had confidence in his own judgment.

In September, the negotiations were completed and Travelers acquired Salomon for $9 billion. Maughan and Dimon became co-CEOs of the new subsidiary now called Salomon Smith Barney. Denham decided to leave the company and returned to his former law firm in Los Angeles, Munger, Tolles & Olson.

Buffett owned 18 percent of Salomon, thereby becoming Travelers largest shareholder, with a 3 percent stake. Not surprisingly, Buffett's public statement on the deal was extremely supportive of Weill. "Over several decades, Sandy has demonstrated genius in creating huge value for his shareholders by skillfully blending and managing acquisitions in the financial services industry," he said then. "In my view, Salomon will be no exception."

Although some called the price too high, overall, given the respective firms' strengths and weaknesses, the deal seemed a good strategic fit. Salomon raised the profile of Smith Barney's investment banking division and created a global profile for Travelers. Until that point, Smith Barney had no international presence and was considered second tier in investment banking. The deal also supplied Smith Barney brokers with more stock and bond offerings to sell. Plus, by balancing relatively stable money management and a commercial banking businesses with Salomon's volatile risk arbitrage trading business, the merger also dampened Salomon's risk profile. Credit agencies raised Salomon's rating, lowering its cost of borrowing.

In many ways, the Salomon deal marked a departure for Weill. He made a point of making a distinction between this deal and those he had done in the past. "The driving force here is not cutting costs," he told the press. "It really is growth, and the entrée into new markets."[21]

Bibliowicz, who had left Smith Barney just before the merger, also said the Salomon deal showed her father was changing. "He's become much more of a long-term thinker," she told the *Times*. She acknowledged that for years Weill had been obsessed with slashing costs, but said that now "he's focused on growth of the company . . . something doesn't have to be down and out for him to take it on now."[22]

Analysts worried that Salomon would be too much for Weill, given the tremendous egos and salaries at the firm. But Weill felt he had enough experience getting people from different corporate cultures to work together to handle the job. Bruce Wasserstein, the legendary mergers and acquisitions specialist, noted in his memoirs that: "In taking on Salomon Brothers, Weill yet again demonstrated his willingness to accept challenges others found too daunting."[23]

The merger of Salomon and Travelers was just one of many financial services marriages in 1997, a period of intense consolidation in the industry. Globalization and technology were shrinking the number of players in the industry to just a handful of truly global firms. As Weill told *Directors & Boards* on March 22, 1998, "At the end of 1997, we had built one of the finest financial services companies in America. . . . But we were looking at a global marketplace, and we didn't really have a position in that global marketplace. And therefore our reason for acquiring Salomon was to give us a jump start to do that, and that's what it's done."[24]

Despite Weill's emphasis on global operations and entering new markets, he moved to cut costs on the homefront, shutting down Salomon's offices and relocating employees to the Travelers headquarters. About 1,500 jobs—mostly at Salomon—were cut.

Harkening Back to Hayden Stone

Weill's run of acquisitions, from Primerica through to Salomon, never veered much from the formula he had employed in the 1970s when he built Shearson. In fact, the nature of the individual deals never really changed much from the Hayden Stone template. Weill continually "merged up," buying bigger companies, occasionally rescuing them when they were foundering, but always seizing the opportunity when they were a little down on their luck.

But there was an important distinction between his two strings of deals. Weill's 1970s acquisitions were all brokerages. As such, his job after each deal was relatively straightforward: cut costs, integrate back offices, and make sure the best brokers stayed. In contrast, his second string of acquisitions encompassed a variety of different kinds of financial services companies. Essentially, each deal filled a different hole in the empire Weill was building. Rather than just getting together with a few associates and making the numbers work, Weill's later deals required more finesse. It took lobbying efforts and public relations campaigns to ensure that regulators and shareholders approved of the deals.

After closing the Salomon purchase, Weill said he felt like he had the final piece in his financial services empire. It turned out, though, that the Salomon deal was just a harbinger of the megadeal to come.

Deal of the Century

Mergers of two huge companies often draw opposition because they create organizations that are seen as just too powerful. One worry is that the new company becomes so large and influential that, if it ever teetered on bankruptcy, the federal government would have to bail it out, much as it did with the airline industry following the September 11 terrorist attacks. The costs of such federal bailouts are inevitably passed on to taxpayers.

A corollary of this "too-big-to-fail" theory is that because companies understand all too well that a federal bailout awaits if business tanks, they are inclined to take undue risks.

This concern was at the center of much of the opposition to the Citicorp-Travelers deal. Consumer advocate Ralph Nader, one of the merger's biggest critics, believed that by allowing the two gigantic financial services companies to merge, the government was essentially granting them state-sponsored immunity from market conditions. Nader called the groundswell of Congressional support for the merger an example of "state capitalism or corporate socialism," when he testified at a Congressional hearing on financial reform just days after the merger was announced. He further argued:

> What we are seeing here is not only explicit, ongoing, often subtle subsidization of the banking industry by federal government agencies, but we are seeing the "too-big-to-fail" approach. . . . So we are dealing here in a sense with Uncle Sam, the ultimate guarantor of a supposedly capitalistic financial sub-economy. That has very, very important consequences.[1]

As it turns out, however, Citigroup has turned the "too-big-to-fail" theory on its head. The truth is that Citigroup, under Weill, is so well-diversified that there seems little chance of it running into crippling financial problems. Citigroup's reach and global nature—two of the reasons people ask whether it's become too large—are actually two of its major strengths. Few companies in the world can boast such geographic diversification, coupled with strength across disparate businesses. Crises that have buffeted the bank in the past—bad real estate loans, poor bets on technology, emerging market loan defaults—would hardly put a dent in today's Citigroup. For example, despite the fact that Citigroup is a major lender to Argentina, the financial crisis there in early 2002 wasn't a serious threat to the company. Citigroup's loan portfolio is just too well-diversified. Even more telling: Despite losses totaling in the hundreds of millions of dollars in the aftermath of September 11, the company reported double-digit earnings gains for the third quarter ended September 30, 2001.

Even at the time of the merger, none of Citigroup's individual businesses was the biggest or most critical in its respective industry. Citibank was not the largest bank, Travelers was not the largest insurance company, and Salomon Smith Barney was not the largest securities firm. The merger of Citicorp and Travelers did not so much increase the concentration of financial power in one place as link three separate businesses that provided very different services and did not contain much overlap.

Due to this kind of geographic and product diversification, Citigroup is, in the end, probably stronger together than if its three main business arms operated as separate entities. To be sure, it is one of a handful of the most powerful companies in the world. But as long as Weill, who avoids risk and maintains tight financial control over operations, is running things, the world may actually be a safer place to do business because Citigroup is around.

Salomon's Arbitrage Group Proves a Problem

By the end of 1997, it was clear that the integration of Salomon and Smith Barney was not going well. Seeds of future management discord were apparent the day of the merger announcement when Jamie Dimon and Deryck Maughan were named co-CEOs in a clear erosion of Dimon's power base. Tensions only grew as Salomon's arbitrage group lost millions of dollars in the months following the merger as a currency crisis in Asia rippled through world financial markets. Salomon Smith Barney reported after-tax losses of $60 million in October, the first month that the combination was supposed to be working on all cylinders.

Weill knew the losses were due to global market volatility. He also knew the addition of Salomon's high-risk, high-reward arbitrage unit would inevitably make the divisions' earnings more volatile. The arbitrage trading division had generated over half of Salomon's profits before the merger.

But there were only so many quarters of losses Weill could take. He had never let fluctuating markets stand in the way of profits before, and he wasn't about to start now. Following several ill-timed deals, such as its $100 million loss betting that

British Telecom would complete its bid for MCI (instead, World-Com won the MCI sweepstakes), Travelers announced it was closing Salomon's New York–based equity risk arbitrage operations.

For a short time, it seemed as if Salomon's London trading desk, which was still generating enormous profits, was safe. But then during the third quarter of 1998 (by which time Travelers had announced the merger with Citicorp), Russia's currency collapsed and then Long-Term Capital, the huge, highly-leveraged Connecticut hedge fund, failed. "All of the world's capital markets began to lock and to distort and so the relationships between the yield curves and the swap spreads became very bizarre," says Maughan in an interview, explaining why trading went so wrong. "And funding shut down and all sorts of things started to go wrong."

Salomon Smith Barney suffered $395 million in third quarter trading losses, a number so huge that Citigroup's net income dropped 53 percent to $729 million, down from combined earnings of $1.54 billion for the two firms in the same quarter the year before. The London trading desk was closed and Salomon, in less than a year since merging with Smith Barney, had lost its defining business. The *Economist* thundered, "Salomon has long been Wall Street's premier bond-trading house. By shutting the arbitrage group, Mr. Weill is ripping out the company's heart."[2]

Indeed, without the trading unit, there was little left to Salomon, says one Citigroup executive. "There was no there, there," he says. For a while, it seemed that Weill had overpaid for Salomon and received little in return.

Maughan admits that the arbitrage trading business had proved more troublesome than Weill had expected. "But Sandy has never complained about that. I mean, he's not happy losing money, understandably, but to his credit he understood what he bought and he lived with it," Maughan says.

Despite the merger's rocky first year and the closure of the New York and London arbitrage operations, most analysts now say the merits of the Salomon deal have been borne out. What Weill mainly got from Salomon is a very powerful brand name that resonated with investment banking clients around the world. That allowed Citigroup to acquire other global investment banks, says Maughan. "It's one of Sandy's great wins, because without the Salomon piece, we could not have [integrated] Schroders, Nikko, and all the corporate banks," he says. Furthermore, Smith Barney alone, without Salomon, wouldn't have been able to grow into the investment bank that exists today, he says.

Weill Mulls Merging with a Bank

There's a theory in the financial world that Weill bought Citigroup to make up for difficulties with Salomon. That's not the case. Even before the Salomon deal, Weill and his Travelers lieutenants were interested in finding a bank to merge with. In the spring of 1997, Weill held a planning meeting in which he and his top executives put together a list of commercial banks with global reach. Citibank was on that list.

In September, even as the press heralded Travelers' $9 billion purchase of Salomon—prompting some to declare that Weill had achieved the pinnacle of his career—Weill was already working on the plan to merge with a bank. In commenting on the Salomon deal, financial services consultant John Keefe inadvertently predicted what was to come. "Under the current thinking, the ideal combination would be a commercial bank with investment banking capability with some kind of retail arm to complete the circle to distribute the products and reach into the consumer market," Keefe told a reporter.[3]

By February 1998, Weill had set his sights on Citicorp. Once he and his team had decided which bank they wanted, it was up to Weill to make overtures to Reed. Most of Weill's confidantes at Travelers thought the deal would go nowhere.

Citicorp: Ripe for a Merger

At the point that Travelers was eyeing Citicorp, it was one of the most profitable banks in the world and a plum prize for Weill. The Citigroup shaped by John Reed had had a tumultuous history. But by 1997, Reed was basking in his achievements. He had led Citicorp back from the brink of dissolution in 1991—when it lost $457 million. In 1995 the bank earned profits of $3.5 billion, the most ever for any U.S. bank, and its stock gained in value by 18 percent. By 1997, Citicorp's international network stretched to 98 countries and the bank was the world's biggest credit-card issuer, with 36 million accounts and 64 million credit cards in use. Citicorp's all-around earnings strength, especially in consumer banking, had helped it weather the 1997 Asian financial crisis. That year Reed announced his intention for Citicorp to have one billion customers by the year 2010, or about one-seventh of that year's projected world population.

That proclamation—while no doubt a "stretch goal" in business speak—hinted at Reed's own growing desire to pull off a major merger that would fuel Citicorp's growth, as well as make the Citicorp name ubiquitous. The health of Citicorp's worldwide brand, in fact, had become a major concern of Reed's in the previous few years. In 1996, he forced out long-time Citicorp executive Pei-yuan Chia, head of the company's consumer business, partly because he felt Chia was not doing enough to boost Citicorp's brand into the same class as companies like Coca-Cola. (Some analysts say Chia was a victim of Reed's tendency to axe up-and-coming executives lest they became a threat to his own job.)

Reed hired William Campbell—an executive at Philip Morris—to burnish Citicorp's image. Campbell, one of the infamous tobacco executives who testified before Congress in 1994 that nicotine was not addictive, took quick action to reinvigorate the brand. He fired the triumvirate of advertising firms serving Citicorp and hired Young & Rubicam, the agency that had handled Philip Morris' account when Campbell was there. He and Reed started giving pep talks and speeches to Citicorp executives about building Citicorp's brand into one as evocative as Disney or Pepsi.

Still, stretch goals and pep talks would not work as quickly as a major deal, and Reed knew the bank would be an attractive partner for another large company. In the fourth quarter of that year, the bank increased earnings by 7.5 percent over the previous year, despite losing $250 million in the Asian meltdown. Indeed, in 1997 Reed held discussions with Weill's old friend Harvey Golub about a Citicorp-AmEx union, but the all-important issue of management structure stopped the deal in its tracks.

"The rumor mill was always that we would be merging with AmEx," says a Citigroup executive who left the firm just months before the merger with Travelers. "Reed was even looking at AT&T. He was always looking at what was going on with AT&T because he thought it would be an interesting technological choice. Travelers was something that was never really discussed."

In February 1998, Reed made a deal with AT&T, purchasing its credit card operation. Then, in late March at a management retreat, Reed told hundreds of Citicorp executives that he was thinking about a major merger, according to the *Wall Street Journal*. The names tossed about in the article were Merrill Lynch and

Standard Chartered, a British bank with operations nearly as global as Citicorp's. Travelers wasn't mentioned as a contender. But the fact is, Reed had already been talking to Weill.

Travelers and Citicorp Talk Merger

Weill approached Reed on February 25, 1998, when the two were in Washington for an annual economics and public policy conference. Weill and Reed had first gotten to know each other in the 1970s while serving on the board of Arlen Realty, a company that had hit hard times and required a lot of attention from its directors. While never close friends, they remained casual business acquaintances. When Weill suggested they get together at the conference, Reed figured that Weill, well known for his philanthropic efforts with Carnegie Hall and the Academy of Finance, wanted a donation of some kind.

Instead, when they met in his hotel, Weill brought up what could have easily been seen as an outlandish idea: a merger of equals between Citicorp and Travelers. Perhaps surprising to Weill, Reed was intrigued. Wasting little time, he asked his vice chairman, Paul Collins, to research Travelers while Reed went on a trip around the world.

It's easy to see why Citicorp executives had to do some research on Travelers. Citicorp, while linked to many other companies, had very few business ties to Travelers. This was true even at the board level, where many deals get done. Citicorp was linked to 29 different companies through various board members, including the three boards Reed served on: Monsanto, Philip Morris, and The Spencer Foundation. But there was no overlap with Travelers on any of them.

This lack of familiarity and mutual acquaintances didn't stop Reed and Weill from acting with amazing speed on the deal.

Reed sent Weill a long fax from Singapore outlining some rough terms for the deal. He returned from his trip and, after just two days of conversations with Weill, wrapped his arm around Weill's shoulder and said, "Let's do it, partner." Weill was stunned the deal had moved so fast.[4] So were a lot of other people. When it became apparent how fast the merger talks advanced, especially after a first few months fraught with problems and management turmoil, it was thought by many that Weill and Reed acted in haste and thought through very few details.

One detail Weill and Reed failed to really think through was how they would manage the company together, and how a successor to the two of them eventually would be named. While it was decided that they would run the company together as co-CEOs, the merger picked up so much velocity so quickly that Weill and Reed never stopped to fully examine just how the dynamics between them would work. It seems they both simply planned on retaining the right to approve or veto all important decisions and didn't think enough about what kind of frustrations the co-CEO system would create for their top managers.

Just as Weill and Robinson presented very different styles years before at American Express, Weill and Reed were also cut from very different cloth. Reed, 59, was known for his tremendous intellect. But he could be distant and aloof, theoretical in outlook and a loner in practice. Weill, 65, was not considered a particularly deep thinker, but was gregarious, surrounded by a network of friends and admirers at Travelers.

In contrast to Weill—whose relentless drive to succeed was legendary—Reed had the mark of a man who didn't need his job that badly. He loved to cook, read, and noodle around with technology. But in his own way, Reed was just as intense as Weill and also shared a reputation for being ruthless. He could quickly lose confidence in protégés he thought weren't measuring up, such as Chia. Conversely, he would cling for dear life to projects he had dreamed up but were clearly failures, like the acquisition of the technology company Quotron, which lost hundreds of millions of dollars before Reed finally gave up on it. "He believed himself to be a great intellect, he was enormously self-confident, but he couldn't stand to have bright people around him," says analyst Richard Bove. "In my view, he was always afraid the guy he was grooming might take his position and move him out."

The fact is, Reed was just as prominent a figure in the business world as Weill, and on top of that, had emerged from several scrapes that would have mortally wounded other CEOs. Reed, presumably, would not be easily pushed aside like some of the CEOs in other companies that Weill had acquired.

Another clear difference between the two men at the start of the merger: They had very different visions for how their co-CEO roles would end. Reed entered into the merger thinking that he and Weill would handle the transition, run the company jointly for some time, and then leave together. He had been CEO for nearly 14 years. Various heirs apparent had come and gone, and now Reed had few potential successors anywhere within Citicorp. Many observers believe Reed was drawn to the merger partly because it provided an exit strategy for him. Jamie Dimon was never specifically mentioned as the successor Reed had in mind, but clearly he was a candidate.

Weill, it would become clear, had no intention of retiring anytime soon. Perhaps early in the talks he thought he and Reed could run the company together for a long time. But many Weill observers think he always planned to eventually take over the reins himself. "I think he went in there with a concept that he would bide his time," says one senior Citigroup executive. "I have no doubt in my mind that from day one he wasn't planning to sit around being co-chief executive officer forever."

Going into the merger, Weill and Reed were both guilty of treating their relationship and its impact on the performance of the new company lightly. Perhaps each knew there would be a messy end to the proposed arrangement, and simply felt the deal was worth it. They were truly forging something new: the long-predicted but never realized financial services supermarket of the kind CBWL's Edward Netter had theorized about over 30 years before. The company would be a major player in consumer banking, investment banking, mutual funds, credit cards, and insurance.

The deal would also produce a legitimate competitor with the world's top banks, which in Asia and Europe weren't restricted from offering banking and insurance products under a single umbrella. They had been combining for years, putting U.S. firms at a competitive disadvantage. Both Reed and Weill wanted to take their best shots at being players on the global stage, and this combination would instantly put them on the map. They also saw the advantage of diversifying their lines of business, making both companies less dependent on earnings from volatile sources, like Salomon's trading operations or Citicorp's Asian emerging markets business.

Then, of course, there was cross-selling. Weill, in particular, still fervently believed that one huge sales force could sell a broad array of financial services to consumers. He wanted bank accounts, mortgages, variable annuities, mutual funds, stocks, and insurance all to be sold by the combined Travelers and Citicorp salesforces. He believed if Travelers and Citicorp were to merge, the people and products would be in place for cross-selling to succeed.

Historically, the lack of cross-selling success for banks was blamed on the federal legislation separating commercial banks from the securities business. Weill, of course, was openly betting that Glass-Steagall would fall in the wake of the Citicorp-Travelers merger. With those regulations gone, he could fully execute his cross-selling strategy for consumer financial products.

Weill also thought that cross-selling could work on the corporate side. Citicorp's corporate bank had relationships with approximately 1,700 institutions. Why couldn't these corporate banking clients be turned into Salomon Smith Barney investment banking clients? Weill also believed cross-selling to date hadn't worked because of poor execution. Just weeks before the merger was announced, he said, "What I had hoped to happen at American Express didn't happen at that particular location, but it didn't mean that my concept was wrong. It was just that the people together weren't able to make it happen."[5]

Reed's motivation from a business point of view was those one billion customers he wanted signed up and the chance to finally parlay Citicorp's brand into one that meant "financial services," as opposed to just banking. According to a Citigroup executive, another aspect of Reed's motivation to aggressively move ahead with the deal was similar to Weill's career-long desire for reliable earnings. He explained:

> In a lot of people's minds, he did the deal with Travelers because he thought Citicorp was going to get into trouble again at some point. By merging with an insurance company, he was acquiring something more stable, an annuity business where you can project what you are going to pay out through actuarial tables. The majority of Citi's business was fee-based and transaction oriented. The Citicorp stock was up and down like a yo-yo. That's ultimately why Reed wanted to do the deal. He was looking to stabilize.

The Epic Deal Is Announced

In the two weeks before announcing the merger, Weill made calls to President Clinton, Treasury Secretary Robert Rubin and Federal Reserve Chairman Alan Greenspan, giving them advance warning that a major deal was coming. Weill and Reed knew the deal violated the 1933 Glass-Steagall Act requiring that commercial and investment banking be kept separate and didn't want to spring the news on Washington. Giving advance notice also enabled Weill and Reed to make their case about why such a deal should be allowed to go through before the public weighed in.

When Weill phoned Rubin to inform him of the plans to merge Travelers and Citicorp, Weill started by saying that he had big news. "Let me guess," Rubin joked, "you're buying the government."[6]

Representatives from Citicorp and Travelers also met with Greenspan. The Federal Reserve Bank had final say on whether the merger could go forward, and Greenspan in the past had been very cautious when talking about Glass-Steagall reform. Executives from both Travelers and Citicorp met with Greenspan about the merger before it was announced. When news of the meetings appeared in the press, Ralph Nader sent Greenspan a letter, urging the Fed chairman to disclose exactly what was said during the meetings. Nader even suggested in the letter that Greenspan's hearing about the merger from Travelers and Citicorp executives before it was made public might have constituted insider information. Fed attorneys countered by saying Greenspan was typically notified of most major financial services mergers before a public announcement was made. Nader didn't push the matter any further.

On April 6, 1998, Reed and Weill announced the record-breaking $70 billion stock swap—a "merger of equals," as the two men took pains to stress. The new entity would be named Citigroup, and the company would retain the Travelers umbrella as its logo. The company adopted the ticker symbol C, given up by Chrysler after its merger with Daimler-Benz. The headquarters would be at 399 Park Avenue, a block or so from the famed Citicorp tower, a shimmering skyscraper with a diagonal roof.

230 KING OF CAPITAL

In a joint statement, Weill and Reed said, "U.S. financial services companies must be able to offer customers the same array of products and services that their international competitors are now free to provide if we are to maintain our nations leadership position around the world. This is particularly critical given the rapid pace of consolidation by global competitors."

Despite the show of unity at the press conference, it was evident that the two CEOs had some homework to do. Reed even stumbled trying to pronounce Primerica, calling it "Prime America." Weill later chided him, "Remember, John, it's not two words." A more substantial example of how few details had been worked out was that Dimon, co-chief executive at Salomon Smith Barney, didn't even know what job he had when the deal was announced. The cross-selling potential of a Travelers-Citicorp merger was clearly on Weill's mind that day. "This is really about cross marketing and providing better products to clients," Weill said, explaining the rationale for the deal.[7]

Right off, the press pounced on the co-CEO arrangement. *Business Week* noted after the merger, "The betting on Wall Street is that the co-CEO arrangement can't last, and that Weill and his close-knit team will eventually run the entire show."[8] Analyst Bove predicted that the Argentine-born Reed would soon be out of the top job and serving a diplomatic role in South America.

Investors and analysts were breathless at the size and audacity of the deal. Citigroup became the world's largest financial services company, with nearly $700 billion in assets and nearly $50 billion in revenues that year. It was the biggest merger in history, dwarfing the $37 billion deal between MCI and Worldcom, which closed a month before (the Citigroup merger would later be dwarfed by the AOL Time Warner deal in January 2000). Travelers shares rose 10 percent the following week, adding $14 billion to the value of the deal and $123 million to Weill's personal wealth, bringing him to the $1 billion mark.

Most public opinion came in favor of the merger. The day after it was announced, an editorial in the *New York Times* referred to "the increasingly unnecessary walls built during the Depression to separate commercial banks from investment banks and insurance companies." The editorial went on to suggest that consumers could be better served by a one-stop shopping approach since they wouldn't be confused by insurance agents offering annuities, banks offering retirement accounts, or brokerages pitching mutual funds. "The fact is that Citigroup threatens no one because it would not dominate banking, securities, insurance or any other financial market," the *Times* said.[9]

Only one thing could get in the way of the deal—the U.S. Congress. Technically, even though Citigroup was a bank holding company, Travelers was the surviving company. The structure of the deal was mandated not by Weill's ego and the power of Travelers—as some people tend to imply—but rather by the law. Only as an insurance company could Citigroup apply to become a bank holding company. As long as the Fed approved their application, Reed and Weill would have a two- to five-year window during which Citigroup could operate as a bank holding company. During that time, if Congress failed to overhaul Glass-Steagall and the Bank Holding Company Act, which banned banks, insurance companies, and securities firms operating under one corporate umbrella, Citigroup would have to be dismantled to conform with the law.

The day after the merger was announced Weill was already working on his legislative and public relations strategy for bringing down Glass-Steagall. He told CNN's Lou Dobbs: "I think we [feel] great about the reaction from the Fed. I think we feel good about the initial reaction from Congress, from both sides of the aisle, and we think this is really the way financial services is going."[10]

Weill's comments to the press took on a more high-minded note. Instead of talking about economies of scale or quarterly profits, Weill spoke about the triumphs of capitalism over communism and the role of American business on the world stage. "Since the collapse of communism, with everybody copying the American way of doing business and following the capitalist system, if you look at the privatization of companies and of pension systems and the development of a middle-class in emerging markets, the opportunities and outlook for a financial services company headquartered in America and looking globally have never been better," Weill told *Euromoney*.[11]

Of course, it wouldn't have been a Weill deal without some fat being cut. Weill and Reed estimated there would be 200 to 300 layoffs among Citigroup's 8,000 corporate employees in New York. Reed predicted correctly that "The biggest impact will be among the top 50 people."[12]

The Changing Regulatory Landscape

While the Bank Holding Act of 1956 allowed banks to operate under a corporate structure with a bit more freedom, Glass-Steagall still made it clear that banks were not to sell securities. By the time of the Citigroup merger, that legislation had become very unpopular.

Throughout the 1980s and 1990s, Congress had made efforts to change Glass-Steagall. Legislators didn't want to be too far out of step with international business trends, and clearly it was in the national interest for American firms to stay competitive on a global basis. Financial services companies spent millions of dollars lobbying lawmakers, who wrote different versions of a bill updating Glass-Steagall, but none ever made it into law. In fact, in the 10 years prior to 1998, each session of Congress attempted to reform the Depression-era regulation, and each time they failed.

The problem was that there were many powerful constituencies with a vested interest in the final shape of the legislation. Lobbyists for banks, insurance companies, and brokerages all wanted the best deal for their industry. For example, in 1997, that year's version of financial services reform had plenty of support in both houses of Congress, as well as among major banks. SEC commissioner and former Weill partner Arthur Levitt testified on behalf of the bill before Congress emphasizing that if Congress didn't act, the current law would just become more irrelevant and more disregarded. Levitt said, in part:

> The development of American financial services has already outstripped the legislative framework that governs those services. The question is no longer whether financial modernization will take place, nor even when it will take place. The only remaining question is how—by banking regulators continuing to enlarge the gaps in the old law or by Congress articulating a more comprehensive vision through a new law?[13]

Securities firms and broker-dealers, however, were unhappy with the 1997 version of the bill, which they thought favored the interests of the banks. For example, the legislation stipulated that banking regulators would be the primary arbiters for financial services companies, even if the securities arm of the company—a business regulated by the SEC—provided more of the company's overall revenue. Lobbyists for the securities firms played a role in quashing the legislation.

Given the political hurdles in getting a law changed, market forces often propel companies in the private sector to act ahead of regulators. Regulators then typically expand their interpretations of law to nominally allow the behavior in question. It was through this back-door method of financial deregulation that in 1987, Citicorp, along with Chase Manhattan and other major banks, began underwriting equity securities. In 1994, Mellon Bank acquired Dreyfus, the mutual fund company. In 1997, Bankers Trust acquired Alex Brown, a brokerage firm.

In 1998, just a week before the Citigroup deal was announced, Congress postponed yet again efforts to overturn Glass-Steagall. But after the deal was announced, Congress decided immediately to reopen debate on the legislation. Hearings were called and less than a day after the announcement, lobbyists for banks, insurers, and Wall Street firms met with Congressional banking committee staffers to retool pending legislation. Senator Alfonse M. D'Amato, the Senate Banking Committee chairman, made it known that he was willing to speed up the process for consideration of the bill.

"We have to strike while the iron is hot," said Roger Levy, a Travelers lobbyist. "This deal is a real live manifestation of how the markets are changing, and that puts the legislation against a different political backdrop than a week ago. We have to take advantage of the current agreement, however fragile, among all of the interested parties. All of these planets are in alignment now in ways they may not be a year from now."[14]

Interestingly enough, Citicorp had taken an aggressive stance against the version of reform being considered at that point. In fact, prior to the merger both Reed and former Treasury Secretary Robert Rubin, who later joined Reed and Weill at Citigroup as a member of the office of the chairman, had opposed deregulation. During the hearings, it was pointed out that Citigroup had flip-flopped in a matter of weeks from opposing the legislation to supporting it.

Reed had never been very interested in banking deregulation, unlike his predecessor Walter Wriston. On this subject, Weill was clearly more Wriston's intellectual cousin than Reed. Wriston had railed for years against the unequal treatment of banks under Glass-Steagall. Reed predicted throughout his career at Citicorp that deregulation would eventually come, but he never pushed too hard for it.

Not surprisingly, consumer groups came out heavily against legislation that would allow mergers of banks and securities firms. Along with Nader, other activists bemoaned laws that would legitimize the existence of megabanks like Citigroup. John E. Taylor, CEO of the National Community Reinvestment Coalition, noted that banks, as they get bigger, tend to charge higher fees and become less interested in loans to small businesses. Although he notes that some good can come out of large bank mergers, he says:

> The bad [side] is that you increasingly create distance between the consumer—the local consumer—and the decision makers in the bank. So products, services, whatever kind of corporate business commitments, consumer commitments increasingly get removed from local geographies.

The Fed Approves the Deal

The euphoria of the merger announcement was short-lived. The late summer and fall of 1998 turned out to be one of the most turbulent times in the history of financial markets. The bad tidings came from as far away as Moscow and as nearby as Connecticut. First, Russia's currency collapsed, exposing the new Citigroup and its emerging market business to huge losses. Closer to home, the failure of the Greenwich-based hedge fund Long-Term Capital Management—which Citigroup was also significantly exposed to—almost dragged down the financial markets. Then there was the dismal performance of Salomon Smith Barney that forced Weill to shut down the Salomon arbitrage groups.

Amid the chaos, some good news finally arrived. The Federal Reserve board approved the merger on October 8, 1998. Without financial services reform, the future of the company was not certain, but at least the merger could proceed for now.

By this point, the deal was worth significantly less. Both companies' stock had plummeted, and the market capitalization of the new company was $37.4 billion after Travelers shares were converted equally to Citigroup shares, down from the $70 billion market capitalization of the deal when it was announced. Citicorp shareholders received 2.5 shares of Citigroup for each share of original stock.

Part of the reason investors punished the stock was uncertainty over financial services reform. At that late point in the year, it was clear there would be no new law passed in 1998. In fact, when the Fed announced that it was approving the deal, it made a point of stating that Citigroup must, within two years, divest itself of nonbanking subsidiaries that provided insurance underwriting, mutual fund distribution, and real estate investment. No one doubted that banking reform, through passage of the Financial Services Modernization Act, would be high on the agenda for the 1999 session of Congress. Weill and Reed would make sure of it.

The First Casualty

Meanwhile, at Citigroup headquarters, Reed and Weill were so decorous and deferential to each other that Citigroup operations chief Chuck Prince describes their early relationship as a "lovefest." They consulted each other on business decisions and would exchange mutual compliments during meetings, extolling each other's virtues. "They'd be sitting there saying, 'John what do you think, you're so good at strategy,' and 'Sandy, what do you think, you're so good at operations,'" Prince says.

Dimon, although not part of the "lovefest," wasn't far removed. Soon after the merger, he found out what he would be doing at the new company. Much as he had at Primerica and Travelers, Dimon assumed multiple roles. He was named president of Citigroup, as well as co-CEO of the brokerage unit, Salomon Smith Barney. Just 42 at the time, Dimon seemed the clear heir apparent to Weill and Reed—or at least that is the way Reed probably saw it.

For Weill, it was a different story. By early 1999, tensions had been growing between Dimon and Weill for some time. There was Dimon's well-publicized run-in with Bibliowicz, and then her departure that left Weill fuming. Also, Dimon, increasingly confident of his own abilities, was more and more second-guessing Weill on various issues, including the appointment of Maughan to lead Salomon in tandem with Dimon. Then, there was the sizable third-quarter losses at Salomon Smith Barney, which happened under Dimon's watch (even if he couldn't be blamed for Salomon's arbitrage failings). Dimon, who for years hadn't been afraid to go to the mat with Weill over issues he felt strongly about, was clashing with his boss more frequently.

Maughan was essentially caught in the middle. "After I arrived, I felt there were some differences of opinion and tensions between Sandy and Jamie, and I did my level best to stay out of it, although that was not easy," he says. "I was co-head with Jamie and we both reported to Sandy and I kept getting pulled into these things. It wasn't that comfortable."

Indeed, on top of the troubles integrating Salomon and Smith Barney, there was now the further complication of Citigroup's corporate bank being thrown into the mix. Weill and Reed handed Dimon, Maughan, and Citigroup's Victor Menezes a daunting task: Get the investment banking and corporate banking divisions to work together as one. Initial efforts following the announcement of the merger had not resulted in much progress.

It turned out that meshing the volatile investment banking division of Salomon Smith Barney with Citicorp's staid corporate lending businesses was leading to more turmoil than expected.

One issue that jumped out at anyone who looked closely was that Salomon's bankers, already reeling from the changes Weill had put in place after the merger with Smith Barney, didn't like coordinating with Citibank on deals. Compensation also became a major sticking point, since Salomon Smith Barney's investment bankers were paid much more than Citicorp's commercial bankers. Salomon and Smith Barney hadn't even had time to mesh their own respective cultures before they were expected to mesh with Citibank's corporate banking business. Dimon and Maughan's rapidly deteriorating working relationship didn't help. It became an open secret that the integration of the investment banking business and the corporate banking business was in disarray.

Shortly after the merger, when tensions were at their height, Weill and Reed brought the management team together for a weekend-long celebration of the merger at the Greenbrier resort in West Virginia. Weill's famous corporate get-togethers with company honchos always included spouses and that had served him well, fostering a kind of family-vacation atmosphere. In this instance, however, mixing family and business made for a combustible combination.

In his profile of Weill in the *New York Times Magazine,* Roger Lowenstein described what Citigroup executives still refer to as "the Greenbrier incident" this way:

The mood at the conference had been tense. Toward midnight, Steve Black, a Dimon friend who had never gotten along with Maughan, offered to dance with Maughan's wife as a sort of peace overture. Maughan failed to return the gesture, leaving Black's wife standing alone. Dimon, who had kept to himself most of the evening, took it upon himself to confront Maughan. When Maughan turned away, Dimon grabbed him by the shoulders, spun him around, popping a button from his lapel, and thundered, "Don't you ever turn your back on me while I'm talking!"[15]

The repercussions of the incident were immediate. On Sunday, November 1, Jamie Dimon had 100 Salomon Smith Barney brokers over to his Park Avenue apartment for brunch when he was called for a meeting with Weill and Reed at Citibank's planning complex in Armonk, New York. When Dimon sat down with Reed and Weill, they told him that things were changing: They wanted Dimon to step down.

Dimon resigned that day and was joined by Black, his friend and lieutenant. Citigroup's stock fell nearly 5 percent at the news as investors rued Dimon's departure. Many employees from the Travelers side had assumed Dimon would succeed Weill and Reed, and were upset he was forced out. Dimon earned a standing ovation from nearly 1,000 traders at Salomon Smith Barney when he walked out onto the trading floor on November 2.

Dimon's departure was very sudden and very public. But it was the culmination of tensions that had long been simmering. In fact, it may have been the inevitable conclusion to a long, stressful mentor-apprentice relationship. Weill and Dimon had worked hand-in-glove for 15 years, longer than the typical half-life for Weill-protégé relationships.

While the blow-up at the Greenbrier was a catalyst, Dimon's main failure was that he was unable to contain the animosity between the risk-taking securities traders and investment bankers from Salomon Smith Barney and the more conservative and bureaucratic commercial bankers from Citicorp. The Greenbrier incident itself proved that Dimon wasn't taking Weill's authority seriously. Weill had warned Dimon and Maughan to improve their relationship. Many also thought that it was just the final straw in a relationship that had frayed since Jessica Bibliowicz left the firm. In the end, instead of offering a new beginning for Dimon, the Travelers-Citicorp merger closed a chapter in his career.

Things didn't get much better for Citigroup when on November 3, just two days after Dimon's resignation, Republican Senator Alfonse D'Amato of New York was defeated by Democrat Charles Schumer. D'Amato was a powerful ally of financial reform and chairman of the Senate banking committee. His loss raised concerns about the chances for banking reform. Without such reform, Citigroup—one day in the not too distant future—would have to sell the Travelers insurance operation. So, in a matter of three days, Dimon had resigned and the landscape of financial services reform had been thrown into disarray.

Dimon's resignation had other unintended effects, such as spotlighting the fact that many Citicorp and Travelers employees were openly rooting for the executives from their respective side. Citicorp loyalists were reportedly jubilant, viewing Dimon's departure as a sign that Reed was more powerful than Weill. One magazine even took the opportunity to take a shot at Weill's cross-selling ideas. The *Economist* wrote, "Rather than cross-sell, the different bits of Citi and Travelers have got cross with each other."[16] Comparisons were made between Dimon's departure from Citigroup and Weill's departure from AmEx in 1985. But Weill told employees in a conference call quoted in the *Wall Street Journal* that "Jamie is going to end up getting a heck of a lot more calls than I did."[17]

Dimon eventually emerged from his forced resignation as a martyr of sorts. The initial pillorying of Weill and Reed in the press led to much praise from Weill of Dimon, and defensiveness from Reed. "This was a unique relationship for more than 15 years," Weill told one reporter. "It was a week I would not want to relive. I think we shocked a lot of people a week ago. And I think we want to create stability and let people get a feeling of where we're going and how we're going to handle things."[18]

Reed basically resorted to the dictum: If we did it, we must have had a reason, so you shouldn't question us. He commented in the same *Times* article that: "Sandy and I are pretty serious people. We're not cavalier, and if we did a reorganization, you've got to assume we did it for semi-reasonable reasons, and it wasn't just, we got up one morning and decided we'd sort of shoot people at random."[19]

For Dimon, things may have worked out for the best. Dimon's resignation was quick and clean, and the Citigroup 1999 proxy statement says that Dimon received a severance package of about $30 million. Today, he is the successful CEO of Bank One. Even Maughan says he sang Dimon's praises to the Bank One board when they asked his opinion. "I think Jamie is a very talented executive," Maughan says. "I was asked repeatedly by board members of Bank One whether they should take him. I recommended him."

Today, Weill and Dimon are friends once again. After all, one never knows when a little mutual self-interest may present itself. Thomas Hanley, an analyst at Friedman, Billings and Ramsey, postulated in a late 2001 report that Citigroup might buy Bank One, partly to solve the thorny question of who will succeed Weill.

Citigroup sans Dimon

The incident at the Greenbrier didn't just bloody Dimon; it affected Maughan as well. He lost day-to-day management responsibilities at the company. He was stripped of his CEO title at Salomon Smith Barney and named, instead, a vice chairman, responsible for strategy and Japan. Victor Menezes and Mike

Carpenter were named co-heads of a joint investment and commercial banking business.

Analysts were underwhelmed at the selection of Carpenter to co-run the investment bank. Carpenter, up to that point, was best known for being asleep at the switch at Kidder, Peabody when the head of Kidder's government bond trading desk dreamed up $350 million of fake profits in the early 1990s.

The task of making all the corporate/investment bank problems disappear by Weill and Reed's deadline fell to Menezes and Carpenter. Menezes was a long-time Citicorp executive with very strong ties to his native India and the Indian business community. Menezes, according to one Citicorp source, "survived by knowing when to keep his mouth shut. He would not take a politically unpopular decision. Whichever way the wind was blowing, he stayed on."

Making the Merger Work

In his book *Joe Dimaggio, The Life of the Hero,* Richard Ben Cramer writes that friends of Dimaggio and Marilyn Monroe said years after Monroe's death that they could never understand why the pair got married, as it was clear they would never get along. But Cramer also wrote that in that place and time, no one else could have possibly known what it was like to face the pressures they faced. In a way, they could find solace only with someone in the same situation.

The partnership of Reed and Weill was similar. The co-CEO's, each of whom had an office on the fourth floor of Citigroup headquarters, seemed to some an odd pairing to run a company together. Yet no one except Reed and Weill knew what it was like to run their respective companies and experience the pressures that came with it.

In a November 15, 1998, story in the *New York Times,* Weill did, in fact, compare the merger to a marriage. "You never really know until you get married what it's going to be like," he said. "And I would say this marriage is off to a very good start. And we lived in the engagement period through one of the most volatile times in the history of financial markets."[20]

After the open management squabbles that had led to Dimon's departure, Weill and Reed made obvious efforts to portray their own working relationship as humming along. "We are getting along fine," Reed told the *Times.* "Better probably than each of us, in the secret hideaways of our brains, thought would be the case."[21]

The truth is, they had plenty of work to do. With Dimon gone, some analysts bearish on the company, and shareholders concerned by the post-merger management shake-up, Reed and Weill concentrated on getting their commercial and investment banks to work together.

Dimon's departure at least achieved an end to the open squabbling that had characterized the relationship between the two divisions. If Dimon could be forced out, it was obvious that further dissension would not be tolerated. Weill and Reed said they wanted any issues resolved by the year's end. In the final months of 1998, it seemed like Citicorp's commercial bankers were gaining the upper hand in how clients would be approached and products would be sold.

Although this development, along with Dimon's departure, appeared at the time like a victory for Reed, it's worth remembering that Weill had begun the process of retooling Salomon Smith Barney well before the merger with Citicorp. The truth is that even though Weill was associated with the investment banking side, he had never really liked the aggressive, transaction-driven investment banking culture. He hated risk and was eager to tame the gunslingers. He liked the 24-hour-a-day banking business, built on long-term relationships with customers.

Meanwhile, Reed started to emphasize succession. Dimon's departure obviously had him thinking about the future of the firm. Reed told the *New York Times* on November 15:

It's extremely important that somebody be groomed. I was working on that with my board before the merger, and I think the merger would simply accentuate it because neither Sandy nor I are kids. Also, I think—and Sandy and I would have a slightly different description, I think—my own view is that it's quite important to the evolution of this merger that at some point Sandy and I step back and allow integrated management to take over.[22]

At the end of 1998, the results of the merger were looking up. Carpenter and Menezes seemed to be working well, the outrage from investors and the press at Dimon's departure had abated, and the market had rebounded.

Through adversity, Reed and Weill had worked together and weathered not only a third-quarter financial meltdown, but also a disastrous first month of the life of the new Citigroup. They had proven they could ride out a rough patch. The next year would reveal what good times meant for their relationship.

Weill on Top

M ore than ever before, CEOs are measured by a single yard-stick: The gains in the stock prices of the companies they run. Improving shareholder value has always been the CEO's chief responsibility, but in the last 30 years or so, as the stock-owning portion of the general population has increased, more people have come to understand that there is one paramount constituent in the business world: the shareholder.

In this light, Sandy Weill is a true star of corporate America. Few CEOs can compete with his track record of increasing shareholder value. Along the way, Weill has demonstrated a willingness to take unpopular or distasteful actions that are in the best interest of shareholders, such as instituting round after round of layoffs, raising banking fees, and whittling back benefit plans. Perhaps inevitably, any criticism of these actions is quieted by the acclaim of investors seeing the results in their stock portfolios. "I've never met anybody like him, and I go back a long way," says Thomas Hanley, a banking analyst now with Friedman, Billings, Ramsey. "He's awesome. In his power, but also in his accomplishments. There's no one in the financial services arena who can quite hold a candle to him."

For the three years after the Citigroup merger, the company's stock price grew 25 percent a year, compared with a gain of just 13 percent for its peer financial companies and only 0.5 percent for stocks in the Standard & Poors 500. David Sowerby, a portfolio manager at Loomis Sayles & Co., which owns Citigroup stock, says that "Sandy Weill is a Hall-of-Famer in the business world. And he gets voted in on the first ballot."

Even executive compensation expert Graef Crystal, who has consistently criticized Weill for his high pay, points out that companies run by Weill have beaten 96 percent of the S&P 500 over the past decade. In fact, Weill typically beats the S&P 500 index by more than two times. "Sandy made a lot of people rich," says Jeff Lane. "The stock deals that he does are terrific deals and they enable people at the time to accumulate wealth."

Weill himself has accumulated plenty of wealth. In 2000, his entire compensation totaled $222.4 million, according to Crystal. Weill has made an annual average of $100.6 million each year for the past 10 years. That's over $1 billion in compensation during one of the longest bull markets ever. In 2000, Weill, like many CEOs, took a base salary of the relatively paltry sum of $1 million (that's the most a company can pay an individual and still deduct it as an expense). But he also received a bonus of $18.5 million, restricted stock options valued at $8.7 million, and a whopping $196.2 million in the value of exercised options. In early 2002, *Forbes* estimated Weill's net worth at $1.4 billion, with the bulk of that in Citigroup stock.[1]

CEO compensation figures, of course, can be misleading. It's not as if Citigroup's board of directors decided in 2000 that Weill should receive over $200 million in pay. Without the $196.2 million in option payments—which he could have exercised years down the road—Weill's 2000 compensation would have totaled the more reasonable-sounding $26.2 million.

Weill has been able to accumulate such a tremendous amount of Citigroup stock thanks to what's known as a "reload" feature in his contract. Basically, that means that when Weill exercises options, a portion of the exercised block of options is replenished. Specifically, he receives one new option for each option he must forfeit to cover the total cost of exercising the options and taxes owed. For example, in 2000, Weill received 20.1 million shares of stock through the exercise of 20.1 million options. Because he needed to give up 17.8 million of his existing shares of stock to exercise these options and pay taxes, the reload feature entitled him to receive 17.8 million new options. Citigroup's stated purpose for this reload feature, which is a compensation device many companies use to retain top executives, is to "maintain the option holder's commitment to Citigroup by maintaining as closely as possible the holder's net equity position—the sum of shares owed and shares subject to option."[2]

Crystal calls this reload feature "Lazarus stock options." "They come back to life," he explains. "Every time he exercises, they give him a new set." Crystal believes that Weill's compensation packages have been too generous, allowing him to obtain so much stock that Citigroup's share price doesn't need to rise very much for Weill to reap major gains. "He has been a terrific performer and builder of companies, he just can't keep his hands off the money," Crystal says. "He is just so wildly overpaid, even for his performance."

Wayne Guay, the accounting professor at the Wharton Business School, says that the number of options Weill exercises in a given year isn't really relevant in determining whether Weill is overpaid. A much more important issue, according to Guay, is whether Weill's total compensation package is tied to his performance and is in line with that of his peers. "But given the company he is running and his ability to create shareholder value, it's not readily apparent who his peers are," Guay says. In fact, Weill's total compensation over the last three years—

roughly $300 million—is but a tiny fraction of the growth of Citigroup's market capitalization. "Presumably," Guay adds, "he's had a lot to do with Citigroup's growth."

Roy Smith, of New York University's Stern School of Business, says that Weill has outdistanced other wealthy CEOs, like Jack Welch and John Reed, because he was essentially an entrepreneur and an owner. In terms of wealth, "Sandy blew right by these guys because he owned the business," Smith says.

When it came time for the Citigroup board to decide whether to keep Weill at the helm of Citigroup or ask him to retire along with Reed, board members no doubt considered Weill's rare ability to keep the share price rising. By that time, after more than 40 years running companies, Weill stood for cutting costs, improving earnings, and raising shareholder value. This track record would put him in good stead when the inevitable showdown with Reed arose.

A New Effort at Cooperation

Early in 1999, the cracks that would lead to the watershed boardroom confrontation between Reed and Weill were still small fissures. Relieved to have the chaos of Dimon's messy departure behind them, the two co-CEOs worked on the challenges inherent in integrating two gargantuan financial services companies. They made joint appearances before the press and said the right things about cooperating and sharing responsibilities. With care and attention, their relationship improved.

It helped that the economy was in an upswing and financial markets were booming, creating enormous profits at Citigroup. After mediocre results in the third and fourth quarters of 1998, the company posted $2.4 billion in revenues from January through March of 1999, making it the most profitable corporation in the United States for that quarter.[3]

These profits, though, had little to do with cross-selling products or synergies between Salomon Smith Barney and the Citigroup corporate bank. To promote cross-selling at Citigroup branches, sales representatives had been told to increase their referrals, as well as open up more accounts, which didn't immediately yield obvious benefits. Another of the company's early forays into cross-selling—an effort to get Primerica Financial Services customers in New York to sign up for Citibank checking accounts—soon languished.

Weill Makes an Immediate Impact

Far more important to Citigroup's bottom line than cross-selling was Weill's trademark efforts to cut costs by eliminating inefficient operations and squeezing benefits. Many of the initial cuts struck hardest at the company's overseas branch networks. Sheena Iyengar, the management professor at the Columbia University Business School who performed research for Reed's academic council, witnessed first-hand the results of the merger on Citigroup's far-flung employees. Iyengar says employees throughout Citibank's international network felt betrayed by Reed, believing he had not only sold out Citicorp's identity in the merger with Travelers, but had granted Weill authority to make cuts in benefits, bonuses, and staff.

When the slashing began, it was even deeper than employees had feared. According to Iyengar, Citigroup branches in Australia were cut from 18 to 3 in one day. Branches in Singapore received sharp cuts, as did those in Latin America. "It was pretty clear in Latin America that there was resentment against Sandy Weill and all the changes, and everyone was whispering that it was really a takeover," says Iyengar. "They were seeing a lot of John Reed cronies being fired and replaced by Sandy Weill cronies. Symbols of Citigroup, including great benefits packages, were being phased out and replaced by items like a stock compensation system. It was clear that John Reed was the less powerful of the two."

Even as cuts were made, the pressure to perform intensified. Branch salespeople had to bring in more business to receive the same bonuses. The company started giving exams to loan officers and other employees in the United States and at various international Citigroup locations. Failing the test could mean losing your job. The complaint echoing throughout Citigroup's international network was that Weill set goals that were unachievable. "The typical little bank teller was being affected by Weill," Iyengar says. "They wouldn't really blame Sandy Weill, but they'd say, 'Things have changed,' and they were angry about it. Weill wanted to increase referrals. Sales reps would have to bring in a certain number of accounts. It varied country by country. He doubled their goals in order to get the same pay and bonus."

Weill also took aim at two of his favorite targets: training and travel budgets. For example, business trips to the United States, held out as rewards for top Citicorp performers around the world during the Reed years, were drastically reduced.

Iyengar concedes that in many cases, the cuts made good business sense. For years at Citicorp, Wriston, and then Reed, had supported the notion of worldwide banking. Whether it was opening new branches in Tokyo or sub-Saharan Africa, Citicorp wanted to be *the* international consumer bank. But according to Iyengar, many of Citibank's branches weren't doing much business in the late 1990s because the local population couldn't afford to bank there.

This was a textbook example of the Sandy Weill school of management. Weill held little nostalgia for Citigroup's glorious past of providing branch banking around the world. When he arrived, he simply closed down unprofitable branches. Workers at the branches obviously opposed the cutbacks. But Citigroup shareholders benefited as Weill jettisoned unproductive branches, helping to boost the company's earnings and stock price.

Meanwhile, Weill brought to Citigroup his lifelong zeal for employees owning equity. In 1999, the firm implemented a new stock compensation program for all employees that included a restricted stock plan and a stock-option plan. The goals weren't simply to get employees worldwide to work hard to increase Citigroup's stock price. They were designed to replace significantly more expensive local country benefits programs. The new program also allowed Citigroup to take advantage of corporate tax breaks that some countries granted to companies that provided their employees with stock compensation plans. Weill has always believed in making his presence felt, and in 1999 he was aggressively putting his stamp on Citigroup.

Reed and Weill Clash

As changes were made at the bank and Weill bolstered his role, Reed had the look of someone less and less engaged. Perhaps Weill had changed Citigroup in ways that Reed hadn't anticipated.

Reed began publicly questioning the efficacy of the merger and certain actions taken by him and Weill. For example, in April 1999, Reed told a Citigroup consumer group conference that losing Dimon was a mistake. Weill was understandably upset about what effect such a comment would have on Mike Carpenter, who replaced Dimon as co-head of Citigroup's global corporate and investment bank, and whose career Weill had personally rehabilitated.

The mutual admiration Weill and Reed had shown for each other in meetings also came to a halt. In fact, the two co-CEOs became openly hostile, according to the *Wall Street Journal,* which described this exchange during one planning meeting:

"Can you quantify the bottom line?" Mr. Weill asked. When Mr. Reed began, Mr. Weill rolled his eyes, said one person who witnessed the exchange. When it was Mr. Weill's turn to speak, Mr. Reed started reading, the person said.[4]

Evidently, Reed and Weill were not even attempting to hide their mutual disdain in the spring of 1999. At a two-day retreat at the El Conquistador in San Juan, Puerto Rico, Weill left just as Reed was arriving, and the two co-CEOs hadn't even bothered to coordinate their comments. While Weill was encouraging in his comments, Reed exhibited unhappiness with the performance of various segments of the company.

In June 1999, the business press began to catch on to the management problems at Citigroup. In its June 7, 1999, cover story headlined "Citigroup: Is This Marriage Working?" *Business Week* reported, among other things, how Saudi Prince Alwaleed bin Talal, the largest shareholder in Citigroup with 4.8 percent, was concerned that Weill and Reed were coordinating with each other less and less.[5]

According to current Citigroup COO and long-time Weill friend Chuck Prince, Reed at the time sincerely believed that since the new Citigroup was such a different company than Citicorp or Travelers, it should be led by someone not identified with either of those companies. "At that time, there was still a lot of 'them' and 'us,'" Prince says. "John believed that he was too associated with Citicorp and Sandy was too associated with Travelers."

It's striking how different were Reed's and Weill's visions of their roles at the company over the next few years. Reed seemed blind to Weill's desire to stay on as CEO. But, Reed may not have known what Weill was thinking, given the extent to which their relationship had frayed.

In fact, the degree to which Weill and Reed worked effectively together seemed to vary inversely with how well the bank was doing. When Dimon was forced out and the investment and corporate bankers were at each other's throats, Weill and Reed patched up their relationship. Starting in April 1999, with the operations of the two companies successfully merged (more or less) and business booming, tensions between the two began to surface. It was almost as if, with business doing well, Weill and Reed had the luxury to focus on their roles at the company, their respective legacies, and whose vision would ultimately become the Citigroup lodestar in the years ahead.

The media began questioning Citigroup's co-CEO arrangement in earnest. On July 1, 1999, an article in the *Financial Post* referring to the bank's strong profits also mentioned doubts about the sustainability of Reed and Weill's relationship, and noted that the succession issue was becoming a wedge between the two. In that article, Michael Mayo, a banking analyst at Credit Suisse First Boston, said that Citigroup represented the Noah's Ark school of management: "As the ark moves forward, sometimes the animals eat each other."[6]

Most likely, Weill decided he was ready to assume full control of the company at some point that summer. He no longer needed Reed's knowledge of the bank or Reed's allies within the bank. Weill knew what he wanted to do, where to make cuts, whom to trust.

A Division of Duties at the Top

Barely speaking to each other by the summer of 1999, Reed and Weill agreed to split up their duties. An internal memo on July 28 announced that Weill would take over the company's operating businesses, while Reed would lead specific organizationwide functions, including Internet strategy, technology, human resources, and the legal department. In theory, the division of duties matched their strengths. Weill was the operations genius; Reed loved to sit back and mull the future of technology and the impact of the Internet. In reality, however, Reed had ceded power to Weill.

Businesses need to make money. At big businesses, operating units bring in the money, and the operating units reported to Weill.

It also so happened that the duties Reed took on were ones that cost the firm money, while Weill's units generated profits. For example, Reed had started and championed e-Citi, Citigroup's organizationwide Internet division, which produced various online banking products. Under the stewardship of Ed Horowitz, e-Citi bled red ink, losing $300 million annually since its inception in 1997. "E-Citi was very typical for Reed," says author and technology consultant Peter Cohan. "It was big and visionary and also hard to figure out what the economic benefit was going to be. It was a bold statement about technology transforming financial services."

For his part, Weill thought each unit should devise its own Internet strategy, if the business called for it. Throughout his career, Weill had spent money on technology, but only when there was a clear return on the investment with speedier, more efficient operations. So, even while Reed was busy promoting e-Citi, it was clear by Weill's comments that he didn't support the project.

Human resources, too, was an area Reed had allowed to become a huge fiefdom under the department's director, Larry Phillips. Weill wanted to reduce the size of the department and put in a cheaper corporate benefits plan.

Lobbying at Citigroup for Modernization

Even as Reed and Weill became increasingly estranged, Citigroup continued to push for passage of the Financial Services Modernization Act. Weill, along with Citigroup lobbyist Roger Levy, was very active in speaking to various constituencies about the legislation.

By 1999, the clock was ticking on Citigroup's two-year window to come into compliance with current law. Citigroup wasn't the only company with a huge stake in financial services reform. Since the Citigroup merger, other companies had merged to form diversified financial services companies (albeit ones smaller than Citigroup), and needed deregulation to be implemented in order to keep their new structure.

Early in 1999, conservative politicians and commentators began worrying that President Clinton would veto the financial reform legislation. Clinton at one point decided to support an element of the legislation that called for protecting the Community Reinvestment Act (CRA), the 1977 Federal law that requires banks to make a certain number of loans and investments in poor neighborhoods. He also wanted reforms in the Federal Home Loan Bank system, another tertiary program affected by the proposed legislation. On February 12, 1999, Treasury Secretary Robert Rubin went before the House to advance the Clinton Administration's argument, opposing the bill in its current form. It was the first salvo in an eight-month battle between the administration, Congress and the banking industry (largely represented by Citigroup) over the bill.

But there was a bigger issue gnawing at Rubin. He was mired in a pitched battle over the legislation with Federal Reserve Chairman Alan Greenspan that would last until Rubin left the Treasury Department in May 1999. "The thing that stalled [the legislation] for the last six months or so was the fight between the Fed and Treasury over who was going to regulate certain things," says Prince. "It was a turf battle. Rubin wouldn't budge an inch. Greenspan wouldn't budge an inch. And neither of them would blink."

Rubin would soon leave the Treasury, but he would not be out of the spotlight for long. Within six months, he would be helping to run the very company that benefited the most from deregulation: Citigroup. In fact, the passage of the law and Rubin signing on at Citigroup would occur just a few weeks apart.

Despite Clinton's threats to derail the legislation if the Community Reinvestment Act wasn't protected, Republican supporters of the bill suspected that the president could be convinced to back the legislation, particularly given his pro-business bent. The Republicans were willing to bet that Clinton did not want to be remembered as standing in the way of legislation that would bring America's financial services system into the twenty-first century.

As winter turned to spring, it was clear that 1999 would be the year for financial services modernization. The proposed legislation breezed through the House Banking Committee by a 51 to 8 vote, and Rubin praised the latest version the next time he appeared before Congress to discuss the bill. On May 5, 1999, he noted that the bill:

> . . . takes the necessary actions to modernize our financial system with respect to Glass-Steagall and the Bank Holding Act. And it takes two other steps that are critical in importance to the administration: It preserves the relevance of the Community Reinvestment Act; and it permits financial services organizations to organize themselves in whatever way they feel best serves their business purposes and their customers.

Rubin had given the bill the administration's green light. If certain improvements were made, Clinton would sign it into law.

Still, in October 1999, neither passage of the Act by Congress nor Clinton's signature seemed a sure thing. During an overnight marathon negotiating session on Thursday, October 21, at a critical juncture in the evening, Senator Phil Gramm of Texas told Levy, the Citigroup lobbyist, "You get Sandy Weill on the phone right now. Tell him to call the White House and get [them] moving or I'm going to shut this conference down."[7]

Weill did, in fact, place a call to Clinton that night. Several last-ditch compromises were made addressing bank compliance with the CRA, and an agreement was reached on the legislation. Hours later, Reed and Weill issued a statement that read, in part:

> We congratulate the leaders of our country for their efforts in hammering out a successful agreement on the last remaining issues surrounding the Financial Services Modernization Act. In particular, we congratulate President Clinton . . . By liberating our financial companies from an antiquated regulatory structure, the legislation will unleash the creativity of our industry and ensure our global competitiveness. As a result, all Americans—investors, savers, insurers—will be better served.

On November 4, the Senate approved the final bill, by a vote of 90 to 8, and the House followed later that evening, with a vote of 362 to 57. Clinton signed the bill into law later that month.

Citigroup was now assured that it could continue business according to Weill and Reed's original vision. In the span of just one year, the co-CEOs had not only created the biggest financial services company in the nation, but they had also successfully changed decades-old laws that prohibited such a merger.

Weill and Reed—particularly Weill—had gotten what they wanted. Citigroup now spanned the globe and was free to acquire virtually any type of financial services company without major regulatory concerns. The last vestiges of restraint had been removed. Only time will tell whether the freedom to acquire new companies and expand into new businesses around the world will ultimately come back to haunt Weill and Citigroup. So far, it hasn't.

Engaging Cuba

Under the joint leadership of Reed and Weill, Citigroup pushed for financial modernization of another type in 1999: ending the 40-year embargo and normalizing economic relations with Fidel Castro's Cuba.

Starting in 1996, Citicorp had been a major presence in the USA Engage Coalition, which endorses business ties with Cuba. On June 17, 1999, Lionel Johnson, Citigroup vice president and director of international government relations, appeared before a U.S. House Committee and urged a "fresh approach" to the use of economic sanctions against Cuba. "We do not have a presence clearly in Cuba," he said. "But we have been in the forefront of the dialogue that has been taking place in policy circles here in the United States to take a fresh approach to the use of sanctions."

Johnson's—and presumably Citigroup's—view seems to be that the United States needed a new approach to enforcing economic sanctions. Johnson said that:

> What [Citigroup has] done with regard to Cuba, I think has to be regarded in the context of our overall efforts to bring some rational thinking and new thinking, a fresh approach to the use of unilateral economic sanctions as an instrument of foreign policy.

One would have thought that Reed and Weill, no matter where they stood politically (Reed is a Republican and Weill a Democrat), would tread lightly in the potential minefield of world events, particularly given the 1990s money laundering scandals at Citicorp and other banks.

Reed at the Money Laundering Hearings

Just a month after the passage of the Financial Services Modernization Act, the Senate began hearings on money laundering by U.S. banks. Citibank had made headlines as one of the biggest offenders in the mid-1990s, before Weill's time. Like all major banks in America, Citigroup maintained what are called private banks, which cater to their wealthiest clients. Private banking is distinguished by the size of the account (usually $1 million or more) and the fact that private banking clients receive one-on-one assistance from a so-called "relationship manager," assigned to manage the assets of that client.

On November 19, 1999, Reed went before a Senate subcommittee that was investigating Citigroup's private banking practices. According to testimony from Congressman Charles Rangel, Citibank's private banking customers included an array of unsavory characters and criminals during Reed's tenure. Rangel said that, at one time or another, Citibank had as clients of its private bank:

> Raul Salinas, brother of the former president of Mexico; now in prison in Mexico for murder and under investigation in Mexico for illicit enrichment; Asif Ali Zardari, husband of the former prime minister of Pakistan, now in prison in Pakistan for kickbacks; Omar Bongo, president of Gabon, and subject of a French criminal investigation into bribery; sons of General Sani Abacha, former military leader of Nigeria, one of whom is now in prison in Nigeria on charges of murder; and Jaime Lusinchi, former president of Venezuela, indicted for money laundering in Venezuela.

There is an interesting aspect to this testimony relating to Weill. Two of the accounts—those of President Bongo and Raul Salinas—were closed in January 1999, just months after the merger. While this may have been coincidental, it would be characteristic of Weill's hands-on management style if when he came aboard, he urged the private bank to clean up its act. Reed hinted at that when he was questioned about any impact the Citigroup merger had in the fight against money laundering. He told the Senate subcommittee, "What we have done is we have sort of raised the awareness." Because of the merger, he said management had, "created a uniform set of policies and procedures across the company."

Weill had shown earlier in his career that he's willing to turn away customers if he believed their actions could put the company at risk (the Hunt brothers, who created so many problems for Bache, for example). It is also noteworthy that while many stars of the financial world burned out amid scandal, Weill has had such a long and successful career on Wall Street in part because he doesn't play fast and loose with the rules. In fact, Weill has surrounded himself throughout his career with people who went on to become regulators themselves, including Arthur Levitt, Frank Zarb, Wick Simmons, and Duke Chapman (who ran the Chicago Board Options Exchange). As Lane notes, "Sandy has always wanted to run a clean shop."

Weill Shores Up His Power Base

Weill had always agreed in theory that he and Reed would step down together once the merger was done and the company was running well. In late 1998, Weill told a reporter when asked about succession: "We have an agreement that we're going to have this place running like a finely tuned machine and doing incredibly well before we go."[8] Clearly, there could be many years and lots more deals before the company would meet Weill's high hurdles.

The problem for Reed, as it turned out, was that he started thinking about retirement soon after the deal was consummated. That explains why Reed, hardly a shrinking violet in his long tenure leading the bank, seemingly had no stomach to fight as

Weill closed branches, retooled worldwide employee benefits and compensation, and took control of the operating units.

Weill sensed Reed's willingness to step down and, as it became increasingly clear that senior management wanted to answer only to one boss, he took the necessary steps to ensure that he would be the one to survive. Weill had become a savvy corporate politician, thanks in no small part to the schooling he received from Jim Robinson years before. At American Express, Weill had been isolated, with no power base and few friends on the board of directors. But now it was Reed who had lost authority for operations and, while he still had plenty of allies on the board, Weill was winning them over.

As 1999 progressed and Weill only became more powerful, Reed continued to cling to the hope that he and Weill would step down together. Reed's vision of events might even have gained support within the management committee and board if not for one critical factor: Jamie Dimon was gone.

Reed's statements early in 1999 that getting rid of Dimon was a mistake turned out to be absolutely correct, as it related to his goal of having the co-CEOs step down together and be replaced by one strong leader. Dimon's departure left no obvious successor. With Dimon in the wings, Weill might well have been forced to leave at the same time as Reed to make way for Dimon.

One senior Citigroup executive believes Weill foresaw that Dimon would have given the board an alternative to choosing him over Reed and this was the main reason he took part in pushing Dimon out of the company. "Any qualms he had about doing that were probably eliminated by Dimon's issues with his daughter," he says. Close associates of Weill's, however, say it was Reed (who had a long track record of firing his heirs apparent) who really forced Dimon out and that Weill, who saw Dimon as a member of his family, would never have made that move on his own.

Weill Reaches Out

By taking control of the operating units, Weill was clearly wrest-
ing the top job from Reed. But he also needed clear allies on the
Citigroup board who would back him when it came to a vote. For
that, he needed to win over several of Reed's appointees. According to one Citigroup executive, Weill apparently outdid
himself in charming Victor Menezes, then co-head of the global
corporate and investment bank. For example, when the two were
in India on Citigroup business, Weill asked Menezes to act as
best man when he and Joan renewed their wedding vows at the
Taj Mahal. Menezes wasn't the only important member of the Citigroup community Weill cozied up to. He also paid a visit around
that time to Prince Alwaleed bin Talal's desert camp in Saudi
Arabia. The prince, while not a board member, held considerable influence as Citigroup's biggest shareholder.

The Citigroup executive believes that Weill the corporate
politician takes so many small, seemingly unrelated steps that
potential rivals don't even realize they've been outsmarted. Unlike his tenure at American Express, Weill was doing a masterful
job of reaching out to various important people and winning
them over. The next one on his list was former Treasury Secretary Rubin.

Rubin Joins the Office of the Chairman

In October 1999, it was announced that Rubin would join the
company as the third member of the office of the chairman
with Reed and Weill. Rubin would also have a seat on the board
of directors. Ostensibly hired so Reed and Weill could discuss
various political and business matters with him and obtain advice, Rubin also brought political connections and international

experience. He was also widely assumed by the press to be a peacemaker between Reed and Weill. Rubin, a former co-head of Goldman Sachs who made $150,000 as Treasury Secretary, negotiated a hefty compensation package during his month-long courtship with Weill. In 2000, Rubin's annual salary, bonus, and stock options was worth about $45 million.[9]

The addition of Rubin was enormously beneficial for Weill. Not only did Weill now have another potential ally, but Rubin was respected on the world stage as a businessman and an effective statesman. Now, Reed could exit and no one would worry that Weill wouldn't have a calm, dispassionate voice within earshot. Rubin was also a perfect choice for Weill because he wasn't interested in running the company day-to-day, and insisted time and again that he had no desire to become the CEO. Having him around may have nonetheless resolved some of the board's concerns about succession. Some analysts believe that if anything were to happen to Weill, Rubin would step in, but only as an interim CEO.

Of course, the most important move Weill could make to win over the board was to run the company well, which he did. Citigroup's overall results were stellar in 1999. The company earned nearly $10 billion, second only to General Electric. In addition, Citigroup met its cost-savings goal of $2 billion that year. The company's earnings were particularly stunning in the third quarter, as it tripled the previous year's third-quarter revenues.

Senior Management Exodus

The positive results were marred by some defections among senior management at Citigroup. In January 2000, Bob Lipp, a long-time friend of Weill's and head of Citigroup's global consumer business, announced he would retire. Sources told the

Journal it was due to his frustration with Reed's involvement in his part of the business. Weill blamed Reed and started to talk more openly about his frustrations with sharing power.[10]

At a management committee retreat at the Boulders resort in Arizona a few weeks later, Reed and Weill received an earful about how frustrating it was to work for the two of them. Roger Lowenstein described the scene in his profile of Weill in the *New York Times* magazine:

> On the second day, [Weill and Reed] went around the room; each manager complained that having two bosses wasn't working. "We can follow any compass," Menezes said, "but we have to know where north, south, east and west are."

In the days following that session, Reed and Weill made an attempt to clear the air. Even with Rubin as peacemaker, Weill and Reed, according to Lowenstein, agreed that the problem couldn't be fixed. Things didn't improve between Reed and Weill when, in late February, CFO Heidi Miller—the highest-ranking woman executive at the company—announced she was leaving to join the e-commerce company Priceline.com. Though she insisted that the Priceline offer was too good to pass up, Weill again blamed Reed.

Boardroom Showdown

In late February, Citigroup's board held a special meeting to address the co-CEO situation. Reed and Weill each gave presentations. In his, Reed proposed that he and Weill leave together and appoint a successor. For his part, Weill lobbied for the job. When the board asked Rubin for his opinion, he said that Weill running the company alone—with Rubin's help—would be better than Weill and Reed both leaving. Board members asked Rubin whether he would accept the CEO position, and Rubin declined.

The meeting went on for hours as the board members discussed different scenarios. At one point, the board asked Reed if he would stay on for a year as chairman with Weill leading the company. Reed declined. Finally, the board came up with a carefully crafted solution: Weill would stay on as the CEO, but would have only a limited amount of time before he would have to come up with a successor. In the carefully worded announcement, the board said Weill, "intends to work with a committee of the board on a plan of succession with the objective of coming up with a successor within two years." Reed would retire. Rubin would stay on in the office of the chairman. *Fortune* wrote of the statement, "There's so much wiggle room in these words that Weill could end up running Citi for years."[11]

Reed Retires

Reed, 61, stepped down on April 18, 2000. Most investors were pleased. Everyone who knew Weill's track record figured that, alone at the top of Citigroup, he would be even more effective at cutting costs and boosting earnings.

Along with even more belt-tightening, something else would also change with Weill at the helm—the rate of acquisitions. It is striking how few big deals Weill did in 1999. With the hard work of integrating the two companies behind him and unfettered by sharing power with Reed, Weill was prepared to set out on a new string of deals.

But before Weill could begin acquiring in earnest, he wanted to scale back or end outright several Reed-driven initiatives that he had never believed in. These ranged from the high profile and big budget project—such as e-Citi—to the virtually unknown, like Reed's academic council. "Within a month of Weill becoming the CEO, the program was shut down with no explanation," Iyengar said of the academic council.

"Now Weill is making clear that Citi has rid itself of Reed," wrote the *U.S. Banker* in September 2000. "Weill is dismantling practically all that Reed had constructed in his final months, in effect, obliterating his former partner."[12]

Weill Leads Citigroup's Global Expansion

In January 2000, a month before the boardroom showdown between Weill and Reed, Citigroup purchased Schroders PLC, a European investment bank. The goal was to build up Citigroup's high-end customer base. Schroders, while a significant acquisition, was also a departure for Weill. Up to that point in his career, he had bought few foreign firms. Any deals with an international flavor tended to be with U.S.-based companies that had international operations, like Salomon Brothers or Citicorp. As he quipped to *Business Week*, "The biggest overseas move I ever made was across the river from Brooklyn to Manhattan." In terms of international experience, he said, "I think it's great if you have the experience of living overseas, but you can learn a lot by listening to people, talking to people, and traveling a lot."[13]

In 2000, Weill caught the overseas' deal bug, facing up to the reality that Citigroup's major growth opportunities were in international markets. In the next 14 months, Citigroup purchased midmarket companies across the world, including credit-card portfolios in Canada and Britain; Bank Handlowy, a Polish retail bank; a 15 percent stake in Taiwan's Fubon Group; and Associates First Capital, which, though based in the United States, had a significant presence in Japan.

It was the Associates First Capital deal that made the most news. Citigroup agreed in early September 2000 to pay $31 billion for the consumer finance outfit, which was based in Texas. Associates started out as a former subsidiary of the Ford Motor Company, established in 1918 to finance sales of the Model T. By 2000, under CEO Keith Hughes, the company's core business was consumer lending. Although the Justice Department was reportedly investigating Associates for alleged predatory lending— a development that could adversely affect the Citigroup brand— the company had a good credit rating and would double the size of the Commercial Credit branch network, which was renamed CitiFinancial.

The deal was vintage Weill. Associates First Capital was undervalued and inefficient at leveraging its sprawling distribution network. Weill saw that if its potential was properly harnessed, Associates could emerge as a huge profit center for Citigroup. The Associates acquisition was also typical of Weill because he simply shrugged off the storm of criticism that followed for purchasing what many believed was a shady organization. Instead of responding to the criticism, Weill talked about how it was an excellent move for—who else?—Citigroup's shareholders.

And, as is often the case, Weill seems to have been right. Once Associates was under the Citigroup "umbrella," the company was subject to much stricter oversight than it had been previously. Associates was revamped and proved a strong financial performer for Citigroup. Plus, it halted some of its most dubious lending practices. "Several of the practices we're most concerned with have thus far been addressed," says John Taylor, president and CEO of the National Community Reinvestment Coalition. "I don't think it would be fair for anybody not to recognize that some good things have happened."

In the midst of this string of deals, in July of 2000, Marc Weill left his position at Citigroup as head of the company's $113 billion investment portfolio. Marc also served on the management committee. According to a *Wall Street Journal* article in November 2000, Marc left to get help with a cocaine dependency.[14]

Ironically, it was only after Reed left that Weill took any steps at all toward giving anyone the kind of attention that would anoint them as a possible successor. Todd Thomson, Heidi Miller's replacement as CFO, was one such person. A 1998 recruit from GE Capital, Thomson carved out the formal deal-making structure at Citigroup. Just 38 when appointed CFO, Thomson essentially served three roles: CFO, head of direct investments, and head of cross-selling efforts. In December 2000, Jay Fishman, who had been with Weill since Fishman was hired as a young executive at Commercial Credit, was named one of two chief operating officers, overseeing finance and risk management. Chuck Prince was named his co-COO, heading up administration and operations.

2001: A Bank Odyssey

The year 2000 ended in triumph for Weill. Citigroup finished the year with earnings of over $13 billion. He had put together a string of successful acquisitions. Most important, Citigroup was his to lead, and he must have looked forward to 2001 with relish.

It started out well. On January 10, 2001, Weill was elected to the board of directors of the Federal Reserve Bank of New York for a three-year term. On May 17, 2001, Weill made another important international acquisition: Grupo Financiero Banamex-Accival (Banamex), Mexico's largest independent bank and brokerage. A main reason for the deal was to attract the business of the 20 million Mexicans in the United States who annually send up to $8 billion home. Oddly, one of the ramifications of the deal was the end—not the expansion—of Citigroup's brand in Mexico. The name Banamex, well-known throughout Mexico, was retained. After a 73-year presence in Mexico, the Citibank name would cease to exist. Mexican President Vicente Fox hailed the Banamex deal as a milestone for his country. Just six years before, Mexico had to be bailed out by U.S.-led efforts after the collapse of the peso. Banamex chairman Roberto Hernandez retained his job and was even given a seat on the Citigroup board.

The Banamex acquisition went far more smoothly than Citicorp's previous Mexican acquisition—the ill fated, pre-Weill Confia deal in 1998. That deal involved a Mexican bank that, just prior to the close of the acquisition, was accused by the U.S. Department of Justice of laundering drug money. (Banamex was also named by the Department of Justice, but to a far lesser extent.) Citibank executives, Confia executives, and the Department of Justice worked out a financial penalty for Confia and the bank was folded into Citibank Mexico.

The spate of international acquisitions expanded Citigroup's reach, but also exposed it to more risk. After the Banamex deal, fully one-quarter of Citigroup's income came from emerging markets, up from 17 percent just two years earlier. As summer 2001 approached, Citigroup was not only weathering an economic downturn that had begun in late 2000, it was thriving around the world.

Citigroup, Post–September 11

During a conference call with analysts in July 2001, the famously risk-averse Sandy Weill explained how Citigroup prepares for the future: "What we do when we think about our company is plan for the worst and pray for the best." Weill had no idea that his expectations for "the worst" would soon be reshaped forever.

Less than two months later, Weill was working in his office on the third floor of 399 Park Avenue in midtown Manhattan when American Airlines Flight 11 crashed into the north tower of the World Trade Center. Weill, who typically rises at 5:30 A.M., reads the papers, and arrives at the office around 7:30, had his office television tuned to CNBC when the plane struck the tower. When Weill saw a second passenger jet smash into the south tower 18 minutes later, he—like everyone else watching—knew that America was under attack.

"The thoughts that went through my mind were incredible," Weill said in a speech to financial services professionals six weeks later. "When I think about September 10 and before, it seems like generations ago—a different life."

Although September 11 traumatized the entire nation, Weill felt the attacks on a very personal level. Six Citigroup employees who had been on sales calls or attending conferences in the towers were killed. As the buildings sickeningly collapsed, Weill surely thought of the occupants of his former office on the 106th floor of the tower, as well as former colleagues who worked at the World Trade Center. Also, the National Academy Foundation headquarters was only two blocks away from Ground Zero.

The fact that Weill prepares for the worst came in extremely handy that morning, when fear and panic spread through lower Manhattan like the billowing clouds of smoke and dust. Exactly four months earlier, the Citigroup investment and corporate bank had simulated the closing of their offices at 388 and 390 Greenwich Street. The simulation included moving staff and equipment to a back-up facility across the Hudson River in Rutherford, New Jersey. It had gone off without a hitch—but then again, it was only a test run.

When actual disaster struck, Citigroup immediately evacuated 16,000 employees from five downtown buildings, including the 2,500 who worked in 7 World Trade Center, which collapsed at 5:25 P.M. after being damaged by debris from the towers. A few employees stayed behind, working all night at the Greenwich Street locations to keep the data and communications systems going.

The next morning, thousands of employees reported to work at pre-ordained back-up sites. Amazingly, Citigroup—including the investment and corporate bank—was open for business the day after the attack. "Our company spent a lot of money for Y2K and put in back-up sites and we never knew how it was going to work," Weill said with pride in an October 23 speech. "The disaster recovery was a wonder to watch."

Weill had other reasons to feel proud of Citigroup's employees and operations in the weeks following the attack. Within 24 hours, two Travelers' catastrophe-response vans were at the disaster site to help provide food, blankets, and medicine to displaced residents. Roseann Keller, a Salomon Smith Barney vice president, spent eight days at Ground Zero with her German shepherd, Logan, joining the search for survivors.

Weill, meanwhile, created the Citigroup Relief Fund, which was seeded with $15 million from the company. It was established to provide college scholarships for the children of the victims and grew in the following months to more than $20 million through donations from Citigroup employees, customers, and clients. Four Citigroup employees in Bangladesh contributed $120 (a small fortune in that country) to the fund. "We felt— and Sandy was very much involved in this decision—there was a tremendous need to look to the future, and the children of the victims are the future," said Chip Raymond, head of the Citigroup Foundation, in the company's internal newsletter. "This was an area that was not being addressed and we felt it was important to do so."[1]

Weill prepared a message distributed over voice mail to all Citigroup employees on September 18, in which he expressed his thanks. "I just feel terrible about the lives that have been disrupted by this, including those of the friends and families of our people who died in the tragedy," he said. "But, what happened afterward is a miracle of dedication and caring."

Weill's Expanding Influence

Following the attacks, Weill assumed a greater presence on the world financial stage than he had before. His comments in open conference calls, speeches, and television appearances reflected his emerging role as a voice for calm in uneasy financial markets. "We will win this battle against 'the evil ones,'" Weill said in a conference call with reporters on October 17.

"And we will make this a better place. That's what it's all about for all of us and that's what our company is about: Helping to create a better standard of living on a global basis and providing the services that go along with that."

Weill also offered his plan for rebuilding lower Manhattan and reducing the risk that a single terrorist attack could again bring the financial center to its knees. He suggested that important financial buildings should be scattered throughout New York City instead of being clustered mainly downtown. He also floated the idea that the World Trade Center site be turned into the home for a new Yankee Stadium. Weill believes that a stadium at the site could serve as the centerpiece of New York City's bid to stage the 2012 Summer Olympics. "It would be a fantastic memorial and it would diversify the economy of the city in a different way without losing anything," Weill said in his October 23 speech to financial executives.

On November 15, in an hour-long CNBC program featuring a roundtable of financial services titans, Weill was optimistic about the economy and the future. "This is a very strong country and what happened was something that nobody expected," he said. He commended the nation's leadership and said its response, "could make this a much better place."[2]

The Financial Impact

Weill has also demonstrated his more pragmatic side since the attacks. The events of September 11 threw global markets into turmoil and catapulted the U.S. economy into recession. In his third-quarter conference call with analysts, Weill didn't pretend that the attacks hadn't weakened the economy and Citigroup's earnings prospects. "When you look at the outlook for the market environment over the next six months, there is no question that we are in a recessionary environment, and that cost-containment and cost-control are going to be an important ingredient in being able to position ourselves for the future," Weill said. "We've always had a focus on cost-containment, and will continue to."

According to the company's own estimates, Citigroup lost approximately $700 million as a direct result of the attacks. That included $500 million in insurance claims from Travelers customers and $200 million in losses due to business interruption, including having the stock exchange closed for four days.

The cost-containment Weill talked about on the CNBC program actually got under way that very day. Citigroup announced that 7,800 workers would be laid off as 2001 wound down, many of them due to duplication caused by the acquisition of Mexico's Banamex. All told, in 2001 Citigroup cut about 12,500 jobs, or roughly 5 percent of its 250,000 employees (a smaller percentage of its total headcount than eliminated by several of its competitors, including Merrill Lynch and American Express). The company continued to whittle back on benefits as 2001 came to a close. In October, the firm ratcheted back on some retirement savings benefits, bringing Citigroup's plan in line with the former Travelers plan.

As a whole, however, the financial impact of the disaster on the company was muted. Citigroup's long-term strategy and revenue growth projections were largely unaffected by the attacks. The company still sets annual growth goals of 15 percent. Citigroup earned $3.2 billion for the third quarter of 2001, a double-digit gain over earnings the year before. Citigroup showed strong growth in its global consumer businesses by remaining a low-cost producer in consumer finance, credit cards and banking. Citigroup's emerging markets earnings (the company defines emerging markets as those economies outside North America, Western and Northern Europe, and Japan) were up

40 percent in the quarter, with a strong contribution from the Banamex acquisition.

As the economy weakened, the analyst community championed Citigroup as a lodestar, pointing out that it was so large, diversified, and well-managed that it could thrive even in a very weak economy. Thomas Hanley of Friedman, Billings, Ramsey & Co. wrote in his November 27, 2001 report:

> Three years since the landmark merger of Travelers and Citicorp, which formed this financial services titan, the new company has emerged as a best-of-breed stalwart in virtually every subsector throughout the financial services spectrum and in every key geographic region around the globe. Underlying this global prowess is the vibrant sales culture that has been instilled by CEO Sandy Weill, which has now permeated the former Citicorp operations.[3]

Indeed, Weill made it clear to the public and Citigroup investors in the fall of 2001 that he fully intended to use the feeble economic environment to make the company stronger. Asked on CNBC what he would "do for an encore," Weill responded: "I would look for us to think out of the box. . . . We could continue to use times that are turbulent to create further opportunities for our company and for our shareholders."[4]

Seizing Opportunity

One opportunity that emerged was the spin-off of Travelers Property Casualty business to shareholders. In late December 2001, Weill announced plans to spin off 20 percent of the company in a public offering and distribute the remaining 80 percent to shareholders. The announcement was vintage Weill. He timed the deal to get a good price. (One effect of the terrorist attack was that it gave property and casualty insurers a chance to raise their premiums, which led to a gain in the share price for those stocks.) And, he invited one of his all-time favorite lieutenants back to run the new company, Bob Lipp.

But what Weill-watchers were really waiting for by the end of 2001 was another big merger. In his third-quarter conference call with reporters on October 17, Weill said, "I think a great preponderance of acquisitions usually happen at extremely good times or extremely bad economic times, much more than they do in average, middle-of-the-road times. I think this would qualify as one of those extreme times."

At the beginning of 2002, many believed Citigroup was poised to acquire American Express, though people had predicted that fitting capstone to Weill's career for years. Still, the timing seemed right. AmEx, which had been struggling even before September 11, had seen its problems compounded when business travel and corporate spending in general subsequently fell off. What's more, its stock price had been falling. Hanley wrote in his report: "On the heels of AmEx's dismal third quarter earnings, we think Citi might be ready to make them an offer."[5] In a follow-up interview, he said, "American Express would fit like a glove."

Despite Citigroup's short-term ability to seemingly brush off—or even see opportunity in—the financial impact of the terrorist attacks, Citigroup still faced several long-term challenges.

Credit Risk and Emerging Market Exposure

Weill has managed to prosper in weak economies before—most notably in the 1970s when he built Shearson. In addition, economic slowdowns typically don't affect all parts of the world at the same time, meaning that global companies can benefit from pockets of growth around the world, even if one region hits a rough patch. On the other hand, the world's economies are increasingly linked, raising the risk of a synchronized slowdown that could significantly harm Citigroup.

Probably the biggest concern in any worldwide economic slowdown is credit risk. In early 2002, the global recession hadn't resulted in an episode similar to the Latin American loan debacle in the late 1980s, the real estate loan defaults in the early 1990s, or the Asian currency crisis of 1997. But Weill remained well aware of worldwide credit risks to his company. For example, in December 2001, Citigroup's exposure in Argentina weighed heavily on Weill as the South American nation was descending into economic disorder, provoking riots on the streets of Buenos Aires.

Hiring and Keeping the Best Executives

Today at Citigroup, Weill needs smart people more than ever. Running a giant corporation is extraordinarily complicated, especially one as global and with as many product lines as Citigroup. As the company has grown, Weill has had to delegate more, which isn't always easy for him.

For example, Weill has had to modify his famously informal style of gathering information. Instead of the monthly planning meetings he grudgingly held earlier in his career, Weill now meets with his top executives every Monday, including the heads of the four main businesses; Robert Willumstad, Citigroup's president, who runs consumer businesses; Michael Carpenter, who oversees the corporate and investment bank; Victor Menezes, who handles emerging markets, and Thomas Jones, who heads investment management at the firm. Each month he meets with the 25 or so executives on Citigroup's management committee. And once a quarter he attends full-day planning meetings for each of the four main businesses. In terms of attracting and retaining world-class executives, it's a must that Weill become better than ever at involving his management team in important decisions.

That's because attrition, especially at the top levels, continued to be an issue for Weill in late 2001. Since November of 1998, Weill has seen several of his top executives leave Citigroup. Some analysts worry about the company's turnover rate among top executives, but others say the company's management ranks remain quite deep.

Cross-Selling and Glass-Steagall Entanglements

There is still scant evidence that Weill's cross-selling plans are reaping the benefits he expects. Even where cross-selling has been successful, it carries potential risks. For instance, Citigroup makes loans (through Citibank's commercial lending division) and provides investment banking services (through its Salomon Smith Barney division) to many of the same customers. That leaves it doubly exposed if that customer goes bankrupt.

This risk came to the fore in late 2001 when Enron, the Houston-based energy-trading giant, collapsed. Citigroup had both lent money to Enron and offered consulting advice in the company's failed effort to merge with Dynegy. The double-exposed Citigroup was left waiting in line (near the front, to be sure, but still waiting) with the other creditors fighting for the scraps left behind in the debris.

Citigroup's size and diversity, however, meant that even the Enron disaster could do minimal damage to its earnings. Citigroup's and other lenders' business dealings with Enron did spark discussion over whether the repeal of Glass-Steagall, of which Weill was a major instigator, was such a good idea. As the *Wall Street Journal* noted in a headline, "Enron's Collapse Raises New Questions about Banking-Deregulation."[6] Economist Robert Smith, president of Smith Affiliated Capital, believes the dismantling of Glass-Steagall created more risk for diversified financial services companies. "I can assure you that all of the protective walls that were there as a function of the excesses of the 1920s have been thoroughly pierced and taken down," says Smith. "There are really no Chinese walls between all these companies."

Foreign Competition

While European and Japanese banks adopted the universal banking model decades ago, most of the world's major banks still don't possess the breadth of products that Citigroup does. But around the world, banks are starting to copy the model created by Citigroup, since the company seems to thrive no matter what curve ball the world economy throws its way. In Germany, for example, the acquisition of Dresdner Bank by Allianz was widely seen as an attempt to replicate Citigroup's balance between consumer and wholesale earnings.[7]

Succession

Another risk to Citigroup is the post-Weill era. What will happen after he leaves? Weill himself is partly to blame for the speculation that has surrounded the naming of his potential successor. In the job-saving deal he cut at the Citigroup board meeting that ended with John Reed's resignation in February of 2000, Weill indicated that he would have a succession plan in place by April 2002. The board must have been appeased when Willumstad was named Citigroup president in January, 2002. But Weill, who turned 69 in March 2002, has shown little interest in stepping down.

On the CNBC "Titans" program, Weill, asked pointedly about his succession plans, gave a version of his stock answer: "We talk about it a lot with our board. It's obviously a board decision, but a company that makes $14 billion a year, plus, and has grown at a 20 percent rate obviously has a lot of very good people. At the appropriate time, one of those good people will be the next person to run this company, and hopefully he or she will do a heck of a lot better job than I do."[8]

But many investors aren't confident that there are many leaders like Weill around anywhere, much less waiting in the wings at Citigroup. Given the size and complexity of the company, they are concerned that only someone as experienced as Weill can handle the job.

While much could change before Weill leaves, it's a fairly straightforward task to pinpoint the pool of people from which his successor would come: Citigroup's management committee, which sets policy and tackles the difficult operating issues for the bank. Prominent members of the committee considered candidates for the CEO job include Willumstad, 56 when named president; the young CFO Todd Thomson; Carpenter; and Menezes.

Willumstad, who runs all of Citigroup's consumer businesses (which generate half its profits) and is also in charge of financial and human resources functions at the company, is the clear front-runner to succeed Weill. But some analysts believe Thomson is also a strong contender. Still in his early 40s, he has assumed a broad range of duties in just a few years. Since joining the company in July 1998 from GE Capital, Thomson has already played several prominent roles: head of global business development, chief operating officer for the global investment management and private banking group, CEO of the global private bank, director of cross-selling efforts and CFO. Some think Weill's plan is to groom Thomson for several years.

There is another way Weill could find a successor—through yet another acquisition. A bid for AmEx, or even Bank One, could yield several interesting candidates. Amex CEO Ken Chenault is one of a handful of executives considered experienced enough to fill Weill's shoes. Then, of course, there's Jamie Dimon, who established détente with Weill over lunch at the Four Seasons in Manhattan in December 1999. There have been some poetic twists in Weill's career: the acquisition of the old guard firm Loeb Rhoades; his recapturing of Shearson from AmEx. But, perhaps a greater irony would be the jilted Dimon taking over the top job at Citigroup.

Weill's Legacy

A list of the most influential corporate leaders of the twentieth century—icons like Chrysler's Lee Iaococca, Coca-Cola's Roberto Goizueta, General Electric's Jack Welch, Wal-Mart's Sam Walton—would include very few financial services professionals.

One of the reasons for this dearth is that, for the most part, banks and brokerages have traditionally offered little incentive for the development of managerial skills. Within financial services, there has been so much opportunity for short-term gain that true executive development has never been emphasized. You're an investment banker in a boom time at a big investment bank? How does a $5 million Christmas bonus sound?

There are exceptions, of course. Walter Wriston, who invented—or rather motivated others to invent—a multitude of new financial services offerings for consumers, is remembered as a visionary.

For his part, Weill has achieved his position in the financial world through a rare ability to sense how the industry was changing and then implement a business strategy that worked for that time and place. Even more than 40 years ago, when Weill was just starting out under the tutelage of Tubby Burnham, he showed a singular interest in how the nuts-and-bolts of the brokerage business really worked, rather than just earning a commission. Through that interest, Weill understood that the brokerage industry was turning toward the individual consumer. He also saw how financial services deregulation would remake the financial landscape.

In an even more recent example of this ability to analyze a given business situation and make the correct decision, Weill is making the Internet work for Citigroup. Maughan says he and Weill "never quite bought the pure online argument" that Reed espoused, and took the technology developed by e-Citi and integrated it into the main businesses. Maughan described the process in a recent interview:

We took e-Citi from $550 million a year in spending to something less than a $100 million. We took a 1,600 head count to 100. But my theory is we do more with less. Today, we have 10 million customers online. We've transformed our corporate banking and our capital markets approach, and we have implemented Internet human resources and other efficiency-raising measures that will yield $1 billion in savings next year. So we took an idea and applied it to a business, as opposed to taking an idea and trying to create an alternative business.

Throughout his career, Weill has been able to turn conditions on their head and score unexpected victories, as he did with Citigroup's Internet strategy.

Will He Ever Stop?

As the leader of a global giant with $1.5 trillion in assets, Weill's station in life would inevitably be diminished if he left Citigroup. For now, however, stepping down is the last thing on Weill's mind. The man who was always looking to prove himself—as a military school standout, a young entrepreneur, a famous dealmaker, and a corporate kingpin—has been preparing for this moment his entire life, and he's not about to remove himself from the spotlight now. He obviously loves his job, and he's just as clearly well-suited for it. At least for the foreseeable future, Sandy Weill surely has more deals ahead.

Introduction: Meet Sandy Weill

1. Leslie Eaton with Laura Holson, "Travelers Chief, at 65, Lands 'The Deal' of a Life of Deals," *New York Times,* April 11, 1998, p. A1.
2. "The Global Billionaires," *Forbes,* March 18, 2002, p. 131.
3. Hoffer Kaback, "Sandy Weill, Pragmatic Dreamer," *Directors and Boards,* March 22, 1998, p. 16.
4. Charles Gasparino and Joann S. Lublin, "Citigroup's Marc Weill to Fight Drug Habit," *Wall Street Journal,* November 24, 2000, p. C1.
5. Dana Wechsler Linden, "Deputy Dog Becomes Top Dog," *Forbes,* October 25, 1993, p. 45.
6. Congressional testimony of Rep. Charles Rangel, November 19, 1999, Senate hearing on investigation into private banking practices.

Chapter 1: The Past Is Gone. The Future Is Limitless

1. Hoffer Kaback, "Sandy Weill, Pragmatic Dreamer," *Directors and Boards,* March 22, 1998, p. 16.
2. Unsigned editorial, "Big Bankers' Gambling Mania," *Literary Digest,* March 11, 1933, p. 11.
3. "More Banks Open All Over the Country," *New York Times,* March 17, 1933, p. A1 (no byline).

4. "OPA Rule Violators Get Court's Warning," *New York Times,* March 8, 1944, p. L36 (no byline).
5. Amy Feldman, "From B'klyn Kid to Wall Street King," *Daily News,* April 12, 1998, p. 28.
6. Judith Ramsey Ehrlich and Barry J. Rehfeld, *The New Crowd* (New York: Harper Perennial), 1989, p. 50.
7. See note 6, p. 50.

Chapter 2: The Best and Brightest

1. Landon Thomas Jr., "Sandy's All-Stars: To Be a Very Important Guy, Surround Yourself with Very Important Guys," *New York Observer,* April 30, 2001, p. 25.
2. Tim Carrington, *The Year They Sold Wall Street* (Boston: Houghton Mifflin, 1985), pp. 35–36.
3. Judith Ramsey Ehrlich and Barry J. Rehfeld, *The New Crowd* (New York: Harper Perennial, 1989), p. 4.
4. Henry Kaufman, *On Money and Markets* (New York: McGraw-Hill, 2000), p. 34.
5. Editors of *Institutional Investor, The Way It Was: An Oral History of Finance 1967–1987* (New York: William Morrow and Company, 1988), p. 366.
6. Jon Friedman, "Sandy Weill Roars Back," *Business Week,* December 4, 1989, p. 88.
7. See note 6.
8. See note 3, p. 52.
9. Tim Carrington, "A Wall Streeter Goes Long on Broadway," *Wall Street Journal,* January 9, 1984, p. 16.
10. Oliver J. Gingold, "Abreast of the Market," *Wall Street Journal,* October 18, 1961, p. 25.
11. John J. Abele, "Cogan, Berlind, Long Unstructured, Gets Boss," *New York Times,* January 18, 1970, p. A1.
12. See note 3, p. 57.
13. William Hall, "An Old Friend of Warren Buffett," *Financial Times,* December 6, 2001, p. 16.
14. Edward Netter, "The Financial Services Holding Company," research report for Carter, Berlind & Weill, August 1967.

15. David Rogers, *The Future of American Banking* (New York: McGraw-Hill, 1993), p. 38.
16. Saul Steinberg, testimony before Securities and Exchange Commission to investigate Leasco-Reliance deal, 1968.
17. Roger Lowenstein, "Alone at the Top," *New York Times*, August 27, 2000, p. 32.
18. Vartanig G. Vartan, "Carter, Berlind and Weill," *New York Times*, May 27, 1968, p. L71.
19. "Primerica: Sandy Weill and His Corporate Entrepreneurs," Harvard Business School, November 20, 1992, p. 4.
20. See note 11.
21. Dana Wechsler Linden, "Deputy Dog Becomes Top Dog," *Forbes*, October 25, 1993, p. 45.
22. See note 11.
23. Editors of *Institutional Investor, The Way It Was: An Oral History of Finance 1967–1987* (New York: William Morrow and Company, 1988), p. 368.

Chapter 3: Hayden Stone: The Prototype Deal

1. Barbara A. Rehm, "Supplement: Best in Banking," *The American Banker*, February 1, 2001, p. 4A.
2. Chris Welles, *The Last Days of the Club* (New York: E.P. Dutton & Co., 1975), p. 172.
3. Tim Carrington, *The Year They Sold Wall Street* (Boston: Houghton Mifflin, 1985), p. 54.
4. Editors of *Institutional Investor, The Way It Was: An Oral History of Finance 1967–1987* (New York: William Morrow and Company, 1988), p. 368.
5. John Seabrook, "Act II," *Manhattan, Inc.*, January 1986, p. 71.
6. See note 2, p. 159.
7. Judith Ramsey Ehrlich and Barry J. Rehfeld, *The New Crowd* (New York: Harper Perennial, 1989), p. 94.
8. *New York Times*, September 27, 1970, CBWL advertisement, p. 81.
9. See note 4, p. 368.
10. See note 2, p. 246.
11. *Manhattan, Inc.*, p. 71.

12. See note 3, p. 74.
13. Dan Dorfman, "Initial Public Offering of One Million Common Shares at $12.50 Each," *Wall Street Journal,* October 5, 1971, p. 25.

Chapter 4: Building Shearson

1. Editors of *Institutional Investor, The Way It Was: An Oral History of Finance 1967–1987* (New York: William Morrow and Company, 1988), pp. 374–375.
2. "Primerica: Sandy Weill and His Corporate Entrepreneurs," *Harvard Business Review,* November 20, 1992, p. 2.
3. See note 1, p. 370.
4. CBWL-Hayden, Stone, Annual Report, 1972, p. 2.
5. "Titans, with Maria Bartiromo," CNBC, November 15, 2001.
6. Tim Carrington, *The Year They Sold Wall Street* (Boston: Houghton Mifflin, 1985), p. 79.
7. John Seabrook, "Act II," *Manhattan, Inc.,* January 1986, p. 71.
8. See note 7, p. 71.
9. Jon Friedman, "Sandy Weill Roars Back," *Business Week,* December 4, 1989, p. 88.
10. Robert J. Cole, "Financial Men Differ on What It Will Take to Lift Wall St. Clouds," *New York Times,* October 7, 1974, p. 57.
11. "Stock-Fee Plan Alarms Wall St.," *New York Times,* August 25, 1972, p. 53.
12. "Hayden and Shearson Planning Layoffs" *New York Times,* June 18, 1974, p. 53 (no byline).
13. Wall Street Journal Staff, "Shearson Settles Three Suits over Topper Collapse for $1.7 Million Total," *Wall Street Journal,* February 25, 1976, p. 12.
14. See note 13.
15. Richard E. Rustin, "Brash Broker; Sanford Weill Runs Shearson with Rigor But an Informal Style," *Wall Street Journal,* August 14, 1979, p. A1.
16. "Shearson Hayden Reports on Profits," *New York Times,* August 21, 1975.
17. Edward Netter, "The Financial Services Holding Company," research report for Carter, Berlind & Weill, August 1967.

18. Wall Street Journal Staff, "Shearson Loeb Gets Spring Fever Again, but Orion Snubs Idea of Courtship," *Wall Street Journal,* May 19, 1980, p. 28.

19. David Rogers, *The Future of American Banking* (New York: McGraw-Hill, 1993), p. 42.

20. See note 1, p. 370.

21. See note 6, p. 86.

22. Tim Carrington, "A Wall Streeter Goes Long on Broadway," *Wall Street Journal,* January 8, 1984, p. 16.

23. Hoffer Kaback, "Sandy Weill, Pragmatic Dreamer," *Directors and Boards,* March 22, 1998, p. 16.

24. Hal Lux and Justin Schack, "Farewell to an Era," *Institutional Investor,* January 1, 2001, p. 75.

25. Vartanig G. Vartan, "Shearson and Loeb to Merge," *New York Times,* May 15, 1979, p. D1.

26. See note 25.

27. See note 7, p. 72.

28. Leslie Eaton with Laura Holson, "Travelers Chief, at 65, Lands 'The Deal' of a Life of Deals," *New York Times,* April 11, 1998, p. A1.

Chapter 5: Deputy Dog

1. Editors of *Institutional Investor, The Way It Was: An Oral History of Finance 1967–1987* (New York: William Morrow and Company, 1988), p. 372.

2. See note 1, p. 373.

3. Jon Friedman and John Meehan, *House of Cards* (New York: Putnam, 1992), p. 96.

4. Tim Carrington, *The Year They Sold Wall Street* (Boston: Houghton Mifflin, 1985), p. 27.

5. Jon Friedman, "Sandy Weill Roars Back," *Business Week,* December 4, 1979, p. 88.

6. Tim Carrington and Daniel Hertzberg, "American Express Co. Tries a Difficult Game in Its Expansion Drive," *Wall Street Journal,* February 25, 1983, p. A1.

7. Speech to the American Bankers Association, October 5, 1981, submitted as part of Congressional testimony on financial services reform on June 27, 1983.

8. Tim Carrington and Daniel Hertzberg, "American Express Names Weill President; Alva Way Moves to the Same Post at Travelers," *Wall Street Journal,* January 18, 1983, p. 2.

9. Howard Rudnitzy, "Tiger by the Tail?" *Forbes,* August 7, 1989, p. 40.

10. David B. Hilder and Tim Metz, "Growing Pains: A Spate of Acquisitions Puts American Express in a Management Bind," *Wall Street Journal,* August 15, 1984, p. A1.

11. See note 3, p. 157.

12. See note 10, p. A1.

13. "American Express's Weill Sells 150,000 More Shares," *Wall Street Journal,* March 8, 1985, p. 16.

Chapter 6: Starting Over

1. Testimony before House of Representatives Subcommittee, 1996.

2. Jon Friedman, "Sandy Weill Roars Back," *Business Week,* December 4, 1979, p. 88.

3. Bill Atkinson, "Man of the Big Deal," *Baltimore Sun,* April 12, 1998, p. 10.

4. See note 2, p. 88.

5. Carol J. Loomis, "Sanford Weill, 53, Exp'd Mgr, Gd Refs," *Fortune,* May 12, 1986, p. 102.

6. John Rockwell, "Weill Recital Hall Opens at Carnegie," *New York Times,* January 6, 1987, p. C13.

7. Editors of *Institutional Investor, The Way It Was: An Oral History of Finance 1967–1987* (New York: William Morrow and Company, 1988), p. 373.

8. Peter Marks, "Tough but Avid Teacher Is Recalled, "*New York Times,* September 25, 2001, p. E1.

9. See note 7, p. 374.

10. Gary Hector, "Breaking the Bank: The Decline of BankAmerica" (Boston: Little, Brown, 1988), p. 269.

11. See note 10.

12. See note 10.

13. Robert J. Cole, "BankAmerica Corp. to Study Weill Bid," *New York Times,* February 27, 1986, p. D6.

14. See note 2, p. 89.

15. Robert J. Cole, "Control Data Unit Gets Weill," *New York Times,* September 13, 1986, p. 33.
16. See note 3.
17. Fred R. Bleakley, "Talking Deals; Weill Issue's Big Following," *New York Times,* November 27, 1986, p. D2.
18. "Primerica: Sandy Weill and his Corporate Entrepreneurs," *Harvard Business Review,* November 20, 1992, p. 3.
19. See note 7, p. 374.

Chapter 7: Back in the Big Leagues

1. Jean Strouse, Morgan: American Financier (New York: Perennial, 2000), pp. 364–365.
2. Robert J. Cole, "2 Leading Financiers Will Merge Companies in a $1.65 Billion Deal," *New York Times,* August 30, 1988, p. A1.
3. "Reed and Technology," *Euromoney,* May 1988.
4. "Primerica: Sandy Weill and his Corporate Entrepreneurs," *Harvard Business Review,* November 20, 1992, p. 5.
5. See note 4.
6. See note 4.
7. See note 4, p. 7.
8. Jon Friedman, "Sandy Weill Roars Back," *Business Week,* December 4, 1989, p. 88.
9. Seth Faison Jr., "Primerica Posts Earnings, Setting Records All Around," *New York Times,* April 14, 1992, p. D5.
10. "Entrepreneur Sanford Weill," *Investor's Business Daily,* May 14, 1999.
11. See note 4, p. 5.
12. Anita Raghavan, "Boss's Daughter Shakes Up the Mutual Fund Industry," *Wall Street Journal,* August 1, 1996.
13. Michael Quint, "Primerica Will Buy Shearson for $1 Billion," *New York Times,* March 13, 1993, p. 35.
14. "Smith Barney-Shearson? King Wile," *The Economist,* March 13, 1993, p. 88.
15. Allen R. Myerson, "Deal Maker Picked to Run Smith Barney Shearson," *New York Times,* June 25, 1993, p. D1.
16. Dana Wechsler Linden, "Deputy Dog Becomes Top Dog," *Forbes,* October 25, 1993, p. 45.

17. Leslie Scism, "The Boss's Daughter and Right-Hand Man Clash—And She's Gone," *Wall Street Journal,* July 3, 1997, p. A1.

18. See note 17.

19. See note 17.

20. Michael Lewis, *Liar's Poker* (New York: W.W. Norton & Co., 1989).

21. Leslie Eaton, "A Wall Street Behemoth: The Strategist," *New York Times,* September 25, 1997, p. D1.

22. See note 21.

23. Bruce Wasserstein, *Big Deal: The Battle for Control of America's Leading Corporations* (New York: Warner Books, 1998).

24. Hoffer Kaback, "Sandy Weill, Pragmatic Dreamer," *Directors and Boards,* March 22, 1998, p. 16.

Chapter 8: Deal of the Century

1. Ralph Nader Congressional testimony, April 12, 1998.

2. "No More Poker," *The Economist,* July 11, 1998, p. 74.

3. "A Wall Street Behemoth: The Industry; Merger Roils a Changing Wall Street," *New York Times,* September 25, 1997.

4. Carol J. Loomis, "One Helluva Candy Store," *Fortune,* May 11, 1998, p. 72.

5. Hoffer Kaback, "Sandy Weill, Pragmatic Dreamer," *Directors & Boards,* March 22, 1998, p. 16.

6. See note 4.

7. Steven Lipin and Stephen E. Frank, "The Big Umbrella: Travelers/Citicorp Merger—One-Stop Shopping Is the Reason for the Deal," *Wall Street Journal,* April 7, 1998, p. C14.

8. Leah Nathans Spiro, "The 'Coca-Cola' of Personal Finance," *Business Week,* April 20, 1998, p. 37.

9. Editorial, "A Monster Merger," *New York Times,* April 8, 1998, p. A18.

10. "Citicorp & Travelers CEOs Speak Out," *MoneyLine* with Lou Dobbs, April 8, 1998.

11. "Can Citigroup Get in Step?" *Euromoney,* May 1998, p. 27.

12. "Shaping a Colossus: The Employees," *New York Times,* April 7, 1998, p. D20.

13. Arthur Levitt, Congressional testimony on banking reform, 1997.

14. "Shaping a Colossus: The Politics," *New York Times,* April 8, 1998, p. D4.
15. Roger Lowenstein, "Alone at the Top," *New York Times Magazine,* August 27, 2000, p. 32.
16. "Citigroup Fall Guy," *The Economist,* November 7, 1998, p. 78.
17. Anita Ragharan and Paul Beckett, "Mentor Breakup: How Jamie Dimon Became a Casualty of Citigroup's Travails," *Wall Street Journal,* November 3, 1998, p. A1.
18. Timothy L. O'Brien, "The Honeymooners Amid the Storm," *New York Times,* November 15, 1998, section 3, p. 1.
19. See note 18.
20. See note 18.
21. See note 18.
22. See note 18.

Chapter 9: Weill on Top

1. "The Global Billionaires," *Forbes,* March 18, 2002, p. 131.
2. April 2001 Citigroup proxy statement.
3. *Dow Jones* staff, "Citigroup's Earnings Easily Top Targets as All Units Show Momentum," *Dow Jones Business Wire,* April 14, 1999.
4. Charles Gasparino and Paul Beckett, "Alone at the Top: How John Reed Lost the Reins of Power to His Co-Chairman," *Wall Street Journal,* April 14, 2000, p. A1.
5. Gary Silverman and Leah Nathans Spiro, "Is This Marriage Working?" *Business Week,* June 7, 1999, p. 126.
6. John Authers, "Citigroup's Odd Couple," *Financial Post,* July 1, 1999, p. C15.
7. Michael Schroeder, "Glass-Steagall Compromise Is Reached," *Wall Street Journal,* October 25, 1999, p. A2.
8. Timothy L. O'Brien, "The Honeymooners Amid the Storm," *New York Times,* November 15, 1998, section 3, p. 1.
9. "Citizen Rubin," Bloomberg.com.
10. See note 4, p. A1.
11. Patricia Sellers, "Behind the Shootout at Citigroup," *Fortune,* March 20, 2000, p. 27.
12. "Sandy's Bank," *U.S. Banker,* September 2000, p. 16.

13. Heather Timmons, "Sandy Weill Wants the World," *Business Week,* June 4, 2001, p. 88.
14. Charles Gasparino and Joann S. Lublin, "Citigroup's Marc Weill to Fight Drug Habit," *Wall Street Journal,* November 24, 2000, p. C1.

Chapter 10: Citigroup, Post–September 11

1. "For the Children's Future," *CitigroupWorld, A Publication by and for Citigroup Employees,* November 2001, p. 8.
2. "Titans" with Maria Bartiromo, CNBC, November 15, 2001.
3. Thomas H. Hanley and Christopher M. Siedman, "Citigroup: A Rock of Stability in Turbulent Times," an analyst report for Friedman, Billings, Ramsey & Co., Inc., November 27, 2001, p. 3.
4. See note 2.
5. See note 3.
6. Carrick Mollenkamp and Rick Brooks, "Fall of a Power Giant: Collapse Raises Issue of 1999 Bank Deregulation," *Wall Street Journal,* November 30, 2001, p. A8.
7. First Union Securities equity research report, June 27, 2001, p. 6.
8. See note 2.

BIBLIOGRAPHY

Auletta, Ken, *Greed and Glory on Wall Street* (New York: Random House, 1986).

Carrington, Tim, *The Year They Sold Wall Street* (Boston: Houghton Mifflin Company, 1985).

Chernow, Ron, *Titan* (New York: Random House, 1998).

Cohan, Peter S., *e-Profit* (New York: American Management Association, 2000).

The Editors of *Institutional Investor, The Way It Was: An Oral History of Finance 1967–1987* (New York: William Morrow and Company, 1988).

Ehrlich, Judith Ramsey, and Barry J. Rehfeld, *The New Crowd* (New York: Harper Perennial, 1989).

Freedman, Samuel G., *The Inheritance* (New York: Simon and Schuster, 1996).

Friedman, Jon, and John Meehan, *House of Cards* (New York: G.P. Putnam's Sons, 1992).

Geisst, Charles R., *The Last Partnerships* (New York: McGraw-Hill, 2001).

Hector, Gary, *Breaking the Bank: The Decline of BankAmerica* (Boston: Little, Brown, 1988).

Kadlec, Daniel J., *Masters of the Universe* (New York: Harper Business, 1999).

Kaufman, Henry, *On Money and Markets* (New York: McGraw-Hill, 2000).

Kilpatrick, Andrew, *Of Permanent Value: The Story of Warren Buffett* (New York: McGraw-Hill, 1998).

Lewis, Michael, *Liar's Poker* (New York: W.W. Norton & Co., 1989).

Malkiel, Burton G., *A Random Walk Down Wall Street* (New York: W.W. Norton & Co., 1996).

Rogers, David, *The Future of American Banking* (New York: McGraw-Hill, 1993).

Smith, Roy C., *The Wealth Creators* (New York: St. Martin's Press, 2001).

Strouse, Jean, *Morgan: American Financier,* (New York: Harper Perennial, 2000).

Thomas, William I., and Florian Znaniecki, *The Polish Immigrant in Europe and America* (Urbana, IL: University of Illinois Press, 1996).

Wasserstein, Bruce, *Big Deal: The Battle for Control of America's Leading Corporations* (New York: Warner Books, 1998).

Welles, Chris, *The Last Days of the Club* (New York: E.P. Dutton & Co., 1975).